Anthony Kilmister remembers

Raymond Chapman

THE Reverend Raymond Chapman, Emeritus Professor of English Literature at London University (with his Chair at the LSE), one of the editors of *The Tufton Review,* a staunch member of the Church Union and a prolific writer died on 5th November 2013, aged 89.

Only weeks before he died Raymond explained to his devoted wife, Patricia, that he had a perfectly good home here [on earth] and a perfectly good home to go to and he didn't want anything in between. God in His great love and mercy granted him that and Raymond died peacefully in his own bed. He was still writing whenever he could and perhaps he just wore out. His funeral service in Barnes, south of the River Thames, on 18th November was attended by a very large number of admirers.

Raymond Chapman, after Oxford and King's College London spent his long academic life at the LSE. With a family background of Welsh non-conformity Raymond "climbed up the candle" and was confirmed as an Anglican at 17 years of age. He was ordained a priest in 1975 and as a NSM served first at St Mary le Strand with St Clement Danes (close to the LSE) and thereafter at St Mary's, Barnes. He could best be described as a Prayer Book Catholic and wrote with great authority on the literature of the Oxford Movement.

Professor Chapman had a great love of the Book of Common Prayer and held high office in the Prayer Book Society. He was also President of the Anglican Society and when it merged with the Anglican Association became President of the Association eventually handing the reins of it on to me.

Raymond was author of so many books, learned papers, articles and the like that I will not attempt to mention even a fraction of them. But his books on Evelyn Underhill, Lancelot Andrewes and Richard Hooker must be the exception.

I remember well my surprise at coming across him and Patricia in the Irish Embassy in London to which I had been invited in connection with a book on the first Transatlantic flight (by Alcock and Brown in 1919). I should not have been surprised for Raymond was Chairman and later vice-president of the Irish Literary Society. He is survived by his delightful Irish wife, Patricia, who is an Anglican too – having been a member of the Plymouth Brethren in her youth.

Tony Kilmister is President of the Anglican Association

FAITH AND REVOLT

FAITH AND REVOLT

*Studies in the literary influence of the
Oxford Movement*

RAYMOND CHAPMAN

WEIDENFELD AND NICOLSON
5 Winsley Street London W1

© *1970 Raymond Chapman*

SBN 297 00219 8

*Printed in Great Britain by
Cox & Wyman Ltd,
London, Fakenham and Reading*

Contents

Contents

To Frederic Hood

Introduction

The revival of Catholic doctrine and practice in the Anglican Church which began in 1833 was, by all laws of probability, doomed to failure as a movement running against the current of contemporary society. It was a protest against increasing State interference in Church affairs, at a time when governmental power over national institutions was generally being extended. It was reactionary in a deeper sense, too, looking back to neglected standards and finding authority in the past instead of in a brighter future of human progress. Its first leaders, devout and compassionate men as they were, had little interest in schemes for social reform and could be charged with concern for ecclesiastical minutiae to the neglect of possible improvements in material conditions.

While the deep, irrational English prejudice against Roman Catholicism was rising to a new frenzy, the men of the Oxford Movement were commending doctrines, interpretations and practices hitherto associated with Popery. The greatest of them changed his allegiance; others preceded or followed him out of the national Church. Those who stayed could be seen as disguised Papists or as unwitting tools of the Pope for the perversion of simple Protestants. Even the critics who could understand the difference between Roman and Anglican Catholicism were repelled by the showiness of derived forms of worship, by the emphasis on practices which made the public devotion seem theatrical and the private ostentatious.

I

More even than this, the leaders of the Oxford Movement were certain where their contemporaries were doubtful, impassioned where they were indifferent. Their scepticism about such matters as the superiority of the present age and the beneficence of parliamentary legislation was aggravated by their seeming arrogance about what they themselves believed. They became an offence for their earnestness and their insistence on telling other people how Christian life should be organized. They stressed the importance of dogma to a generation which had inherited a religious attitude resting on kindness, contentment, attention to immediate duty, obedience to lawfully constituted power. The Evangelicals had already made themselves unpopular by asserting that these things alone were not enough for a Christian. Now the new teachers came saying that precise items of theology were important, that salvation might depend on the acceptance of beliefs handed down from the earliest days of Christianity. They seemed to stand against everything which the popular interpreters of religion offered, as cheerfully expounded by Martin Tupper in 'Of Creeds':

A pure life, a liberal mind, an honest and good heart –
This is the threefold cord bent upon the anchor of religion;
If either of these strands be rotten, that bark is found in peril,
Nigh to be drifted on the reef, when as its hawser parteth:
Void of purity in morals, faith is but a hypocrite of words,
Charity cannot dwell with a mean and narrow spirit,
And there is but little hope, failing integrity of purpose;
Faith, hope, charity, the triple-twisted cable of religion,
In a mere creed there is no salvation, no happiness in articles or
    dogmas,
No real safety for the soul in the best cold code of forms;
Though thy theology be logical, and thy scheme most orthodox,
Though thy sect be of the straitest, thy chain from the fathers of the
    strongest,
These are none of them the comforters to bring a man peace at the
    last,
These are not the elements of heaven in the soul:
Holiness that hath no evil memories, kindliness lovable to all,
And cheerful trust toward God, will outweigh all creeds.[1]

Such polarized opposition of formal dogma and the good life was contrary to what Newman, Pusey and Keble believed and expounded. For them right doctrine and right conduct were inseparable. Yet these men had a deep and far-reaching effect on their time. The revival which they began did not totally triumph, though much for which they fought has since become the common practice of moderate Anglicans. What that revival could give, to hostile critics as well as to sympathizers, has left its literary record. The gifts were great for those whose spiritual lives were newly directed; they were not negligible for those whose doubts and fears were given a visible target to attack. The Tractarians were called narrow and dogmatic, but their non-attachment to many problems of secular society made them able to show that these immediate concerns were not the whole meaning of life. They stressed a wider and longer view which could sometimes ease the pressures of the here and now. The Victorian dilemma needed the long as well as the short view for its resolution.

The highways of Victorian life, and the byways too, often led into literature. Growing literacy and new opportunities for reading helped to canalize the contemporary debate. The novel in particular argued the case for and against every question, with that sense of mission which could inspire great writers and single-minded propagandists. The Oxford Movement produced its own flood of imaginative writing, some of it long forgotten except when research disinters it for examination. Like all minor and occasional literature it has its own illuminations to offer, and it has found interpreters.[2] Gresley, Paget, Armitage, Sewell and many more put the new ideas into the form of fiction.

There are others who, if not all in the great tradition of Victorian literature, brought distinctive talents to religious issues. These were not propagandists who saw in literature a convenient way of spreading belief; rather was their imaginative response to life affected by what had been happening at Oxford. What they had to say, to their time and to ours was something more than could spring from obsession or bigotry. Because their vision was wider they could grasp the social as well as the personal significance of this strange and alien theology. The novelist and the poet needed to express things which a generation before had been the property of tracts and devotional books. The language and imagery of religious experience demanded new formation: the statement became more difficult as the religious situation moved from the assured to the tentative and provisional.

The Oxford Movement impinged on society and was consequently noticed by many of the great Victorian writers. For the majority the revival was an objective phenomenon, to be mentioned sympathetically or satirically as part of the total scene but not taken into the whole personality. Disraeli pinned some of his hopes on a revitalized Church of England as part of the Young England drive against Whig encroachment. What he learned from his Cambridge friends in the political world was in some ways akin to Tractarian teaching, but irreconcilably different in emphasis. The Church as a supernatural society might be valuable in the restoration of hereditary power, but the attraction was superficial and based on notions which were not in the mainstream of the religious movement. After the secessions to Rome, Disraeli turned away and lived to become a bitter enemy of later Ritualism.

Trollope may seem to be more closely involved, but his concern does not go to the heart of things. His clergy may be party men, but their supposed allegiances do not stamp their characters. Grantly is strong for Church rights against the attacks of Parliament, but he does not seem aware of his function as a priest in the Apostolic line. Arabin comes to Barchester from the Oxford home of controversy, but he shows little more sacerdotal feeling, openly calls himself a Protestant, and gets a good deanery at a time when men of the Tractarian party were seldom in line for preferment. Mrs Proudie is staunch for Protestantism and against such signs of Popery as weekday services and reference to saints' days, but her lively appearances in the novels do not give us much sense of what it really meant to belong to the extreme Protestant wing of a Church in conflict.[3] This by no means depreciates Trollope as a novelist; he simply used some of the dramatic possibilities of the theological dispute without deeply feeling its attractions and tensions.

Dickens gives us Mrs Pardiggle, whose unfortunate children 'attend Matins with me (very prettily done) at half-past six o'clock in the morning all the year round, including of course the depth of winter'.[4] Though his genius is at its highest in

4

the bricklayer's monologue which echoes and answers Mrs Pardiggle's vapid questions, there is nothing in her delineation to suggest the realities of the new Anglican piety. Her devotional habit is simply the exaggeration of an observable trait to particularize a creation: Dickens's great gift, and sometimes his undoing. His mind was not theologically inclined, but his insight could express the deeper anxieties of his time in casual and undeveloped references. He can offer and throw away some of the common charges against followers of the Oxford Movement. The accusation of neglecting social reform in the cult of ecclesiology, the English dislike of ostentation in worship and a Victorian sense of unease imaged in terms of personal cleanliness – all these appear in the brief introduction of Mrs Pardiggle's friend, 'an extremely dirty lady . . . whose neglected home . . . was like a filthy wilderness, but whose church was like a fancy fair'.[5]

Others were more deeply marked by the realities of the movement. Charlotte M. Yonge and Christina Rossetti each found, for all the differences of situation and temperament between them, a possibility of sacrifice and dedication made with a good heart and in a higher service; a faith-centred life that went beyond compensation for the frustrations of middle-class spinsterhood. For others there was in the movement that vein of tragedy usually lacking in novels and plays that tended to melodramatic oppositions. Those like Newman who changed their allegiance, those like J.A.Froude who were spun off from the centre of belief, were changed not only in themselves but in their total relationship to society. Those like Kingsley who reacted strongly against the movement were forced either to make a more coherent statement of their opposition or to reveal their own inadequacies – many, including Kingsley, did both. Some passed through a brief period of enchantment which left its mark on them after other preoccupations had come to the fore. Some, born too late for the first flood of enthusiasm, could discover an Anglicanism better able to command their love and respect.

The omissions from a study of this kind are inevitable and open to dispute. By concentrating on those who expressed themselves mainly or significantly through accepted literary forms, I have given only slight attention to such an important castaway of the movement as Mark Pattison. Newman's two novels and his *Apologia* are discussed, but little is said of his theological contribution before or after his secession except as it illuminates the wider effects of the movement. I have not devoted space to the poetry of Isaac Williams because he was, though a lovable and holy man, not a very good poet. Keble might *just* get in as a poet alone, but his influence on others makes his place secure; there is no comparable result from the contributions of Newman and Froude to *Lyra Apostolica*. The conversions to Roman Catholicism of Patmore and Hopkins, although inevitably touching men whom the Oxford Movement had itself touched, were not in the main line of that movement.

A study of writers who show an emotional and imaginative involvement in the movement will understate or even ignore things which might be of the first importance to the social historian or the interpreter of religious and philosophical ideas *per se*. The great social work undertaken by the second generation of Anglo-Catholics has little place here. Lowder, Mackonochie, Stanton and Headlam were great men; but their greatness was of a kind different from that of the Tractarians and its interpretation was less often literary.

The movement itself changed with time, even as it helped to change the life of faith. The Church of England in the years when the *Tracts for the Times* were coming out was different from the Church which saw the publication of *Essays and Reviews*. Pusey and Keble lived to be alarmed by the latter, but their teaching found new and freer interpretation in *Lux Mundi*. R.W.Church as Proctor defended Tract 90 and lived to give qualified approval to *Origin of Species*.[6]

Although the revival showed itself capable of continuance and adaptation, it was the early years which seized the imagination and to which these studies will constantly return. The first Tractarian ideals, rather than the later Puseyism, were those that found fullest literary expression. The twelve years between Keble's Assize Sermon and Newman's secession became the source of inspiration and of legend. In the troubled Oxford of that period the faithful could find the fount of joy, the opposition could trace the roots of evil, the disillusioned could mark the loss of security. The next Oxford generation would measure their own time critically against the years of the giants. With the lapse of time, men would think it greatness to have been close to the heart of change, so that Archbishop Trench could mistakenly believe that he had seen Newman at Hadleigh; and Hawker in his Cornish parsonage could fancy that he had sat in the common room with the Tractarian leaders. The power to enrich imaginative life through intellectual controversy speaks for a rare quality in both the controversialists and their interpreters.

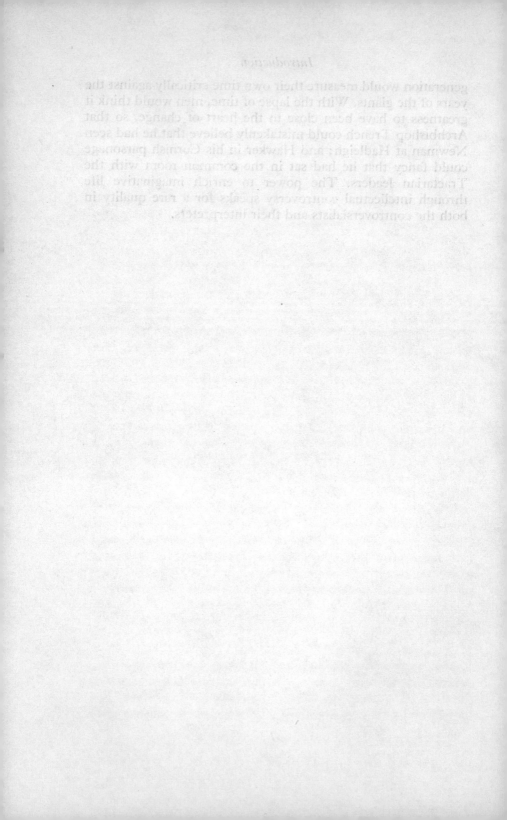

I

The Background of the Movement

The temptation to contain human complexities in simple images is nowhere stronger than in matters of religion. The churchgoing Victorian, puritan and fundamentalist, is an image that has resisted the revaluation of nineteenth-century society more successfully than most. In popular estimation that society existed in an age of faith, to be viewed with nostalgia, contempt or indifference according to the presuppositions of the modern observer. The image may contain as much truth and as much error as most generalizations. The religious temper of the Victorians showed itself in protest and revolt as well as in acceptance.

That religion penetrated the thinking of the age in many of its aspects is not in question. The Victorians were openly concerned about religion. The previous century, chastened by memory of religious strife at home and awareness of worse overseas, had played a quieter note. To be 'enthusiastic' was an offence against that politer mode of conformity where

> To rest, the cushion and soft dean invite,
> Who never mentions Hell to ears polite.[1]

Yet the enthusiasts like Wesley and Whitefield brought a resurgence of faith to their own age and passed on its legacy to the next. They were an offence to those for whom reason was more worthy than passion, for whom the areas of agreement

9

were to be broadened and those of dispute minimized or ignored.

Both the enthusiast and the latitudinarian found new voices in the nineteenth century: so did many others who previously had lingered inarticulately on the fringes of society. There were heard objections to Christianity stronger and more widespread than before, but these too often had an essentially religious temper. Most of the great doubters and agnostics believed that basic values had been betrayed by formalized religion and they sought rather to assert those values on a new basis than radically to change them. They reacted with distaste to the cruder manifestations of anti-Christian feeling which accompanied Continental scepticism. Like the eponymous hero of *Robert Elsmere*, one in retreat from the orthodox position could be hurt when his new associates mocked the faith which he had left. To understand at all, it is necessary to enter into the belief that religion matters, in all its shades and affiliations. It is a hard exercise for the modern humanist who has dismissed religion as irrelevant, as hard perhaps for the modern Christian who can accept as commonplace the issues which were bitterly fought over not so long ago.

No date, no accession, no publication, can mark a decisive break between one age and the next. Theological ferment increased but older attitudes lingered. The young Queen reacted against the slack morality of Regency years but also retained the distrust of extremes in religion. Guided in the early years of her reign by Melbourne, to whom studied moderation was a creed, she was never at ease with the stronger manifestations of that piety for which her own household became the exemplar. Both temperament and the demands of her position kept her from favouring any but the moderate; Evangelicals and Anglo-Catholics alike roused her distrust. Many of her subjects felt the same and, like Kingsley's old squire, would curse the Methodists, 'under which name he used to include every species of religious earnestness, from Quakerism to that of Mr Newman'.[2]

Other men, including Kingsley himself, could rather rejoice in the excitement that was being aroused by religion. A multiplicity of new ideas and practices might bewilder the old, but large-scale production was pleasing to those who found their age a challenge. The idea of progress, with Britain in the lead, demanded experiment before the ideal was attained:

What a chaos of noble materials is here – all confused, it is true, polarized, jarring, and chaotic – here bigotry, there self-will, super-stitition, sheer Atheism often, but only waiting for the one inspiring Spirit to organize, and unite and consecrate this chaos into the noblest polity the world ever saw realized![3]

Beyond conformity or enthusiasm, the objector could be soci-ally as well as personally insecure. An agnostic's little girl would remember all her life the feeling of deprivation at not going to Sunday School with other children, and the castaways of the Oxford Movement would keep up the practice of family prayers long after their own orthodox belief had gone.[4]

In public as well as family life religion was a strong preoccu-pation. One can scarcely conceive a modern newspaper editor keeping a list of the London clergy with notes on their theo-logical tendencies.[5] Or a popular novelist, and one for whom popularity was studied, taking for granted his readers' interest in religious affairs as part of the social background:

The story was thoroughly English. There was a little fox-hunting and a little tuft-hunting, some Christian virtue and some Christian cant. There was no heroism and no villainy. There was much Church, but more love-making.[6]

Something more has to be realized if we would enter fully into the mind of that age. It was not only the basic acceptance of Christianity that mattered, for two men might each profess to believe every word in the Bible yet consider the other utterly wrong on matters of interpretation. Although the ecumenical spirit was slowly emerging by the end of the century, we have come so much farther in the last generation that we may have a mental block about the *odium theologicum* which raged in the Tractarians as strongly as in their bitter opponents. Goodwill in one section of the community and indifferentism in another are both disabilities in studying the importance of denomina-tions. For the divisions of religious allegiance were social as well as religious. To change was to affect cultural life, reading and leisure, to be largely severed from one's past, often to lose the comfort of family and friends when they were most needed.

Conversion could not remain a private affair: it involved the whole of a man's immediate circle and, for a man of Newman's position, the whole of society. Even one whose profession was not the Church but the Law could set down for his own consideration among reasons for not becoming a Roman Catholic, 'hesitation at separating myself from every relative I have'.[7]

We shall meet a great deal of the hostility to Rome in what follows and we have to accept its reality at the time. One of the things which brought the Oxford Movement into public concern was the fact that it made secession a living possibility. By raising questions about authority and true catholicity, it developed Papal claims from a distant horror to one near at hand. The fear and antagonism were, of course, old enough. Folk memories of Marian persecutions and Elizabethan plots, kept alive by a secular as well as an ecclesiastical anathema on Guy Fawkes',[8] mingled with the consideration that the Pope was a foreign potentate whom no trueborn Englishman could serve. The few Roman Catholic families at the beginning of the nineteenth century tended to keep to themselves, thankful if they could escape the penalties which the law still laid on the practice of their faith, a handful in infidel territory where no hierarchy was established.

Catholic emancipation came in 1829, largely as a political move to assuage the growing discontent in Ireland after the Union of 1800 had denied hopes of national independence. The chief immediate beneficiaries were the English Roman Catholics who were now admitted to full citizenship in most respects. Political measures did not bring a change of heart, as Victorian reformers were to learn in other fields. The emergence of Roman Catholics into the full light of day made it possible to accept them as reasonable human beings. There was still suspicion of their clergy and bitter hostility to the idea of a Protestant seeking the Roman yoke. To be a crypto-Papist was a terrible thing, an accusation that could be levelled with deadly effect by religious opponents. It was even, however improbably, alleged of the Prince Consort when he was suffering from general unpopularity in the country.[9] To some extent, emancipation led to an exacerbation of anti-Roman feeling, particularly when some of the younger generation began to look for closer links with Italy and to urge the establishment of a territorial hierarchy.

Hostility became hysterical when a significant number of lay and clerical converts moved to Roman Catholicism around the middle of the century. Hitherto the Papists had been virtually confined to old families which had passed on the faith, foreign denizens and immigrants, and the growing number of Irish settlers. Now it seemed that thoughtful and devout men could pass from one allegiance to another. They did so at the cost of personal anguish as well as private hostilities and public obloquy. The problem of ultimate religious authority gave to the Oxford Movement a deep vein of tragedy. There was a special tension for men who had been brought up to see religious attachments as the simple polarities of good and evil.

For the majority of Englishmen there was little desire either to understand or to accommodate the differences between Protestants and Romanists. General sympathy would be with the kind of parson who 'did not want to be reconciled to the Church of Rome; he wanted to make all Roman Catholics turn Protestants, and could never understand why they would not do so'.[10] Proximity and the real possibility of secession led to more fear, as Newman could point out to a 'zealous Catholic layman' in 1841:

> Suspicion and distrust are the main causes at present of the separation between us, and the nearest approaches in doctrine will but increase the hostility, which, alas, our people feel towards yours, while these causes continue.[11]

Newman, alone of the writers of *Tracts for the Times*, went over; those who remained suffered the charge of being dishonest or stupid tools of Rome. The fever did not abate until the century was nearly over; it ranged from the almost lovable mania of Borrow with his gibes at 'old Mumbo-Jumbo' to the tolerant amusement of Sydney Smith who could sympathize with the wrongs suffered by Irish Catholics yet sneer at their 'bargains for shirts and toe-nails of deceased saints – surplices and trencher-caps blessed by the Pope'.[12] At all levels it betokened more fear than theological dispute, the need for a national scapegoat, and the 'dogged hatred of Popery which lies inarticulate and confused, but deep and firm, in the heart of the English people'.[13]

'Frustrate the machinations of Popery, whether within or without the Church' was the prayer of an Evangelical family in 1849.[14] For them the meaning of 'the Church' was as unequivocal as it had been for Fielding's chaplain: 'When I speak of religion, I mean the Christian religion; and not only the Christian religion, but the Protestant religion; and not only the Protestant religion, but the Church of England.'[15] Yet the power of that Church over the nation as a whole was declining, until by the middle of the century not more than half the churchgoing population was at an Anglican place of worship.[16]

The Protestant dissenters had often been mocked for their apparent excesses or despised for their narrowness, but they had escaped the smear of potential disloyalty to the Crown which had stuck to Roman Catholics. They abounded in those virtues of industry, sobriety and honesty to which the age paid homage. The repeal of the Test and Corporation Acts in 1828 lifted from them most of the civil disabilities from which they had in theory suffered, although for many years there had been an annual indemnification of offences against those laws. Also there were many Protestant dissenters who found no difficulty in assenting to the Articles and appearing at Anglican services so long as they were free also to hear more congenial preaching. The Methodists indeed scarcely regarded themselves as a separated body and felt, as Wesley had done, that they were a special part of the Church of England. As time went on, however, the Methodists tended to produce new sects which would emphasize their differences from the Establishment.

The older dissenting groups held themselves more apart. Baptists and Congregationalists were for the most part socially and educationally poor; their belief in each local church as a self-governing entity hindered progress until they formed national unions. For the early part of the century they lived and worshipped within the constrictions memorably depicted by Mark Rutherford. Yet there was fervour and deep consolation as well, and great names of the past to be recalled with pride.

Further out theologically were the Unitarians, drawn partly from seceders from the Church of England but also from the

English Presbyterians rejected in 1662. Despite their Socinian denial of the divinity of Christ and the Trinity, they were generally regarded as reasonable dissenters. Only the theologically perceptive were inclined to put them outside the orthodox pale, and even these did not class them as dangerously as Papists. A moderate High Churchman could write to a young man applying for a post in a Unitarian-sponsored hostel:

I do not see that this employment need bring you into hurtful intimacy with Unitarians. There is no reason why we should not know Unitarians. I have been well acquainted with some myself.[17]

Unitarianism collected some of the drifters-through from orthodoxy to agnosticism. Francis Newman was disappointed at their credulity when he first came among them but he defended them against prejudices which were excluding their writings as rigorously as the Roman Index.[18] Their intellectual status declined, but it was something to have been associated with names like Hazlitt, Gaskell and Martineau.

As the old sects grew more moderate and hence more respectable, new movements foreshadowed a crop of wilder unorthodoxies later in the century. Edward Irving achieved a spectacular success in the thirties when he claimed special revelation to found the 'Catholic Apostolic Church' and to ordain a new ministry in preparation for the Parousia. Carriages blocked the approach to his church in Hatton Garden as the fashionable world came to hear the 'speaking with tongues' which unfortunately produced no clear interpretation. The movement survived into the present century and was a precursor of the conflicting claims of Theosophy, Christian Science, Mormonism and the spiritualism which fascinated Elizabeth Barrett Browning, drove her husband to wrathful satire and even drew a leading Catholic layman to 'spirit rappings' in the course of which he talked with a 'Buddhist spirit in misery'.[19]

These excesses came later, but they grew from a period in which the Church of England, though still entrenched, was heavily embattled. The clergy were disposed to feel secure in their own position in face of dissent or infidelity, but the more intelligent were coming to realize that complacency was ill-founded. Their Church had emerged from conflict and controversy in the sixteenth and seventeenth centuries. Its long reign with the full protection of the State was drawing to a close: there were challenges which struck at the roots of its being and which were to bring great gains out of seeming loss.

The gloomy picture of the spiritual state of the Church of England just before the Oxford Movement began has been too strongly drawn, particularly by apologists of that movement. The worst was over by the time the Tractarians became articulate about the situation. One may compare the evils of industrialism, which were still bad but past their worst when they became matter for the polemical novel. The Oxford Movement was the principal but not the sole element in the Anglican revival. Both the support which it won and the opposition which it aroused were the products of a situation in which religion mattered. Men like Newman, Keble and Pusey were serious Christians disputing with other serious Christians. The lack of fervour in the Church of their young days was the result of the deliberate distrust of enthusiasm as much as of slack indifference. The Oxford Movement was a deeply religious movement in a religious age.

Nevertheless, the criticisms of the Church, from inside and from outside, had some basis. The case against was put strongly by J.A.Froude, who had grown up in a clerical household, became involved with the Tractarians and eventually cut away from his Anglican allegiance. His diatribe is in a tone which many others adopted, and it is not totally unjust. Froude understood the tensions and pressures better than most men, though he wrote out of a personal suffering in which the bad examples seemed to outdo the good.

What a sight must this age of ours have been to an earnest believing man like Newman, who had an eye to see it, and an ear to hear its voices? A foolish Church, chattering, parrot-like, old notes, of which it had forgot the meaning; a clergy who not only thought not at all, but whose heavy ignorance, from long unreality, clung about them like a garment, and who mistook their fool's cap and bells for a crown of wisdom, and the music of the spheres; selfishness alike recognized practically as the rule of conduct, and faith in God, in man, in virtue, exchanged for faith in the belly, in fortunes, carriages, lazy sofas, and cushioned pews; Bentham politics and Paley religion; all the thought deserving to be called thought, the flowing

tide of Germany, and the philosophy of Hume and Gibbon; all
the spiritual feeling, the light froth of the Wesleyans and Evangelicals; and the only real stern life to be found anywhere in a strong
resolved and haughty independence, heaving and rolling under the
chaff-spread surface. How was it likely to fare with the clergy gentlemen and the Church turned respectable, in the struggle with enemies like these?[20]

Here are themes and words that will come up often in our
exploration – the clergy rich, time-serving, ignorant; the easy
accommodation of utilitarian secularism; the threats of new
German rationalism and old British scepticism; the shallow
emotionalism of the Evangelical section. How valid, as a total
concept, was the attack on a 'foolish Church'?

Although the diversities within were not yet fully developed
or strongly marked by outward practice, the Church of England was not monolithic. In the early years of the Oxford
Movement she seemed to be 'a bundle of religious systems
without number'.[21] For the majority there was no problem in
falling in with the requirements of the Book of Common
Prayer as interpreted in the most Protestant sense. The emphasis in public worship was on preaching rather than on sacrament. Celebrations of Holy Communion were infrequent and
without ceremony: usually four times a year though sometimes
more often. There is evidence, however, that 'Sacrament Sunday' brought a large congregation in many parishes and
that the attitude was reverent on the part of both priest and
people. The simplicity of form was compensated by that
decency and orderliness which are fundamental concepts in
Anglicanism.

There is evidence of the other extreme too, of instances of
pluralism whereby a man could hold more than one benefice
and draw the main revenues for the cost of an underpaid curate
too overwhelmed by financial worry to give much pastoral
care. Then, as always, the Church had her scandals as well as
her saints. The significance of what happened in Oxford from
1833 does not rest ultimately on either extreme. It depends
largely on the fact that the Anglican clergy, good, bad or unfortunate, were almost all united in their acceptance of the
Church of England as a Church established by law. The ultimate protector and the supreme legislator was the Crown. The

Church had the right to tithe and to oversee the flock, with the concomitant duty to obey enactments legally made.

Some clergymen took their duties more seriously than others; few indeed thought of themselves as priests in the Apostolic order, endowed with spiritual powers and obligations which might conflict with their role in the established system. Not all had sought ordination simply as a means of earning a living, but few indeed had seen it as a sacramental seal on a divine calling. How could it be so understood when there were no theological colleges, when the examination of ordinands was rudimentary or non-existent? Consider the clergy of Jane Austen, men not shown as generally contemptible: Mr Collins is an unusually nasty piece of work. Yet they inspire little respect beyond that given to their social position. Edmund Bertram is at some trouble to explain that he has chosen to be a clergyman and is not entering on the profession purely for family reasons, although Miss Crawford is unconvinced and sees him as 'fit for something better'.[22]

To regard the Church as a part of the national system, a profession within which both the privileges and the obligations of the national law operated, was to take a 'Low' view. Neither 'High' nor 'Low' in regard to churchmanship had the connotations of doctrine and practice which were later associated with them. The general, conformist view of the Church of England was Low; its opponents sometimes called it Erastian. The belief that the Church should be subject to the ordinances of the State might find philosophical justification in Selden and Hobbes, with pragmatic approval in a general desire for lawful order and a distrust of sects.

The High Churchman counted himself an equally loyal citizen but was more inclined to stress the rights of the Church as an abiding institution which the State had not created. He looked with some favour on the example of the non-jurors who had been deprived for refusing the Oath of Allegiance to William III. Without being greatly exercised by any residual Stuart claims, he found strength in the Caroline divines who had promulgated a theory of the Church within which Anglicanism had an honourable identity and who had regarded their ministry as something more than a Crown licence to preach.

However, High Church was a comprehensive and sometimes vague description. It could include those whose main claim to it was the Tory resistance to Whig encroachments on ecclesiastical privilege but who were otherwise content with the standard practice of the State Church. The more theologically minded of the High wing could nevertheless hold that their priesthood was within the Apostolic Succession on which Newman based the appeal of the first of the *Tracts for the Times*. This doctrine appeared, for instance, in Daubeny's *Guide to the Church* (1798) and Van Mildert's Bampton Lectures (1814). The group known as the Hackney Phalanx or the Clapton Sect, led by Joshua Watson, took a view that foreshadowed the early Tracts, though those who lived to see it were mostly repelled by the Romeward movement of Newman and others. A High Doctrine of the Church as a divine society rather than a department of State was held by believers as distant from the Tractarians and from one another as the Evangelicals and the Noetics.

The Whig Low Churchmen in fact did not have things all their own way even before 1833; and theological principles were intertwined with politics in the years leading up to the new movement. The fact that many High Churchmen accepted views expressed in Laudian days inclined them towards a Catholic interpretation of their churchmanship, with an opposition to Rome that was bigoted but better reasoned than other Protestants could produce. When the increasing challenge of secular control became urgent, the underlying theological principles were emphasized and brought into public controversy. Hurrell Froude and John Keble both grew up in clerical families where traditional High Church principles were held, and on this basis, different though they were in temperament, built a structure that altered the face of their beloved but threatened Church.

High and Low alike, the clergy were not well placed in public esteem. The wealth and temporal assets of the higher dignitaries had grown and were emphasized by the poverty not only of the lay working class but of many of the ordinary priests; though some of the parochial incumbents were rich men. The bishops were members of the House of Lords, where their presence seemed to symbolize the radical view that clergymen in general were State hirelings, the oppressive allies of the landowning class. When John Sterling described the parson as 'a black dragoon in every parish'[23] he may have provoked laughter among his contemporaries at Cambridge but he said something that many in the nation would approve. The muttering became a roar of fury when the bishops, with only two exceptions, voted against the first Reform Bill. 'It was not safe for a clergyman to appear in the streets,' Sydney Smith recalled when the crisis was past.[24] In Bristol the Bishop's palace was burnt; a dead cat was thrown at the Archbishop of Canterbury in his coach; stones and insults were hurled even at humbler members of the clergy. The popular dislike of anything that emphasized the special position of the priesthood was another cause of hostility to the Tractarians in the years to come.

For Churchmen did not cease to be targets for hostility when the Reform Act was eventually passed. The new Parliament of 1832 was indeed much less reformed than some had hoped and others had feared; but it was in a reforming mood. There had been a taste of what could be done through the legislative process, and the reactionary attitude of the majority of the clerical Establishment was not forgotten. A series of attacks on ecclesiastical privilege began.

The Church from which issued the *Tracts for the Times* was a Church under fire. In 1832 Lord Henley, Peel's Evangelical brother-in-law, produced his *Plan of Church Reform*. He proposed, among other things, the redistribution of revenue by reducing cathedral and collegiate establishments, the removal of the few remaining disabilities on dissenters and the formation of a commission to manage Church income and property. The Ecclesiastical Commission was set up after the report of the Ecclesiastical Duties and Revenues Committee which investigated the matter in 1835 and 1836.

Thus the Church of England was dragged protesting into the new age, to undergo the typical nineteenth-century process of agitation followed by inquiry, report and legislation. Various legal measures were passed which reduced the huge gaps between the highest and the lowest clerical incomes, rooted out the worst cases of pluralism and produced better parochial stipends at the expense of some rich prebends. What inequality remained can be seen in the pages of Trollope two decades later.

At the same time the native Irish got a certain oblique revenge for centuries of suffering. The Anglican Church in Ireland was in a peculiarly vulnerable position once the Whig attacks had begun in earnest. She had the status and privileges of establishment while numbering only a small fraction of the population as her flock. Closer scrutiny of the anomaly came as more intelligent Englishmen turned their interest towards Ireland – some from a simple love of justice, others from curiosity about a country where Roman Catholic dominance in faith could be observed without leaving the British Isles. The retreat from orthodoxy of both Francis Newman and J. A. Froude was hastened by their experiences in Ireland.

The Irish Catholics, mostly poor and ignorant through little fault of their own, were valuable to those who looked for any stick with which to beat Papistry. The fact of Protestant control over the government and economics of the country was conveniently ignored. Yet the contrast between the wretched state of the peasants and the comparative wealth of the English Church in their land was not always seen complacently:

> The revenue of the Irish Roman Catholic Church is made of half-pence, potatoes, rags, bones and fragments of old clothes; and those Irish old clothes. They worship often in hovels, or in the open air, from the *want* of any place of worship. Their religion is the religion of three-fourths of the population! Not far off, in a well-windowed and well-roofed house, is a well-paid Protestant clergyman, preaching to stools and hassocks, and crying in the wilderness; near him the clerk, near him the sexton, near him the sexton's wife – furious against the errors of Popery, and willing to lay down their lives for the great truths established at the Diet of Augsburg.[25]

The questioning which these contrasts caused brought the whole idea of Establishment in consideration. Was the Irish parson preaching to stools and hassocks so much worse than the English one who seldom preached in his parish at all? A beneficed clergyman, a prebendary, a bishop, could defy almost any attempt to remove them for inadequate performance of duties. The age was not so tolerant of sinecures as the previous one had been.

Some clergy too were beginning to wonder if the link with the State was entirely beneficial to the Church. The whittling down of temporal power gave new importance to the indelible nature of priesthood. What had sustained the despised Romanists through the penal centuries? Could a Church in fact be stronger, holier, more spiritual, without the hand of Government poised to crush as well as to protect? Questions like these were being asked in Oxford and elsewhere.

While many of the reformers were loyal churchmen seeking to improve a corrupt situation, others saw in legislation the means of undermining the Church of England. She seemed 'ripe for dissolution'[26] in the view of Jeremy Bentham, who carried most of his disciples with him in the opinion that traditional religious institutions were outworn, useless, an offence against efficiency and the general tidying of society. He struck a blow against the older universities, Oxford in particular, when he helped to found the new University College in London which soon became 'the monument, totem and temple of the forward-looking, anti-classical, non-Anglican reformers'.[27]

Open atheism was still unfashionable even in the House of Commons, as Bradlaugh was later to discover. Already, however, objections were being more freely voiced against the assumptions of Christianity rather than against this or that Church. As the most powerful institution, the Church of England was the most sharply attacked. The attackers came in many shapes and colours, united only in the belief held by James Mill that the '*ne plus ultra* of wickedness . . . was embodied in what is commonly presented to mankind as the creed of Christianity'.[28] Many of those in the raionalist line of Locke and Hume had kept up a cynical outward conformity while established religion was accepted with little question and were now emboldened to more open dissent. Others had adopted one of the several varieties of Deism – a creed as productive of sects as the Trinitarian orthodoxy which affronted it – ranging from belief in moral government of the present world to vague postulation of a withdrawn First Mover. The Industrial Revolution had brought sufferings that produced a tough anti-clerical pragmatism in men like Robert Owen. There was the moral objection, voiced by Paine and echoed in the next generation, against the faith that seemed to depend on fear of 'a God who kept a hell prison-house'.[29] There was the challenge, as yet slight but steadily growing, of a more confident and mechanistic science. And, still little known outside the company of a few theologians like the young Professor Pusey, there were the probings of German rationalist criticism.

With such challenges and uncertainties it was no wonder that many Anglicans felt that anxiety about the future which was to haunt them and their successors all through the century. Not only the disenchanted believed that the Church of England had barely escaped alive: fifty years later, Newman's brother-in-law looked back to the time just before the Oxford Movement began, when:

> Every party, every interest, political or religious, in this country was pushing its claim to universal acceptance, with the single exception of the Church of England, which was folding its robes to die with what dignity it could.[30]

Yet it was not a question of loyalty or opposition to a moribund institution. The attacks showed that there was less indifferent religious acquiescence than there had been fifty years earlier. On the more positive side, the Evangelical revival had changed the appearance of Christianity for many people.

The Evangelical view was not the dominant Victorian mode of faith; nor was it totally opposed from the start to the Oxford Movement; nor was it confined to a single denomination. It was general in the nonconformist churches but had substantial support in the Church of England. Methodism had started as an attempt to evangelize the Church of England, but Wesley had been excluded from some Anglican pulpits for his Arminian view that the benefit of Christ's redemption was freely available to all. Strict Evangelicals, both churchmen and dissenters, followed Whitefield in the austere Calvinist belief that some individuals were elected to salvation and that for them alone Christ had died.

A change of religious temper came over the country towards the end of the eighteenth century. There was a new seriousness, caused partly by the Napoleonic threat and the concomitant domestic troubles, which prepared the way for the earnest Victorian agnostic as well as for the Anglo-Catholic revival.

Fear of atheism, militant and destructive in the pattern of the Jacobins, made a link between dissenters and Anglicans. Divines of all churches sprang to the defence of Christianity with the learned publication of 'evidences' to assert the inalienable truth of their faith. Yet the Evangelical revival was, unlike the Oxford Movement, never primarily a clerical matter. Indeed, it did little to exalt the position of the clergy, and some of the most influential Evangelicals like Wilberforce and Shaftesbury were laymen.

The Evangelical emphasis was on personal salvation by acceptance of Christ's saving power. After conviction of sin and a realization that unaided human nature was in a state of total depravity, there should be repentance, a humble acknowledgement of justification in Christ, followed by assurance of pardon and of perseverance to final salvation. This encounter between Christ and the individual soul could be mediated by no person or institution, though preaching could open the heart to conversion. Sacraments were effective not for any power inherent in them or in their minister but as tokens of what Christ had done and commanded. Salvation could be merited by no works: the insistence on faith alone brought a danger of antinomianism to the weaker brethren. The great philanthropists of the movement, and the lives of humbler men and women too, proved that the Evangelical could be active in love. The highly individualist doctrine put emphasis on self-improvement and duties of thrifty activity which accorded well with the temper of the age – and perhaps helped to form that temper. A sense of social responsibility soon developed. Nevertheless, there was a danger that spirituality would neglect the intellectual demands on human nature and 'leave it a fallow field for all unsightly weeds to flourish in'.[31]

It is not to be supposed that the whole nation experienced an Evangelical conversion. Many people were repelled by the negative side of the movement – its puritanism, its exclusionist attitude, its tendency to self-congratulation and smugness. The Evangelicals were strong sabbatarians, and what they gave humanely by keeping Sunday as a day of rest they took away by making it a day of gloom. They could seem reactionary enemies of the working man who had no other chance for recreation but who found the doors closed and the chance of travel restricted.

To oppose sabbatarianism became a proof of opposition to the whole Evangelical principle. Francis Newman as a boy was upset when his father commanded him to copy a letter on Sunday and his refusal was supported by his elder brother. J.A. Froude recalled how people had worried themselves about what was or was not permissible on Sunday – letters could be read but not written, serious books were accepted, but not novels or newspapers. Places of entertainment were closed; London museums and art galleries did not open on Sundays until 1896.

Another Evangelical feature was the support of missions. The establishment of new missionary bodies helped to shake the old Anglican societies from their torpor and consequently to produce a period of unedifying sectarian squabbling in the mission field. In contrast, an early blow for ecumenism was struck by the Evangelical British and Foreign Bible Society with its dual secretariat of an Anglican and a dissenter. The opposition could find in attention to heathens abroad yet another sign of indifference to sufferings at home, an image immortalized by Dickens in the chaotic state of Mrs Jellaby's family. Yet missionizing at home was active and often criticized. Exeter Hall in the Strand was a centre of Evangelical preaching, in which Irish clergy and laymen played a prominent part. Their natural eloquence, applied to militant Protestantism through their minority position at home, gained them fame or notoriety. One of the few points on which Kingsley and Newman were ever in agreement appears in their attitude to the characters of O'Blareaway in *Yeast* and O'Niggins of the Roman Priest Conversion Branch of the Tract Society in *Loss and Gain*.

The greatest influence of the Evangelicals in institutional religion was exercised when their spiritual fervour had waned and the observation could be made that: 'Preached in the pulpits of fashionable chapels, this religion proved to be no more exacting than its "High and Dry" rival.'[32] Their very success had tended to make them static within the framework of specific organizations. They were probably at their strongest as a national pressure-group between 1850 and 1860, when the

Evangelical Sumner was Archbishop of Canterbury and Palmerston was the political leader. The divisions in the Anglican Church following the Oxford Movement, and the excesses which marked some aspects of that movement in the second generation helped to bring new respect for Evangelicals. The assertion of the Protestant position and the desire for firmer links with nonconformity were natural for those who feared that the alternative was a further drift to Rome. By 1870, Matthew Arnold marked the decline:

> The Evangelical clergy no longer recruits itself with success, no longer lays hold on such promising subjects as formerly. It is losing the future and feels that it is losing it. Its signs of a vigorous life, its gaiety and audacity, are confined to its older members, too powerful to lose their own vigour, but without successors to whom to transmit it.[33]

Though they might be influential, the Evangelicals were never widely popular. They came to see themselves as the divine answer to Puseyism, but they were deplored by many staunch English Protestants who continued to regard as dangerous all extremes in religion. Broad Churchmen like Kingsley who hated Roman and Anglo-Catholics were equally scathing about Evangelicals. Frances Trollope painted a bitter picture of an Evangelical clergyman in *The Vicar of Wrexhill* (1837). Her son, though as we have seen not very theologically penetrating, found Evangelicalism a blanket condemnation for the Proudies and Slopes. Dickens brought out humbug and cant in Evangelical terms with Stiggins and Chadband. No major novelist of the period had a good word to say for the extreme Evangelical.

The novelists expressed what was widely felt: 'the British public feared Puseyites and despised Evangelicals.'[34] There was a general assumption, almost as potent as the folk-myths about Roman Catholics, that the Evangelical discourse masked hypocrisy, complacency and greed. The nature of their profession made it easy to accuse the Evangelicals of spiritual selfishness. At Oxford their stock was very low by 1830 and they could easily be discounted as holding no firm theological position.[35] Yet the Oxford Movement owed much to those who cared enough about religion to be unpopular for its sake and who provided a climate of moral seriousness in which other emphases could grow. The Evangelical spirit was highly susceptible to abuse by charlatans, but it also produced some of the noblest Victorians. It is worth remembering that Pusey once said: 'I love the Evangelicals because they love our Lord.'[36]

Despite the gloom of some of her adherents and the exultation of her opponents, there was still life in the Church of England when the Oxford Movement began. The strength to fight back against the growth of infidelity was provided by Evangelical fervour and by the High Church assurance of a city not built with hands. The backward longing for the days of Caroline Anglican ascendancy could produce something more than nostalgia, and Romantic enthusiasm for the Middle Ages brought an exaggerated but encouraging notion of a society in which faith was universal and the Church powerful. Although the Romantic Revival was to be blamed for the trappings of later Anglo-Catholic extremists, it had also helped to bring new religious orientations. Borrow could sneer at Scott's effect on 'Charlie over the waterism' and his glorification of Stuart legitimism. Newman never ceased to look on Scott's novels as an anticipation of some aspects of the movement:

The general need . . . of something deeper and more attractive than what had offered itself elsewhere, may be considered to have led to his popularity; and by means of his popularity he reacted on his readers, stimulating their mental thirst, feeding their hopes, setting before them visions, which, when once seen, are not easily forgotten.[37]

The older Romantic poets had their place in the genesis of the movement, though the younger generation were regarded as sadly fallen into disbelief and immorality. Wordsworth's late rediscovery of loyalty to the Church of England could not fail to be encouraging to those like Keble who regarded his poetry with admiration amounting almost to reverence. Wordsworth was not a systematic thinker; he found in the Church a means of particularizing, with all the associations of dignity and tradition, the more general and mystical spirituality of his earlier years.

Coleridge was intellectually tougher and his influence was correspondingly more widespread. Through Maurice he became a source of Broad Church inspiration which reached its height after the first impetus of the Oxford Movement was over. But on that movement too he had his effect, most of all perhaps through his insistence on the absolute need of the individual for faith rather than the production of reasoned 'evidences'. His respect for historical development and his concept of a universal, supernatural Church as distinct from the national 'clerisy' that might not necessarily be Christian, all gave backing to the anti-Erastian school. Here was the doctrine of a Church which had neither been created by the State nor could be changed by it in a moment of time.[38]

A more political warrant for High Church claims came from the new Toryism, derived again partly from Coleridge and from Burke, which offered more respect to the Established Church in a reuniting of ancient national strands against the divisive force of Whiggery and mercantilism. The relationship between Church and State was forcing itself on the attention of all thinking men in those years. Some saw the answer in the kind of syncretism which Arnold proposed in his *Principles of Church Reform* (1833), a truly Christian State whose national Church should comprehend all believers except Socinians, Quakers and (of course) Roman Catholics. The leaders of the Oxford Movement saw in this proposal the confirmation of some of their worst fears.

From fears as well as from hopes there grew a revival which changed the face of the Church of England and touched in some way all who retained any concern with the Christian faith. Anglicans found themselves members of a Church with claims more lofty than the old 'High and Dry' adherents had ever thought to make; Roman Catholics, in the euphoria that followed Emancipation and then the restoration of the hierarchy, were compelled to defend their claim to unique catholicity; Protestants of all denominations had to think harder about the positive nature of their protest and the distinctiveness of their confessions.

There were gains and there were losses, for individuals and for Churches. For many who stood firm there grew a new vision, of something scarcely to be recognized in the Church of their youth. Thus it appeared to one who, guided by a leader of the early movement, claimed for herself neither sanctity nor heroism:

It spoke of the glorious company to which they belonged: of the Angels at their side; of the Saints made perfect, who were their brethren; of the whole Catholic Church praying with them and for them; of the Comforter within their hearts; of the Brother who is touched with a feeling of our infirmities; of the Father whose hand is ever over us. Dreary and dark the world around might be, but the path of the righteous would only be a shining light, shining more and more unto the perfect day.[39]

How different from the attitude of Mr Harding, that kindly and respected old clergyman, who 'performs afternoon service every Sunday, and administers the Sacrament once in every three months'.[40] The tensions between those views of the Church of England made the Oxford Movement necessary and inevitable.

2
Twelve Years

The preaching of a special sermon before His Majesty's judges at the opening of an Assize was but one of the many ways in which the links between Church and State were maintained. The Oxford Assize Sermon on 14 July 1833 was given in the University Church of St Mary by John Keble, Fellow of Oriel College. A cynical auditor might have noted that the date was that of the fall of the Bastille in 1789, the root of many woes for Tories and High Churchmen. If he had listened attentively to the preacher he would have had more thoughts on the irony of the occasion.

Keble's Assize Sermon made little immediate stir in the sleepy Oxford of the long vacation; but it was as notable in its way as the display of Luther's theses or the assassination at Sarajevo. Occasions are important as foci of deep and complex causes, and these were plentiful in 1833. Keble spoke for many in the Church of England, of different shades of opinion, who were dissatisfied with the increasing encroachment of governmental power on Church affairs, impatient of the way many people regarded the Church as a polite adjunct to social life, and alarmed by the attacks of dissenters and atheists. Keble touched on these matters and fulminated, if the word is appropriate for that gentle but fearless man, against indifference in religion:

Under the guise of charity and toleration we are come almost to this pass; that no difference in matters of faith, is to disqualify for our approbation and confidence, whether in public or domestic life. Can we conceal it from ourselves, that every year the practice is becoming more and more common, of trusting men unreservedly in the most delicate and important matters, without one serious inquiry, whether they do not hold principles which make it impossible for them to be loyal to their Creator, Redeemer and Sanctifier? Are not offices conferred, partnerships formed, intimacies entered upon – nay (what is almost too painful to think of), do not parents commit their children to be educated, do they not encourage them to intermarry, in houses on which the Apostolical Authority would rather teach them to set a mark, as unfit to be entered by a faithful servant of Christ?[1]

'National Apostasy' was the title under which the sermon was later published, with a prefatory note that 'the calamity in anticipation of which [it] was written' had come to pass. Ten Irish bishoprics had been suppressed by Parliamentary authority, contrary to the wishes of the English and Irish episcopates. It was, like many issues which the Oxford Movement was to raise over the coming years, an unfortunate choice for resistance. The power of the Church in Ireland was, as we have seen, indefensible, but for men like Keble this Act was an example of that national sickness which produced disrespect for bishops and forgetfulness that they were 'successors of the Apostles'. A High doctrine of the Church was no novelty to Keble himself:

He ever held and taught to the end what he had received from his father's teaching – that to take from God or His Church that which had in any way been consecrated to Him was sacrilege.[2]

Behind him stood not only those clergymen like his own father who looked to the Caroline tradition but also more recent churchmen like Alexander Knox and John Jebb who saw the Church of England as a particular guardian of Christian truth, avoiding the errors of Rome and of dissent.[3]

Sermons are usually soon forgotten and every preacher knows only too well that the parable of the Sower is highly apposite. Keble had no expectation of the consequences which were to flow from his words; the lost leader of the movement wrote many years later: 'I have ever considered and kept the day, as the start of the religious movement of 1833.'[4] Keble canalized something which was already swelling to flood: the sense of crisis in Church affairs, the urgent need to stop the erosion of ecclesiastical status and make primary again the notion of a divine society. 'Those who can recall the feeling of those days,' one contemporary wrote, 'will at once remember the deep depression into which the Church had fallen, and the gloomy forebodings universally prevalent.'[5] Yet disquiet might not have risen into action had not four clergymen met ten days after the Assize Sermon at the rectory of Hadleigh in Suffolk. Three of them are little remembered today, but their names deserve honour from all who see any lasting significance in the Oxford Movement. They were the Rector of Hadleigh – H.J.Rose, a Cambridge man who had already brushed with Pusey over the dangers of German rationalism; William Palmer, of Dublin and at that time of Oxford, perhaps the outstanding liturgical scholar of the time; Arthur Perceval, the son of a peer, a former pupil of Keble's and a royal chaplain.[6]

The fourth participant was a young Fellow of Oriel, another of Keble's past pupils and now his colleague. Richard Hurrell Froude, a man of ebullient temper and personal charm, 'a bold rider, as on horseback, so also in his speculations',[7] was the type to inspire more cautious minds with the religious enthusiasm that their generation as a whole distrusted. He was a child of the Romantic period, impatient of the eighteenth-century distrust of extremism which was still prevalent – and not least in Oxford. His influence over greater men has reasonably been called 'the true genesis of the Oxford Movement',[8] and he himself left posthumous record: 'If I was ever asked what good deed I had ever done, I should say that I had brought Keble and Newman to understand each other.'[9]

Froude combined the traditional High Churchman's view with a new vision. His father was an archdeacon who had imbued him with the principle of opposition to the Erastian idea but had not encouraged further theological speculation. While most High Churchmen honoured the Caroline and Elizabethan divines, Hurrell Froude looked back beyond the Reformation to the centuries when the Catholic Church of the West was undivided. A new cult of medievalism had flowered in Romanticism; it revealed to Froude an age of faith and Christian living when the Church was greater than the State. His friends in the new movement did not go so far; but the revival was to derive much of good and of ill from him. He played his part in the growing myth of medieval glory, potent in different ways over Anglicans, Roman Catholics and agnostic socialists.

In another way, too, Froude was prepared to go beyond the others. While they were concerned – more and more as time went on – to prove the true catholicity of the Church of England, he wanted to find out exactly where catholicity had been preserved and where it had been lost. In pursuit of that quest he was willing to deny assumptions that the others took for granted; he broadened the cause and also endangered it. He drove himself with the manic recklessness of the consumptive and left a troublesome legacy after his death. He lacked the quiet sanctity of Keble and the deep inner commitment of Newman. Beneath the show of vigour he was a tormented character, full of the tensions and scruples which the movement was to engender in many then young or yet unborn. As he fought with himself, he fought with the outward enemy as well, rejoicing in the clash of battle between Church and State.

The Hadleigh conference might have produced no more than conferences are apt to do. The four who met there had the idea of forming an association of churchmen to resist State encroachments of the kind which Keble's sermon had attacked. It came to nothing, beyond addresses to the Archbishop of Canterbury in the following year which supported those principles with a substantial number of clerical and lay signatures. These gave further proof that the Church of England was not totally sunk in Erastian torpor. But whatever encouragement it may have given to Archbishop Howley, this indication of loyalty did not suggest that anything new and exciting was afoot. Yet it helped to give a sense of solidarity which could strengthen what had already begun at Oxford after Froude returned there from Hadleigh.

Oxford in 1833 was a reassuring place for loyal or timid members of the Church of England. 'Oxford was emphatically definite, dogmatic, orthodox, compared even with Cambridge.'[10] Within her confines she was an epitome of those powers and privileges towards which jealous eyes were turning at Westminster. Matriculation, graduation and fellowships were limited to Anglicans, or at least to those who would sub-scribe to the thirty-nine Articles. Each college had its chapel at which a certain number of attendances were compulsory for undergraduates in residence. All the great moments of the academic year had religious orientation with their special formularies, their bidding prayers or sermons. Unhappily, the less satisfactory side of the national Church was reflected in the light pressure of these duties on the majority. Termly communion was compulsory and was often followed by excesses of eating and drinking which shocked the more serious, whether High or Evangelical. 'It did not seem . . . strange or a profanation that a whole mixed crowd of undergraduates should be expected to go on a certain Sunday in term, willing or unwilling, fit or unfit, to the Sacrament, and be fined if they did not appear.'[11]

Yet out of the conformism, the sinecures, the amassed revenues from old endowments, a new spirit was already growing. There were Fellows to whom faith was true and serious, some of whom became leaders in the new movement. Matthew Arnold saw Oxford forty years later as producing 'more knowledge, more light', but lacking the great personalities of his undergraduate days.[12] For the majority of his contemporaries, less gifted with high seriousness, Oxford in the thirties was a grand finishing school before emergence into adult life. Its purpose was to consummate what his public school had done for the young man; not to knock back, as Max Beerbohm said, the nonsense which that school had knocked out of him.

The very topography of the place seemed to insulate it against the entry of new and alarming ideas. It was still 'that Oxford in which it was a principle of the President of John's that there should be no houses between their college and the country'.[13] There were virtually no suburbs; the coach rolled across Magdalen Bridge after passing no more than a small huddle of houses around St Clement's. But the coach was soon to give way to the railway and Oxford was to be dragged more and more into the new world of quick communications where privilege was going out and reforms were coming in.

Not that Oxford had done nothing to reform herself already. Oriel College had led the way towards elected fellowships by examination, with continuous recruitment of the brightest young men from all colleges. Some, like Hartley Coleridge, did not survive beyond their probationary year. Others remained, to cause unforeseen divisions in the college which had chosen them. Keble was one of the Oriel Fellows, already a respected figure in Oxford when the Assize Sermon was preached. He had a brilliant academic record, a double first at the age of eighteen and the winning of both the Latin and the English essay prizes. His reputation had become national as a religious poet with the publication of *The Christian Year* in 1827. Like Froude he was a High Churchman by upbringing, a man suspicious of the current liberal morality which placed stress on particular good works and made people satisfied with a 'shadow of religion' to the neglect of those eternal values which should govern conduct.[14]

It was fitting that Keble launched the Oxford Movement which, for all its dynamism and all the changes of personal commitment which it brought, was essentially backward-looking. He was the product of a quiet country parsonage, a man whose knowledge of England was limited to Oxford and the rural south, a priest who had no patience with speculation and for whom doubt was sin. 'Truth was a master to be served, not to be criticized; it was like the ark which he dreaded to touch with unconsecrated hands.'[15] Yet he had great gifts which were equally significant for the movement: a deeply sacramental sense, a sanctified Romanticism which found the presence of God in all material creation. He had experience of parish work and carried Tractarian ideas back into parish life in the early years. Newman revered him and came to love him; when Keble shook his hand on his own election to Oriel, 'I seemed desirous of quite sinking into the ground'.[16]

Keble's pupils during his tutorship at Oriel had included as well as Hurrell Froude, two bright young men called Robert Wilberforce and Isaac Williams. All three, who had come to know and love their tutor on vacation reading parties as well as in college, represented different aspects of the movement. Wilberforce, a son of the great Evangelical, was destined to pass through the Tractarian years and across to Rome, causing one of the family splits which brought tragedy into the complexities of religious allegiance. Williams, who always believed that his conversion grew from his association with Keble, remained in Anglicanism and defended its catholicity by delving into the history of the ancient Celtic Church.

With such affection, such general respect, it is not surprising that Keble was mentioned for the Provostship of Oriel which fell vacant on the appointment of Whately as Archbishop of Dublin. He did not hold even his admirers to the point of voting for him: Newman summed it up when he wrote, 'We are not electing an angel but a Provost'.[17] Keble was not the man to hold an administrative helm through storms of controversy. His true quality was recognized when he was elected Professor of Poetry in 1831. Thus the Assize Sermon was the work of a man known for good influence, already seen to have strong views about the question of Parliamentary power over the Church now that the House of Commons was open to members who need not be Anglicans. For him the Church of England was part of the Holy, Catholic and Apostolic Church, and it was intolerable that she should be ultimately governed by a legislature 'the members of which are not even bound to profess belief in the Atonement'.[18] In 1835 he married and returned to parish life; he was out of Oxford when the movement was at its height, but he had helped to start something which in many ways outran his expectations and his desires. He had led some of his contemporaries and juniors to a position from which revival could grow: the Anglican claim of 'the best possible title' to carrying on the commands of Christ, 'provided always that nothing heretical or otherwise immoral be inserted in the terms of communion'.[19]

For a man of Keble's background these matters were axioms to be defended rather than proved. For others, however, they were revelations, and it was these men who took the movement away from extreme High Churchmanship in the old tradition. As well as Froude and Keble, there were Oriel Fellows who were thinking and caring deeply about the condition of the Church. One of them was John Henry Newman, who had been elected in 1821 after a brilliant examination which made nonsense of his poor performance in the Schools. His childhood had been not in a country parsonage but in a London family where business worries and failures were more usual topics of conversation than theology.

Yet, in common with many who came under Evangelical

influence, he had experienced as a boy the sense of conversion
and the assurance of salvation. A schoolmaster, Walter Mayers,
had directed his reading and started him on the quest for
religious truth which led him at last to Rome but not even then
to the end of seeking. Oxford fed still more the appetite for
religious inquiry, and gave employment to a man who drove
himself hard and would follow through a problem at whatever
cost to himself or to his friends.

Newman had just returned from travelling abroad in July
1833. The journey had been started with Froude for the sake
of the latter's health, but Newman too had fallen ill and come
near to death. What he saw in Italy confirmed his prejudice
against Roman Catholicism but gave him an uneasy sense that
there was more to this foreign Church than Englishmen generally supposed. While he was recovering from sickness, there
came to him a conviction that he had work to do at home. He
was ripe for the warnings of Keble and the exhortations of
Froude. Newman was a man who believed in destiny,
sanctified as the Will of God.

Yet this new certainty was a confirmation rather than a
sudden epiphany. Oxford had been working its influence on
the middle-class Evangelical and had begun to turn him into
the leader of a movement that would change the aspect of
religion in friend and foe alike. From being 'in a loose and
rough way . . . counted among the few Liberals and Evangelicals in Oxford',[20] he was becoming a strong defender of Church
privilege and a supporter of tradition. As a man with the
Evangelical experience of conversion, able to understand the
party which at that time gave the only real force that English
Protestantism possessed, he was starting from presuppositions
different from those of Froude and Keble.

They had already given him an understanding of High
Church principles. Whately, the Provost of Oriel when Newman became a Fellow, had taught him the principles of logic
and how to apply them to such matters as Church Establishment. From the rough shaking of Whately, a great sheepdog
of a man who drove home his teaching by force of personality,
he came to the smoother influence of Hawkins. The new Provost slipped under Newman's guard of Evangelical individualism the notion of tradition, of a body of doctrine handed on

through the continuing Church and not dependent on subjective experience for its preservation. Hawkins taught him also the doctrinal importance of the historic creeds.

Newman, however, was bringing to the new revival qualities which he had not learned from either his elders or his contemporaries. Darkness and tragedy in the life of faith were realities to him. In his sermons and his writing, then and always, he stressed the cost of believing, the probability that perseverance would bring suffering. For all the changes and developments that he underwent, he never shed the sense of personal encounter, the self-examination that verged on morbid introspection, the sense of numinous awe, the thirst for holiness in this world. These were aspects of faith not peculiar to the Evangelical temper, but it was in Evangelical circles that they were most often heard discussed. Newman's gift was to take them from the realm of loose, undirected piety and subject them to the discipline of a great intellect.

The combination was irresistible for the young men with whom he was in tutorial and pastoral relationship. The challenge of difficulty brings response from young people, especially in a society where the prevailing tone is optimism to the point of complacency. Those who followed him might lose the comforts as well as the gloom of Calvinism, exchanging assurance of salvation and final perseverance for faith which clung to the Church and her sacraments in a pilgrimage through a world that was dark, threatening, uncomprehending. For, like many Evangelicals, Newman already highly valued sacramental life. He was taking Holy Communion fortnightly when he was an undergraduate, a degree of devotion which his parents thought excessive.[21] It was not surprising that a young woman noted in her journal a few years later, when the Oxford Movement was at its height: 'Have been reading Newman's Sermons. They have made me feel afraid.'[22]

For a man who distrusted the comfortable way in religion, the easy association of Church and State was irksome. His opposition to the complex of attitudes known as Liberalism was equally grounded in dislike of the assumption that all things were well and tending to become better. The Protestant emphasis in the Church of England was beginning to seem arrogant in its reliance on individual interpretation of the

Bible, coupled with a minimum of submission to ecclesiastical duties. A Church that put so much faith in the essential goodness of the individual and allowed him to find his own way to truth must be lacking in sanctity. Yet the Church of Rome seemed to crush the individual by a weight of organizational and doctrinal compulsions. To make a triumph out of seemingly insoluble dilemmas was Newman's greatest gift to the Church that he later joined, and a valuable legacy to the Church which he left.

The Fellow elected to Oriel in the year after Newman was Edward Bouverie Pusey. He shared the High Church tradition in which Froude and Keble had grown up, but in a different environment. He came not from the country parsonage but from a rich lay family with aristocratic connections. He thus had secular as well as religious reasons for disliking the new tendencies in politics and the erosion of traditional privileges. Newman, admiring his goodness and devotion, distrusted him as a stern opponent of the Evangelical party. Pusey was already one of the outstanding scholars in Oxford by 1833. He was Professor of Hebrew, and in pursuit of information on that language, as yet little studied in England, had travelled to Germany. There the new Biblical criticism had excited rather than dismayed him and he had returned to defend it against more cautious conservatives like Rose of Hadleigh.

Pusey was destined to become the leader of the Oxford Movement after Newman went; his name would become its name, to be revered or execrated above most names in England at that time. He would be suspended from preaching for doctrine contrary to his Church; he would retract many of his views about German theology. All of which seemed in 1833 to be a very unlikely future for the brilliant, shy, devout young don who played no part in the first months of excited activity after Hadleigh.

Those months were active largely because Hurrell Froude did not have the temperament that was disposed to wait for loyal addresses and associations. He wanted to do something at once, and to do it in a way that would bring his ideas to wider notice. This was a time when the printed word was gaining more respect and greater circulation than ever before. Literacy and leisure were slowly increasing; book-production was becoming cheaper and more efficient; better communications were carrying material for reading to all parts of the kingdom. The appetite for reading grew with the possibility of its satisfaction, so avidly that the privileged who took reading for granted were set thinking. The power of the printed word was seen as a potential threat to stability as well as a hope for general progress.

While the hack publishers produced a spate of cheap, sensational literature, the serious-minded were joining battle to win the new army of readers. The Benthamite Society for the Diffusion of Useful Knowledge was as zealous in its dissemination of secular learning as was the Religious Tract Society for the theological. Therefore, men like Froude concluded, why not use these new resources and assault the minds of the learned as they in turn assaulted the minds of the poor? It was true that religious tracts had a bad name among High Churchmen, arising from 'the pertinacity of good ladies who pressed them on chance strangers, and who extolled their efficacy as if it were that of a quack medicine'.[23] Yet the Church of England could be called to a sense of urgency in these dangerous times by a judicious series of tracts. Let them be called, then, *Tracts for the Times*.

The first of the series was written by Newman and appeared in September 1833 under the forbidding title, 'Thoughts on the Ministerial Commission, respectfully addressed to the clergy'. It had only four pages, but with the concentrated intellectual power expressed in lucid prose that only Newman of the Anglican party could have written. He published it anonymously – 'I am but one of yourselves – a Presbyter' – and warned his fellow-clergy of the dangers that were threatening the Church. 'The times are very evil,' he wrote, admonishing them to support their Bishops, the successors of the Apostles – although if it became necessary 'we could not wish them a more blessed termination of their course than the spoiling of their goods and martyrdom.'

It was not the kind of commendation that the Bishops would welcome; and the doctrine of the Apostolic Succession was little more palatable to them. This emphasis on sacerdotal power, derived by presbyters from episcopal ordination and by bishops from an unbroken line of consecration back to

Apostolic times, was at variance with the notion of clergy commissioned to preach and perform other services within an established Church. Yet it was no more than the Ordinal of that Church claimed to do and authorized to be done. In rousing the clergy to their perilous state, Newman was forcing them to look at the nature of their office and authority. He thereby started the first serious examination of the Anglican distinctive position to be undertaken since the seventeenth century.

More tracts followed rapidly; Newman was joined in their production by Keble, Froude and his lay friend, John Bowden. The young dons rode about distributing their work to country rectors who found themselves called to accept a status which they had almost forgotten or never fully understood. Bishops were not only recommended for martyrdom but were reminded that they had a power conferred by no legislative assembly. Laymen too got hold of them: 'they gave a system to my High Church proclivities; I thought the reasoning conclusive,' one of them wrote.[24]

The tracts took on new force when Pusey was persuaded to write the eighteenth, about the practice of fasting. He was not yet fully committed to the new movement and he insisted that the tract should be signed with his initials to distinguish it as an individual production. The departure from complete anonymity was combined with his immense learning and his repute as a sound and temperate man. The tracts gained new status; from clever squibs they were becoming mines that would upheave the whole of the English Church. Ancient questions of dogma and practice were brought out of the study and into the daily life of Anglicans. The leaders of the movement were being called Tractarians, a name which spread from them to their supporters and their principles.

In Oxford and beyond, both approval and opposition grew. The moderate view, expressed in retrospect, shows what the Tracts could do for those neither within the movement nor repelled by it:

Without being a 'Tractarian' I always thought we were under an obligation to the writers of the Tracts, for having maintained (and indeed effected) a greater reverence for our Liturgy, our Creeds, our Sacraments, and our Bishops; and that they wasted the great opportunity, brought about by themselves, of raising our low notion of what is meant by 'The Church' – by shooting *beyond the mark*, and by forcing things (in some respects desirable) too far, too fast, and in too arrogant a tone.[25]

This was written long after the movement had suffered its losses and changed its early course. In the Oxford of the thirties there was some excuse for an arrogant tone, while the influence of the Tracts was enhanced by the preaching of Newman as Vicar of the University Church. Few talents are more fleeting, few more potent at the time than those of the great preacher; and the evidence of friends and enemies agrees on Newman's quality in the pulpit. Softly but with penetrating power, rapidly but with long pauses between his sentences, he made his listeners think about neglected truths rather than new ideas. In vain did hostile Heads advance the hour of evening hall; undergraduates would rather miss their dinners than Newman's sermons. Many admirers have left record of his power; let one speak who was far from sympathetic to him:

After hearing those sermons you might come away still not believing the truths peculiar to the High Church system, but you would be harder than most men if you did not feel more than ever ashamed of coarseness, selfishness, worldliness, if you did not feel the things of faith brought closer to your soul.[26]

With his dogmatic appeals to the clergy and his pastoral power over undergraduates, Newman was now one of the most influential men in Oxford. But his influence was not unchallenged, even in his own college. Newman, Keble, Pusey and Froude were a powerful quartet; yet the Liberalism which they hated found some of its most intelligent theological expression in the Senior Common Room which they shared. Those who had applied critical and logical minds to Church affairs before the Tractarian movement began were called the Noetics. It was mainly they who had made Oriel eminent among the colleges and begun the serious thinking which helped to clear the way for the Tractarians. They formed nothing so definite as was produced by the tighter loyalty of the latter. They had in common only the desire to question and reappraise.

The Noetics were neither latitudinarian nor sceptical,

though their opponents thought them to be both. They had a sense of the value and status of the Church which was high, if not always so High as that of Keble and Froude. They were loyal to that Church, but with loyalty that was prepared to look at awkward challenges, to accept that doubting was not in itself sinful, to practise cautiously what we should now call demythologizing. A young man who went to Keble with doubts about the complete accuracy of all parts of the Bible might be told that he was in a state of sin; if he went to one of the Noetics he was more likely to be soothed and told not to worry about such things as the chronological inconsistencies of the Old Testament. A good Christian could regard Noah's Ark as a myth and the story of Joseph as 'a beautiful poem'.[27]

The latter dictum was that of Thomas Arnold, a contemporary of Keble in his undergraduate years at Corpus Christi College and the Fellow of Oriel to whose place Newman had succeeded. He was now Headmaster of Rugby, where he was striking a pattern that would change the English public schools. His teaching, with its ecumenical outlook and its emphasis on practical good works, made him seem the diametrical opposite of Newman. Serious-minded young men were likely to fall under one influence or the other: 'the leader of the Movement took us all his own way; all that is who were not Arnoldized.'[28] Newman had been sufficiently irritated by Arnold's liberal views to ask, 'But is *he* a Christian?'[29] Such remarks would be repeated and did not improve relations as the theological argument grew hotter. The open clash which established Arnold as one of the arch-foes of the Tractarians came in 1836 when he attacked them in an article headed 'The Oxford Malignants'.[30]

Arnold expressed the fears of many who thought that the Tracts were becoming dangerous and going beyond Anglican loyalty. The ostensible reason for his article was the behaviour of the Tractarians over the new Regius Professor of Divinity. This was a Crown appointment dealt with by the Prime Minister, who was then the latitudinarian Whig Lord Melbourne. The post went to Hampden, whose Bampton Lectures in 1832 had been critical of tradition in the Church. There had been little comment at the time, but the new wave of power emboldened the Tractarians to oppose his appointment on the grounds of heresy. It was an ill-timed and uncharitable move, with the suspicion of personal motives from the fact that Hawkins had sent pupils to Hampden after a quarrel with Newman about the proper functions of a tutor. Any unorthodox views expressed by Hampden seem to have emanated largely from Blanco White, another Oriel Fellow, who was passing through the Church of England on his journey from Romanism to Unitarianism.

The Regius Chair itself was not open to attack from within Oxford, but an underhand blow could be struck by depriving the Professor of his voice in the selection of preachers for University sermons. A motion to this effect was introduced into Convocation, which was packed with supporters of both sides in contrast with its usual calm and ill-attended disposal of routine business. The motion was thrown out when the Proctors gave their traditional but seldom-used veto. One of Arnold's pupils wrote in delight and admiration:

> Arnold has written a Hampden defence pamphlet . . . what glorious fellows those Proctors are for stopping that furious Convocation . . . doubtless these High-Church Newmanitish people will try to get the Proctors' power of a veto done away with.[31]

The day would come when the Newmanitish people would be glad of that same veto; in the present case they got their way under new Proctors a month or two later. Like so many crises in the movement, the occasion was unwisely taken and proved that the opposition too had strength. As a protest against State interference in Church affairs it was a continuation of the warnings which Keble had uttered in 1833. More, it united groups which were soon to fall farther apart than ever. The Evangelicals at Oxford mostly supported the Tractarians in the Hampden affair, against the liberals and Erastians.

The Evangelical revival had created a climate in which other religious movements could grow, and the Evangelical clergy could welcome many things in the early Tracts. The sense of a supernatural order, threatened by laws passed by men who might have no Christian conviction, was dear to them as well. The Tractarians said little with which they would disagree, until there came increasingly stronger emphasis on the Church as an institution, and on the sacraments as modes of salvation rather than extensions of the individual conversion experience.

For the Tracts were becoming longer, more detailed, more insistent on particular beliefs. Pusey's three successive tracts on baptism ran to a whole treatise, adducing views which set him squarely within the new movement and went against the tenets of popular Protestantism. The series which had started in defence of a threatened Church was now making claims for the power of that Church which few of her members could yet accept. At the same time a new periodical, the *British Magazine*, was publishing Tractarian ideas to an even larger circle of readers.

The supporters of Hampden, battered but not defeated, rallied with accusations that the Tractarians were tending towards Papistry. Their devotion to strict orthodoxy, their sacramentalism, their apostolical view of the Priesthood, their eagerness to hunt out heresy, all seemed manifestations of what good English Protestants had been taught to hate. The men of the Oxford Movement, in that generation and in the next, suffered from the common hatred of Rome. Although Wiseman, later the head of the restored hierarchy, had spoken against them, it could be said that the Tractarians were not reformers of the Church from within but had dangerous separatist tendencies. They would drive men to Rome or spread Popish ideas within the English fold.

At this time Newman still saw himself as defending his Church against the corruptions of Rome as much as against the onslaughts of Liberalism. It is true that in 1836 he wrote *Romanism and Popular Protestantism*, which pressed the need for more care and scruple in controversy instead of blind bigotry. But in the same year he pressed also the appeal to antiquity which was to lead him and others into unexpected paths. With Pusey and Keble he began editions of the early Fathers of the Church. For the Tractarian leaders, these were products of an undivided Church, valuable to Anglicans as supporting claims to catholicity that did not depend on acknowledgement of the Bishop of Rome as Pope. For people who held that the Fathers were Popish and that pre-Reformation theology was inconsistent with sound Protestant doctrine, even these scholarly offerings were suspect. There began the whispers, about Newman in particular, which grew louder year by year:

> . . . that I was a 'Romanist' in Protestant livery and service; that I was doing the work of a hostile Church in the bosom of the English Establishment, and knew it, or ought to have known it.[32]

Others again were not so certain about the depravity of Romanism. Hurrell Froude was looking critically at the English Reformation and talking with something like contempt about its leaders. Was it right to condemn the medieval Church because one rejected modern Papal claims? Indeed, could even those claims to authority and sole catholicity be altogether ignored? Men like Keble could see that the Roman question 'was becoming the great shadow that hung over us'.[33] Then the Tractarians made another error of judgement. A reverent attempt to honour a friend's memory brought them into worse opprobrium than anything they had yet published.

Hurrell Froude died in that tempestuous year, 1836, worn out by the controversy which he had loved but which had been too much for his diseased lungs and weakened frame. His papers were entrusted to Newman and Keble for publication. It was common practice, and remained so to the end of the century, for the close friends of a man who had made some mark on public life to issue a memorial containing his letters and unpublished works. Usually the pious result sold by subscription, evoked some obituary comments and was forgotten. The appearance in 1838 of the *Remains of the Late Reverend Richard Hurrell Froude* caused a storm that did not subside for many years. Nothing could have been more calculated to arouse the hostility of the country than the two volumes of Froude's letters and journals. Many of the things which were to be charged against Anglo-Catholics, sometimes justly and sometimes not, were set out in cold print. Here were the inordinate scruples, the attempts at asceticism and mortification, the hints of secret temptations which attracted even while they repelled.

The great Tractarians were in some ways innocent to the point of stupidity; or rather, their ignorance of uninformed but commonsense reactions was normal in Oxford dons of the

time but culpable in men who were trying to change the condition of the national Church. It was one thing for those who
had been intimate with the provocative, charming young
clergyman to receive letters from him which remarked 'I am
becoming less and less a son of the Reformation' or 'the
Reformation was a limb badly set; it must be broken again to
be righted'.[34] For those who had not known him, these ideas
from a clergyman of the Established Church, doubly sworn to
loyalty by his order and his Fellowship, seemed to prove that
the darkest hints about the Tractarians were true. 'Its pre-
dominant character is extraordinary impudence,' Arnold commented after reading the first volume.[35] Others were even less
charitable, and more seriously disturbed. Newman and Keble
had shown how removed they were from the temper of their
average fellow-countrymen. Their preface had emphasized
Froude's Anglican loyalty, but his own words seemed to make
them liars as well as traitors. They who could remember his
tricks and his enthusiasms, who could still hear his laughing
tone in the outrageous epigrams, had sadly misjudged.

There were some who welcomed the publication for its
anti-Reformation sentiments. Froude enlivened the Oxford
Movement posthumously as he had in his life, encouraging its
extremists to go to greater lengths. The English Reformation
heroes had been attacked by Lingard from the Roman Catholic
position, and by Cobbett from the anti-everything position,
but an Anglican assault on defenders of the Protestant resistance was something new. The opponents of the movement in
Oxford thought that the time for a test of loyalty had come. A
public demonstration of support for Reformation principles
would check the headstrong and force the leaders either to
climb down or to stand revealed as foes to their own Church.
A proposal was put in hand for a memorial to the Marian
martyrs who had suffered in Oxford itself. Newman, Keble and
Pusey refused to subscribe though aware that they were being
pushed into a more aggressive position than they desired. The
Martyrs' Memorial was erected, ironically in the neo-Gothic
style that was soon to be a mark of Catholic architecture, and
there it remains today in token not of one religious controversy
but of two.

Now that the Roman issue was in the open and the battle

fairly joined, the Tractarians found new strength. They lost some waverers but attracted new supporters who were ready to take up the more daring challenge. Newman was the unquestioned leader: 'In the spring of 1839 my position in the Anglican Church was at its height.'[36] The revival which he headed was no longer a purely Oxford affair. The Tracts were finding lay as well as clerical readers up and down the country. Even the august pages of *The Times*, hostile to all things savouring of Romanism, tended to be friendly – admittedly influenced by the fact that the editor's brother was a Tractarian sympathizer. Many years later Newman would recall that: 'Not to mention the excitement it caused in England, the Movement and its party-names were known to the police of Italy and to the backwoodsmen of America.'[37]

More important for its immediate future, the teaching of the movement was being heard in parochial life. From being a party group among the clergy, it had already come to be an influence on ordinary men and women in their daily lives. Keble had gone back to life as a parish priest and there were many lesser but equally dedicated men who had gone down from Oxford with a new sense of pastoral duties:

Undergraduates in due time took their degrees and became private tutors themselves. In this new status, in turn, they preached the opinions which they had already learned themselves. Others went down to the country and became curates of parishes. Then they had down from London parcels of the Tracts and other publications. They placed them in the shops of local booksellers, got them to newspapers, introduced them into clerical meetings, and converted more or less their Rectors and their brother curates.[38]

Some of this eulogy must be seen as the product of hindsight and nostalgia. But though Tractarian parishes were a small minority, the influence of the Oxford leaders was coming to be felt in new attitudes to parish visiting, the religious education of the poor, the preparation of children for Confirmation. Even more significant was the infiltration of Tractarian ideas into religious homes, often on fertile ground prepared by Evangelical stress on the propagation of sound faith within the family. Under a cover of fiction, Hurrell Froude's younger brother described what was taking place:

Just as I was leaving off being a boy, we fell under a strong Catholicizing influence at home, and I used to hear things which were strange enough to my ear. Faber was put away out of my studies; Newton was forbidden; and Davison, that I thought so dry and dull, put in his place. Transubstantiation was talked of before me as more than possible; celibacy of the clergy and fast days were not only not wrong, but the very thing most needful.[39]

The Oxford Movement had started as an extension of the High doctrine of the Church in opposition to State control. In considering the rightful claims of the Church it had been necessary to consider also her true nature. From that consideration there had emerged ideas and practices which had hitherto been confined in England to the small band of Roman Catholics. When Anglicans joined in the credal assent to a Catholic and Apostolic Church, the Oxford men made them remember that they were claiming membership of a Church going back to the Apostles, from whom power to celebrate valid sacraments had been passed in unbroken line to the modern clergy. The English parson could celebrate Holy Communion not as a memorial only but as bringing the Real Presence to those who knelt to receive. He could remit or retain sins: he could exercise powers influencing salvation. It was this kind of authority, more precious than incomes and endowments, which made Parliamentary control seem sacrilegious.

Therefore the Tractarians urged churchmen to recognize that true authority lay not in Parliament but in the episcopate. Newman was humbly respectful to his Bishop even on the increasingly frequent occasions when they were theologically at odds with one another. 'Our Bishop is our Pope,' he declared,[40] uttering an idea as distasteful to most of the Bishops as it was to the nation as a whole. It was dangerous too: once the question of authority was raised, many eyes would turn towards Rome where authority was claimed and exercised without hesitation. Even at the end of the century, loyal Anglicans were still urging their Bishops to accept their real power and not bow to democratic pressure: 'the Church of England rests upon *authority* . . . and on AUTHORITY will it be maintained.'[41]

Thus the duty of the layman was not solely or even principally to go to church, join in the psalms and responses and listen to the sermon. The Eucharist was seen as the most important

49

service: although the Tractarians themselves did not favour non-communicating attendance, their younger disciples were beginning to explore the possibilities of 'High Mass'. Private confession, permitted and indeed enjoined by the Prayer Book for unquiet consciences or in sickness, was being more widely urged. Men like Keble did not try to enforce it,

> . . . or even wished for it to be used unless the need for it were felt . . . he expressed disagreement with the teaching of the 'advanced' school on this subject, speaking strongly of the unreality to which he thought it had given occasion.[42]

The advanced school, however, came to arouse some of the worst opposition to Anglo-Catholicism by offering confession as a strongly desirable preparation for all communicants.

Much of the trouble came from the break with Catholic practices which had taken place in the Church of England. Those who now discovered that the essential catholicity of that Church had not been lost and ought to be manifested had no model except in contemporary Roman Catholicism. The High Churchman who a few years previously would have taken his stand on the Caroline divines was now delving into medieval annals or peering at the usages of his abhorred Roman brethren. The Tractarian leaders were not ritualists and added very little to the normal practice of the time: it was in interpretation rather than in externals that they found their strength. But those who had trotted beside them were beginning to move ahead. Vestments and altar lights, crossing and genuflection, were appearing as the hallmarks of catholicity. To neglect them meant a refusal to claim the rightful Anglican heritage. Hostile observers saw only an unintelligent aping of Rome and a retreat to superstition:

> Whatever be their aim, they have lost themselves in the empty chaff of outer ceremonies, and seem to think that God, who is a spirit and must be worshipped in spirit and in truth, can be amused like a child with a rattle and a straw, that he is small enough to delight himself with theatrical dresses, theatrical positions, and a return to the semi-pagan ideas of Rome, rather than the simple truth of the gospel.[43]

With such sentiments Newman in 1840 would largely have agreed. But doubt was creeping in as his studies of patristic

theology gave him the uncomfortable idea that the Anglican
Church might be in the position of the early heretics against
whom Rome had maintained the orthodox truth. Then Wiseman wrote an article in the *Dublin Review* which openly compared the Anglicans to the Donatists. A quotation of the words
of St Augustine, '*Securus judicat orbis terrarum*', beat into
Newman's mind and made him wonder if his position was
tenable. 'By those great words of the ancient Father, the
theory of the *Via Media* was absolutely pulverized.'[44] But this
was not yet the end for him and he set out to meet his own
doubts together with the attacks of opponents on both sides.

The movement itself was changing character as the suspicions of Romanizing grew. The Tracts were being regarded
less favourably and the new disciples did little to alleviate fears.
In Oxford itself a number of young dons were lending the
kind of support which must lead to tragic splits. Their loyalty
to the Church of England was less firmly rooted than that of
the old High Church leaders, their suspicion of Rome was less
strong. They did not share the scholarly reticence of their
elders but were determined to make themselves heard in the
country.

The most remarkable among them was W. G. Ward, who
was in some respects a successor to Hurrell Froude. Young,
lively, eager to be liked but equally ready to shock, he differed
from Froude in an important respect. He was less concerned
to defend the catholicity of the Church of England than to find
for himself the home of true catholicity as proved by marks of
holiness. He had been a follower of Arnold until Froude's
Remains brought him into the new movement, to which he
contributed the convert's zeal which he was later to show in
the Roman Church. He brought too a warm sympathy for the
poor which was to be found in the next generation of Anglo-
Catholics as well as in the Christian Socialism of Maurice and
Kingsley. He sought for sanctity, and the quest was taking
him away from parallels with the undivided patristic Church,
away from medievalism and closer to the modern Roman
Catholics. Here too he was a long way from Froude, for whom
the post-reformation Papal developments were, equally with
the Protestant, a betrayal of his beloved Middle Ages. Meeting
Wiseman in Rome, Froude had decided that there was no

hope of reunion 'without swallowing the whole Council of Trent'.[45]

Newman was beginning to withdraw from the centre of these controversies. His charge of St Mary's gave him also the small parish of Littlemore, about three miles from Oxford, where he had built a new church in 1836. He was spending more time there, leaving St Mary's to his curate. In 1842 he retired to Littlemore in the hope of finding peace to work out his true position. For in the previous year he had 'received three blows which broke me . . . from the end of 1841, I was on my death bed as regards my membership with the Anglican Church'.[46]

One blow came from his intensive study of the early Church which had already made him uneasy. As he examined the Arian controversy, it seemed to him that the Arians were like the more extreme Protestants of his own time, the Anglicans were like the semi-Arians, and Rome was in the position of monolithic authority and orthodoxy which she still claimed. His gift for analogy now threatened his own security: he had appealed to history, and history had returned an unexpected and unwelcome answer.

The second blow, weaker in itself, struck further at a shaken loyalty. There was a proposal, approved by the Government to establish a bishopric in Jerusalem in collaboration with the Lutheran Church of Prussia, for the pastoral care of all Protestants in Palestine. It was another affront to the Tractarian view, drawing the Church of England closer to those without the Apostolic Succession. Once again the State was taking on ecclesiastical privilege, establishing sees as merrily as she had abolished them in Ireland.

Heavier than either, more damaging to the whole movement, was the fortune of the ninetieth and last of the *Tracts for the Times*. In an effort to justify Anglican claims to catholicity, Newman turned his attention to the thirty-nine Articles to which all the national clergy had to assent, and which were also to be subscribed by members of the University of Oxford on matriculation and graduation. They were generally accepted as controverting any suggestion that the Church of England was other than a Protestant Church in complete opposition to Rome. Newman bent the whole force of his intellect to prove that the Articles were directed against abuses in popular Romanism and not against any orthodoxy of the undivided Church.

It was another example of Newman's lack of practical wisdom and his ignorance at that date of the deep Protestant bias of the majority of English people. He wrote to strengthen the waverers in the Romanizing party, to show men like Ward that their new-found love of what was Catholic need not drive them to the feet of the Pope. Yet a justification of purgatory and intercessions, even though set out in the sweet reasonableness of Newman's fine prose, was bound to rouse fury.

The storm that followed publication was greater than the one over Froude's *Remains*. Four Oxford tutors delated the Tract and the Heads of the colleges followed their lead by an almost unanimous condemnation. Bishop Bagot of Oxford declared against it; Newman offered to conclude the Tract series provided the last one was not to be withdrawn. He put upon it his reputation in the Anglican Church, surely knowing and perhaps partly hoping that he would lose. In Parliament and in the London clubs, in country rectories and dissenting chapels, Tract 90 was condemned – and the author with it. The nation did not want to be convinced that the Prayer Book teaching was Catholic and that the Articles 'may be subscribed by those who aim at being Catholic in heart and doctrine'. 'This has made a great row ... pamphlets are appearing in shoals,'[47] young Arthur Clough wrote to a Cambridge friend. As for Newman himself: 'I saw indeed clearly that my place in the Movement was lost; public confidence was at an end; my occupation was gone.'[48]

Meanwhile, Ward was not convinced that his Church had been proved adequately Catholic. His publications became increasingly critical of Anglicanism until in 1844 he produced a long and tediously written volume with the title, *The Ideal of a Christian Church, considered in comparison with Existing Practice*. He was not content to demonstrate that the Roman Catholic Church alone had kept the marks of catholicity but went on to declare gleefully that he and others held office in the Church of England while holding and promulgating Roman doctrine. Here was the severest blow yet dealt to the whole Tractarian idea, admitting and actually rejoicing in the charges which opponents had been trying to prove.

Froude had been beyond the reach of reprisal when his *Remains* were published. Ward was a ready sacrifice for all that the Tractarians had done or appeared to do. Once again a large meeting of Convocation assembled: the machinery which had been used against Hampden was now set moving by the opposite party. It was not Ward's book alone that was on trial in the Sheldonian, that bleak day of frost and snow in February 1845. There were proposals to condemn his book and, a childish attempt at revenge, to deprive him of his degrees and senior status in the University. There was a further motion of censure on Tract 90, long after its publication. Ward spoke eloquently in his own defence; the *Ideal* was condemned by a large majority and his own deprivation was passed by a smaller one. Then the motion was put for the condemnation of Tract 90. As if the Hampden affair had to be imaged in every detail of irony, the proctors exercised their veto before a vote could be taken. That night the junior proctor of the year wrote home to his mother:

The only thing to relieve the day has been the extreme satisfacttion I had in helping to veto the third iniquitous measure against Newman. It was worthwhile being Proctor to have had the unmixed pleasure of doing this.[49]

Newman still had his supporters, especially among the younger men. Ward was cheered and the Vice-Chancellor snowballed as the Convocation dispersed; but the great twelve years of the Oxford Movement were drawing to their close. The secessions to Rome were increasing and the Established Church was fighting back with more severe reprisals. Pusey had already suffered two years of suspension from preaching for a sermon delated as heretical, although he had been allowed to make no defence. The years of suspension, deprivation and legal prosecution against his followers were beginning. In his old age, the junior proctor who had stood loyal to Newman remembered the unhappy time:

It was the day of the violent on both sides: the courtesies of life were forgotten; men were afraid of being weak in their censures, their dislike and their opposition; old friendships were broken up, and men believed the worst of those whom a few years back they had loved to honour.[50]

Ward was received into the Roman Catholic Church soon after his condemnation. Others soon followed him: Oakeley of the Margaret Street chapel in London went in October, 'the first to realize the capacities of the Anglican ritual for impressive devotional use'.[51] It seemed as though the prophecies of opponents were justified and that the Oxford revival could lead only to Popery. Still Newman remained.

The ties that held him to the Anglican Church were loosening one by one. At Littlemore he had found neither the physical solitude nor the spiritual peace for which he had hoped. Rumours that he was starting a monastery had brought everyone, from heads of colleges to undergraduates, to spy on him. His last sermon before the University had been preached in February 1843, a month after he had published an article retracting some of his strongest words against Romanism. In the following September he had resigned from St Mary's and retired into lay communion. He preached, for the last time as an Anglican, at Littlemore that month. It was at once an indictment and an appeal, as he took his formal leave of the Church which he had tried to revive and which was slowly driving him away:

> O my Mother! My Mother! How is it that those who would have died for thee fall neglected from thy bosom? How is it that whatever is keen in intellect, or patient in investigation, or energetic in action, or ardent in devotion, or enthusiastic in affection, remains unused by thee? Why are they forced to stand idle in the market-place, whilst with ready hands and eager hearts they are eager to toil for thee? How is it thou hast no words of kindness, no sign of encouragement for them, but that those suspectest, or slightest, or scornest, or fearest them, or at best dost but endure them?[52]

Every hurt of the last ten years had left its mark, as he had tried to follow his quest towards the truth. Two years of struggle remained before he resigned his Oriel Fellowship, and all knew that the time of waiting was nearly past.

The suspense with which Newman's final act of withdrawal was expected, in Oxford and throughout the country, was remarkable even for that time when a change of religious allegiance was far more than a private decision. The years following Keble's famous sermon and the Hadleigh meeting

55

had brought into greater prominence the problems of authority in faith. Out of the suffering and the triumph, the hope and the despair, a point had been reached for new departures. The night of 8 October 1845 meant that things would not be the same again with the Tractarians, their successors or their enemies. Through a heavy storm there arrived at Littlemore Father Dominic of the Passionists, an Italian who had come to England in response to a conviction that he had important work to do north of his native land. He received John Henry Newman into the Roman Catholic Church.

It was over; and the whole nation seemed to sigh with relief, or triumph, or despair. Newman was gone, Froude dead, Keble obscure in a rural parsonage. Only Pusey of the first Tractarians remained active, and he now emerged as the leader of the loyalists, to gain new stature and respect as well as new obloquy when the mantle of Newman fell upon him. Others at Oxford proved themselves capable of courage to develop: Charles Marriott, Richard Church and James Mozley took Tractarian principles forward to the next phase at the University, while Keble and other priests whose names are forgotten carried them into the parishes. Others thinking Pusey too close to Rome, followed men – like Samuel Wilberforce, the new Bishop of Oxford – who were more eclectic in their application of these principles within a moderate position. There was none with Newman's great intellect or charismatic power, though there was holiness and devotion in many. To outsiders, Newman's secession seemed a decisive blow to the new movement. Even in Oxford itself, from the moment of Ward's condemnation, 'It was more than a defeat, it was a rout.'[53]

Where the Tractarians mourned, others rejoiced. 'How silently Newman has glided over *to his own place*,' Charles Kingsley wrote to a friend.[54] Indeed, the liberal and Broad Church principles were furthered by the event: *Essays and Reviews* loomed ahead. The importance of Newman's personality and of his decision did not affect only his friends. One who drifted from support to be highly critical of the movement recalled:

It is impossible to describe the enormous effect produced in the academical and clerical world, I may say throughout England, by one man's changing his religion. But it was not consternation; it was a lull – a sense that the past agitation of twelve years was extinguished by this simple act.[55]

It seemed so indeed; but the real agitation was beginning. To the end of the century and beyond, the controversy of those twelve years was refought and developed, bringing many to a new view of their faith. Others less in sympathy would yet find in the revival their own comfort or disquiet.

3
A Tractarian Parish

The loss of Newman marked the end of the Oxford Movement in its first phase, when the controversies had been manifested chiefly in clerical and academic circles. Its principles had already been carried into wider fields; sympathizers and opponents might be ranged on each side of a parish boundary or divided within a single parish. The progress of 'Puseyism', as it had come to be generally known, made national as well as local news. The most sensational aspects in the later forties and fifties were reported, satirized, exaggerated: the extension of ritual and ceremonial, the revival of private confession, the establishment of religious orders, all of which seemed an unwelcome submission to priestly dominance over the individual layman.

Too often Puseyism became a focus of that growing antagonism to established religion and clerical power which had been manifested at the time of the first Reform Act. Any church-centred controversy could bring out the destructive fury of the 'mob' – a perpetual dread of the middle class and a reality for those concerned with the preservation of order.

While rioters were wrecking and cursing in East Grinstead, in Exeter and in Pimlico, Tractarian ideas and practices were taking root in less spectacular ways. The influence that was slowly to change the Church of England and to restore a more Catholic interpretation of her functions was often neither urban nor extremist. From its inception, there had been a division of emphasis and intention in the movement. Even Froude and Keble, both the products of clerical homes where High Church principles had been accepted, had come to look in different ways at their missions. There was the type, of which Froude was one, who was prepared to press on with experiment and investigation, to discuss and test new ideas in the search for true catholicity. Whether that principle was to be found in the neglected past or the unexplored present, or in both, was yet to be determined. The true Church would be known by its marks of holiness: for Newman, Ward and many others these turned out to be in the Roman obedience.

Others were concerned rather to emphasize those aspects of Anglicanism which seemed to contain the full Catholic spirit, overlaid though it was by false accretions and political interference. It was to free and reinvigorate the Church that they resisted Erastian demands and appealed to the older English divines. The Apostolic Succession, the creeds and sacraments of the primitive, undivided Church – these had never been lost, though their integrity was now in danger. Keble numbered himself among those who so believed, committed by family tradition and by personal conviction:

> The Kebles were all of them men of the old-fashioned High Church orthodoxy, of the Prayer Book and the Catechism – the orthodoxy which was professed at Oxford, which was represented in London by Norris of Hackney and Joshua Watson; which vehemently disliked the Evangelicals and Methodists for their poor and loose theology, their love of excitement and display, their hunting after popularity.[1]

In 1845 John Keble had been for ten years Rector of Hursley in Hampshire. His vocation hereafter lay in that rural incumbency from which he had for a time been drawn away only because he hoped that the work of an Oxford tutor could also be pastoral. He continued to do the work in which he believed, maintaining those ideals of priesthood which he had defended at the time of his Assize Sermon and in the early Tracts. He had stood firm, but those twelve years had battered him. After Newman went, 'cheerfulness was there, but it was the cheerfulness of patience more than of hope, or rather the hope was of faith, not of sight',[2] and it was said that the marble bust of

Newman in his study was now covered with a veil.[3] Keble had virtually withdrawn from the Oxford scene by 1841, though he was Newman's confidant still. He had been confirmed in his own belief that a pure Church must be a suffering Church:

> Pusey and Newman were full of the wonderful progress of the movement, whereas I had been taught that the truth *must* be unpopular and despised, and to make confession of it was all that one could do; but I see that I was fairly carried off my legs by the sanguine views they held, and the effects that were showing themselves in all quarters.[4]

It is not easy to imagine Keble being swept off his legs, though Froude had for a time taught him to fight hard. In his quieter way, and with that vein of tragedy always in his teaching about the Christian life, he came to exercise an influence which the Church of England needed at the parish level. He was resolved to see the principles of the movement made effective in daily life, even though the common rooms of Oxford might reject them. In this task he had three advantages, one of which was the result of happy accident. His teaching and writing carried the stamp of the charm and quiet sanctity which had delighted his contemporaries at Oriel. He was known throughout the country as a religious poet admired by many who did not share his theology. And he had a parishioner who was developing a remarkable talent for novel-writing.

His success came from a full use of the opportunities which a country parish offered. The rural areas still gave habitation and employment to a large proportion of the English people, though as early as 1838 Henry Wilberforce could observe the beginning of what would be beyond dispute by the end of the century: 'From an agricultural we have become, in great measure, a commercial and manufacturing people . . . villages have swelled into towns, and towns into mighty cities.'[5] The country parson was still at the centre of a more fully integrated community. He might have trouble with his squire and perhaps with his churchwardens, but he was unlikely to meet violent or concerted opposition. Those who did not like his ways might slip away to the nearest dissenting chapel, but they were more likely to accept any innovations with the same acquiescent grumbling that had carried their ancestors through the perplexities of the sixteenth and seventeenth centuries. If the parson met trouble, it would more likely be as a member of the gentry, threatened by the rick-burning and machine-wrecking labourers whose riots John Keble had witnessed as a young man in his father's parish.

The typical parish church had changed little since the beginning of the previous century. Its large central pulpit, its high-backed pews with tables and even stoves in the most privileged, its gallery where a few local players would provide music – all these stressed the importance of comfort, exposition and sermon rather than of sacraments.[6] Here a man like Keble could hope slowly to bring a new emphasis into public worship, finding a response slower but more lasting than the febrile enthusiasm of undergraduates. He could expound ideas of the Church which had been imperfectly understood or never realized. His national reputation could give encouragement to those who had held their High Church ideas timorously and in apparent isolation. The great men of the movement would even be seen in the parish, so that the rumours of doings at Oxford suddenly became real.[7]

In the hamlet of Otterbourne near Hursley there was at least one family for whom Keble's teaching 'seemed nothing new, only the full consequence of what they had always learned'.[8] Charlotte Mary Yonge came from a home where the old High Church principles were accepted, as they had been in Keble's own family. In her childhood she first met Keble, 'with awe and reverence', as the famous poet. Thirty years of respect and influence began not with a sudden conversion but with a predisposition to his teaching. She was to gain much from him, to give perhaps even more by her advocacy in fiction of his cause.

At fifteen I became a catechumen of Mr Keble's, and this I would call the great influence of my life did I not feel unworthy to do so; but of this I am sure, that no one else, save my own father, had so much to do with my whole cast of mind.[9]

'I became a catechumen' – the phrase with its precise technicality reflects the new importance of confirmation and the relationship with the parish priest. The sense of humility and the utter devotion to parents are also things that her novels later manifested. 'One did not merely look at him externally as a great man, but he became part of one's own life.'[10] It is easy enough to dismiss Charlotte Yonge's devotion for Keble as the reaction of a frustrated spinster with a father-fixation. Yet wiser judgement may take into account Oxford testimony to the tutor whom Newman regarded as 'the first man in Oxford', the loved master of Froude, Wilberforce and Williams, the man who hid his copy of Law's *Serious Call* instead of leaving it on view for admiration.

The ideas which he had championed at Oxford were now to be tested parochially and passed on to the wider world through his female disciple. He taught her, as he taught the simple village children, with the pessimism about worldly hopes that went deep in his belief. 'He gave me two warnings,' Charlotte recalled after his death:

The one against much talk and discussion of church matters especially doctrines, the other against the danger of loving these things for the sake merely of their beauty and poetry – aesthetically, he would have said, only that he would have thought the word affected.[11]

It was a long way from the Oriel common room and from the antics of the extreme Puseyites who teetered between Rome and the new aestheticism. The Oxford Movement won many of its successes through that dissatisfaction with the age which some of the best minds were beginning to feel. It could fill a gulf between ideal and reality by offering reasoned pessimism instead of despair, other-worldy hopes in an ordered visible system, a discipline that sanctified inescapable sacrifices.

These ideas and opportunities were to be made more widely known through the novels of the woman whose spiritual master was himself a creative writer. Charlotte Yonge wrote the domestic type of fiction which became the dominant mode, replacing the older sensationalism and 'silver fork school' until it gave way to a demand for a different type of realism. Keble was a poet in the derivative and moribund style of the late Romantic period.

Keble's poems, published as *The Christian Year*, do and yet do not stand as a manifesto of the Oxford Movement.

They are Tractarian in their attachment to the Book of Common Prayer: each was written for a Sunday or Holy Day. They are Tractarian in their direction towards the disciplined personal life which was aided by following the ecclesiastical year, and in their emphasis on sacramental services. On the other hand, the volume appeared in 1827 and contained pieces from as early as 1819, so it was a forerunner and not a product of the movement. More important, the sentiments are Evangelical as often as the interpretations are Catholic. Hurrell Froude's typical comment on its publication was a fear that the author would be taken for a Methodist.[12]

The combination of Evangelical aspirations with regular churchmanship and the sacramental life was irresistible to many who were seeking that very balance for themselves. The poems were absurdly overpraised both by serious critics and by those humbler folk who bought the book and, like Arthur Pendennis and his mother, 'whispered it to each other with awe'; a demand built up which took it into more than ninety editions before the end of the century. Yet it had a quality which even those who were not Keble's contemporaries would recognize in later years:

The book which, in the present century, has had the greatest sale of all others is John Keble's Christian Year, and why? Because, across the poetic Fantaisie of flowers and woods and winds and hills, we trace the passion-play of a suffering, self-denying life and death.[13]

The Christian Year won admiration also from men hostile alike to Tractarian discipline and Evangelical piety. Thomas Arnold, whose friendship with Keble began before the days of the Oxford Movement and outlasted its antagonisms, knew some of the poems before the volume was completed. 'It is my firm opinion that nothing equal to them exists in our language . . . if they are not published, it will be a great neglect of doing good.'[14] John Morley said that in Keble's poetry 'the Church of England finds her most affecting voice'.[15] Even for A.E.Housman, years later, 'Keble is a poet: there are things in *The Christian Year* that can be admired by atheists.'[16]

There were of course dissenting voices, from Roman Catholics and from Evangelicals who found Keble's doctrine too slack. Others, seeking to resist the claims of the Tractarians by damning all their works both past and present, could include it in a general condemnation:

> Burbidge is very savage about the Lyra Apostolica, and is writing a review of it, the Christian Year and the Cathedral which he says he will send to every periodical in search of admission. I do not know what are the grounds of his wrath, but whether it be from their partisan character which superinduces slang and cant in various modifications or from the forced character of the church system generally they cannot produce good poetry.[17]

Although modern judgement strives to separate the criticism of content from the criticism of presentation, no such distinction was generally made or even desired when Keble wrote. Religious poetry started with a strong advantage or disadvantage as it agreed or conflicted with its readers' views. Keble's poetry appealed to the majority: 'the devout among the Anglican middle classes came to value it as dissenters valued *Pilgrim's Progress*.'[18] Burbidge was right in seeing that the poets of the early Oxford Movement did not write for the sake of poetry itself. They had ideas to promulgate, minds to influence, souls to save.

The criticism that the 'forced character of the church system' prevented their writing good poetry raises issues which will appear in later considerations. It is true that many of the most serious Victorians did not feel themselves to be free agents in the exercise of literary talent. The power to influence others, and the duty to use that power responsibly, were not limited to Tractarians or to any Christian group; George Eliot was concerned as deeply as Charlotte Yonge about consequences.

The thinking behind *The Christian Year* is expounded in the lectures given by Keble as Professor of Poetry at Oxford between 1832 and 1841. Lectures delivered in Latin and dealing with pagan or Old Testament writers might not seem to be the fittest apologia for the poet of the Book of Common Prayer. Yet in lectures and in poems there is manifested the ideal of Romanticism subordinated to the tenets of Tractarianism. When Keble spoke of the sincerity that must go into all great poetry, he was combining a Wordsworthian aim with his own conviction that right thinking and moral excellence always went together: 'a simple and sincere mind declares itself by almost exactly the same manifestations, whether in poetry or the common talk of daily life.'[19]

Yet poetry was to be no flow of personal emotion, valuable by reason of being deeply and sincerely felt. It was no mere exercise in language, no aid to self-understanding, no raid on new and perhaps forbidden experience. These things were part of the Romantic legacy to some later phases of poetic creation. For Keble the only sincerity which mattered was the kind that would shun excess and give expression to proper sentiments without over-conscious artistry:

> The central point of our theory is that the essence of all poetry is to be found, not in high-wrought subtlety of thought, nor in pointed cleverness of phrase, but in the depths of the heart and the most sacred feelings of the men who write.[20]

Poetry is to be, in T.S. Eliot's phrase, not a turning-loose of emotion but a release from emotion. Religious sentiment is not loose feeling but a discipline growing from exercise of the will – a notion dear to the Tractarians and frequently urged on Charlotte Yonge's characters. Both heart and desire should be controlled lest they rule the character and set the pursuit of happiness above the pursuit of truth.

The notion of 'reserve' had been developed by Isaac Williams in the eightieth of the *Tracts for the Times* – 'On Reserve in Communicating Religious Knowledge'. A decent reticence about discussing sacred doctrines and using holy names was a thoroughly Anglican concept; but the odium of the time construed it as Jesuitical and tending to dishonest concealment. Williams was canvassed as Keble's successor in the Chair of Poetry but hostility made him withdraw in favour of the Low Church candidate Garbett. The elective post was even then the centre of party feeling, though without the antics which have more recently characterized it. As far as poetic ability went, even a great admirer of Williams had to admit that 'his power of expression was not always equal to what he wanted to say'.[21]

John Keble practised in poetry the reserve which he admired in personal life. *The Christian Year* is restrained, almost cold in comparison with the outpourings of Evangelical hymnologists. Yet the coldness gives way to a sense of humility and reverence on deeper reading. For Keble there was abiding truth in the Centurion's 'Lord, I am not worthy':

> For ever, where such grace is given,
> It fears in open day to shine,
> Lest the deep stain it owns within
> Break out, and Faith be sham'd by the believer's sin.[22]

To which the faithful interpreter adds her gloss:

There is often a tendency to reserve in strong devotion, and a dread of profession, lest by outrunning practice it should give occasion to the enemies of the Lord to blaspheme.[23]

Again, the poem for the fourth Sunday in Lent:

> E'en human love will shrink from sight
> Here in the coarse rude earth:
> How then should rash intruding glance
> Break in upon *her* sacred trance
> Who boasts a heavenly birth?
>
> So still and secret is her growth,
> Ever the truest heart,
> Where deepest strikes her kindly root
> For hope or joy, for flower or fruit,
> Least knows its happy part.
>
> God only, and good angels, look
> Behind the blissful screen –
> As when, triumphant o'er His woes,
> The Son of God by moonlight rose,
> By all but Heaven unseen.

Charlotte Yonge's comment here is important for our understanding of more than the single poem:

Reserve, reverent reserve, was ever a characteristic of the teaching of the school of divines of which the 'Christian Year' was the first utterance. Those who had gone before them, in their burning zeal to proclaim the central truth of the Gospel, had obtruded it with little regard to the season of speaking or the frame of mind of the hearer; and moreover, there was a habit of testing the sincerity of personal religion by requiring that its growth should be constantly proclaimed and discussed with great fullness of detail.[24]

The emotional rant and the introspection of the undisciplined Evangelical, satirized by many Victorian novelists, was never more smoothly or more gently dissected. One of the contributions of the Oxford Movement was the substitution of calm evaluation for fiery 'testimony', of disciplined sacramental life for subjective assurance. Yet there were areas in the national experience that called for extremism rather than moderation; nor was reserve always productive of charity towards other opinions.

The need for personal discipline and the subordination of self-will were not conspicuous in the Romantic image of the poet. The Tractarians admired Wordsworth, moved by his swing from revolutionary radicalism to a stout defence of English traditions. Keble gave Wordsworth high praise in the oration when an honorary degree was conferred on him at Oxford in 1839. The older poet is said to have praised *The Christian Year*; he cannot have recognized it as the work of a disciple. Keble views the natural world with firm theological convictions: 'the whole of creation exists to help men to get into the closest possible contact with God.'[25]

To see all Nature as a perpetual sermon of divine love may give new significance to descriptions of natural beauty. Unfortunately, the language of the sermon is not the language of poetry. The theological message is liable to fall into diction derived from broad sympathy with a poetic school but not assimilated to the precision of doctrine which was essential in Tractarian thinking. Keble's generation had not solved the problem of language for religious poetry. For instance, the poem for the Tuesday in Easter Week begins with an apostrophe of the snowdrop, reminiscent of those aspects of Wordsworth which we should prefer to forget:

> Thou first-born of the year's delight,
>> Pride of the dewy glade,
> In vernal green and virgin white,
>> Thy vestal robes array'd:
>
> 'Tis not because thy drooping form
>> Sinks graceful on its nest,
> While chilly shades from gathering storm
>> Affright thy tender breast;

67

Nor for yon river islet wild
    Beneath the willow spray,
Where, like the ringlets of a child,
    Thou weav'st thy circle gay.

The development by way of childish innocence towards thoughts of the Resurrection is too obvious and too tritely expressed. If Keble avoided some Romantic excesses, he did not escape the bathos and the forced image. Hopkins had a point when he commented: 'the Lake School expires in Keble and Faber and Cardinal Newman.'[26]

The style and diction of the older Romantics could influence those who disliked the attitudes of the younger. Keble, predictably, had no time for Shelley and Byron who seemed to have abused their gifts:

He, merciful and mild,
As erst, beholding, loves His wayward child;
When souls of highest birth
Waste their impassioned might on dreams of earth,
He opens Nature's book,
And on His glorious gospel bids them look,
Till by such chords, as rule the choirs above,
Their lawless cries are tun'd to hymns of perfect love.

(Fourth Sunday after Epiphany)

Thus Nature has a sacramental as well as a didactic function: general revelation leads by Grace to the special revelation of Incarnation through the Church. Lest the reader have any doubts about these wayward 'souls of highest birth', Charlotte tells:

We believe that the temptation to contemplate vice and to love the excitement of the study of passion, to which these verses primarily referred, was that afforded by Byron's poetry; and that the last lines expressed the hope that could not but be felt, that such a change in the unhappy poet would come while it was not yet too late.[27]

Even when the 'unhappy poet' had passed beyond human judgement, censorious Philip Morville found his poetry 'bad food for excitable minds', at least in respect of 'his perversions of human passions, not his descriptions of scenery'.[28]

Leaving aside these attitudes, there is more in *The Christian Year* to repel than to attract the modern reader. The style is erudite and allusive, drawing on the Bible, the Fathers, the Caroline divines and the Greek classical writers. The diction is often heavily Miltonic without the Miltonic grandeur: a survival of Keble's undergraduate enthusiasm for Milton which suggests that his later disclaimer – 'I've no love for that poet'[29] – was based on doctrinal rather than poetic grounds. There is little music and the visual imagery is conventional.

Yet, derivative in style and constrained by the doctrine of religious reserve, the volume reveals a great deal of the man and of the movement which he helped to begin. He came to feel embarrassed by its success and to fear that it gave him an undeserved reputation for holiness. It was perhaps to avoid such identification that he wrote the later and inferior *Lyra Innocentium* under the guise of poems for children. In fact this book shows an extension of his theological beliefs, under the influence of the more thoroughgoing Tractarians. Written mostly between 1841 and 1846, the poems of the *Lyra* show a more advanced sense of ritual and ornament in church services. The devotion towards the Blessed Virgin did not pass unnoticed at the time of publication, and even at the end of the century an editor was finding it necessary to explain that Keble was warning children 'against adoration or the thought of an Immaculate Conception'.[30]

The success of *The Christian Year* may have caused Keble to write the poem beginning:

> When mortals praise thee, hide thine eyes,
>   Nor in thy Master's wrong
> Take to thyself His crown and prize;
>   Yet more in heart than tongue.[31]

It certainly moved him, a few years later, to tell Charlotte Yonge after the reception of *The Heir of Redclyffe* that a successful book could be the greatest trial of a lifetime.[32] For her part, she regarded *The Christian Year* as the greatest memorial of her master. Her published commentary sometimes stretches itself in relating his work to his life, as when the St Mark poem is suggested as a foreshadowing of the brief reunion of Newman and Keble in 1865:

> Since not Apostles' hands can clasp
> Each other in so firm a grasp,
> But they shall change and variance prove.
>
> Yet deem not on such parting sad
> Shall dawn no welcome dear and glad.

Sometimes her purpose becomes more apologetic than expository. The Gunpowder Treason poem was written 'at the time when scarcely even the most Catholic-minded English churchman could speak of Rome other than abusively'. In the same poem, Keble is defended against any charge of denying the Real Presence in writing:

> O come to our Communion Feast:
> There present, in the heart,
> Not in the hands, th'eternal Priest
> Will his true self impart.[33]

Yet Charlotte Yonge did not and does not exist as a shadow of Keble. She wrote nearly a hundred books and became a novelist of national and international repute. The direct exposition which appeared in her comments on *The Christian Year* is subordinated in her novels to the presumptions about character and situation. She showed in fiction, as Keble showed in his incumbency, what the Oxford Movement could do in Anglican life without either causing violent upheavals or controverting its own doctrine of reserve. She was no shadow, but she was a very faithful and humble disciple.

She constantly discussed her writing with Keble and his wife, and submitted to his censorship with no recorded murmur. Keble warned her against her first idea of putting Philip Morville in fear of insanity during his solitude, and 'mentioned instances in which the suggestion of the idea had done serious harm to excitable persons already in dread of that visitation'.[34] He continued to be her spiritual mentor, in ways that typify the extremes of Anglo-Catholicism for good and ill. On the one hand there was the childish scrupulosity, which her own characters so often reflect, with which he told her to prick holes in a piece of paper to keep count of the number of times she became impatient; on the other, that tolerance and charity coupled with a firm sense of his own right belief, which inspired his views on Roman Catholicism:

No doubt we could ask Roman Catholics many questions they could not answer, and they could ask us many which we could not answer; we can only each go on our way, holding on to the truth which we know we have.[35]

Charlotte remembered such teaching even to her last year of life, when she wrote *Reasons Why I am a Catholic and not a Roman Catholic*. This little pamphlet does not give the impression of a writer who had charmed thousands of readers over a generation; it is a commonplace apologia for those principles which greater minds had fought over and which were now increasingly appearing in popular form. Yet it is a reminder of those early days when the Roman question was threatening many Anglicans; for all its gentleness, it shows a hostility to the Roman Church greater than many Anglo-Catholics of the late century were inclined to express. Its main thesis is the Catholic sufficiency of the Church of England, the belief which Keble had never ceased to hold and promulgate. 'Our veteran Churchwoman', as the editor called her, believed that 'some recent secessions to Rome were those of persons who had never been taught what the Church of England really holds'.[36]

This was Keble's way of thinking. Charlotte shared his suspicion of both the Roman Catholic and the extreme Anglican ritualist. The increase of ceremony did not seem to her conducive to devout worship and her later works contain a good deal of disapproval – satire is not a word applicable to her treatment – of vestments, chants and ornaments. Clement in *The Pillars of the House* grows out of his youthful ritualism and improves as a pastor while he loses his preciousness. Much earlier, in *Heartsease*, Emma Brandon's desire to restore an old priory is seen as a superstitious dread of sacrilege; her attachment to the idea leads her to disobedience to her mother and almost into the arms of Rome. Her faithful friend and counsellor Theresa Marstone actually secedes to Rome, fortunately after her hold has weakened. Otherwise, 'such intelligence might have unsettled Emma's principles as well as caused her deep grief'.[37] She is spared too from the machinations of Mark Gardner, whose pose of extreme Anglo-Catholicism nearly succeeds in concealing his wild (though unspecified) badness:

71

It was all ecclesiastical aesthetics, and discontent with the present system, especially as regarded penitence; by and by, when his hold should be secure, he would persuade the heiress that she had been the prime instrument in his conversion, and that she had gained his heart.[38]

Such dark suspicions might have come from any of the anti-Puseyite novels of the fifties. Charlotte's theology did not venture far beyond what was taught in the parish of Hursley; her last pamphlet shows no acute or developed theological thinking. She wrote novels in the style most popular at the time: novels of family life, suitable for reading by families similar to those depicted in her pages. The very fact that novels were being read at all by religious and earnest people – though still not by the more rigid nonconformists and Evangelicals – was an indication that this form of literature had struggled through opposition and distrust to achieve a serious status.

With no contribution to the direction of the novel, no special technique, no developing theology, what is there to set her apart from the many female novelists whose quiet lives and personal convictions could furnish stuff for books once popular but now forgotten? Is there any reason for rating her above Margaret Oliphant, Elizabeth Sewell, Mrs Craik? It is not the sheer amount of her work, impressive though it is.[39] It is not the aspects which brief histories often notice, for these can be paralleled often enough in her contemporaries. On the level of discernible conduct she shares the attitudes of Broad Churchmen and Evangelicals, to say nothing of the vague Dickensian ethic of the good heart. The Tractarians did not innovate much on questions of personal behaviour: the disputes were seldom about the validity or even the interpretation of the formal Christian morality. Tom May's awful sin, which sets him on the downward path for a time with drink and evil companions, is his failure to own up when he spills ink on the schoolmaster's book. 'It is concealment that is the evil, not the damage to the book.'[40] Charles Kingsley would have heartily approved the sentiment. Guy Morville's continual struggle to control his hereditary temper is only a more sophisticated version of the warnings against lack of control which pepper the pages of nursery and school books of the time.

The more spectacular episodes in her novels are those which

every novelist with an eye to popularity was using. Mrs May's violent death at the start of *The Daisy Chain*; the end of Mrs Nesbit after the fire in *Heartsease*; the invalids who dominate family life and provide models of patience or warnings against selfishness; the mysterious appearance of babies without suggestions of sex – all these are common enough in the mid-Victorian novel and represent preoccupations of the age for which there were complex causes. Charlotte Yonge does not show herself a rebel or an innovator when she depicts them. She is not at odds with her age to the extent that one would expect either of a Tractarian follower or of a talented woman who achieved popularity and even fame. Female emancipation has little place in her books, either openly or by implication. Rachel Curtis in *The Clever Woman of the Family* reads unwisely and suffers doubts but is soon put right by the good clergyman Mr Clare. Her doubts are left as vague as those of Norman May in his Oxford days – or as those of Mrs Gaskell's Hale in *North and South*; and Clare is remarkably reminiscent of Keble.

Where Charlotte Yonge breaks away from the mainstream of the domestic novel is in the place which she accords to the Church of England as a visible and vital force. The moral problems, the deaths, the sufferings, the victories, are lifted out of the realm of vague goodness and given the framework of Anglican discipline. The Church is the back-scene against which her trivial and her major happenings alike are set off. It is the principal factor that remains consistent in her work, right through from the theme of building a new church in *Abbey-church* to the fortunes of the Underwoods in *The Pillars of the House*. It is not enough to be good, not enough to be wary of consequences – though Charlotte did not quarrel with either of these ideals. Yet right conduct is not fully right if it is wrongly motivated and undirected. When Kate and Emmeline in *The Castle Builders* start parish visiting and teaching poor children, they are doing indisputably good work. But because they have not come under the direction of the parish priest but under a committee which includes dissenters among its members, they find it hard to uphold their principles.

With Charlotte Yonge, the Book of Common Prayer becomes a regular companion to the Bible for the regulating of fictional characters' lives. The services of the Church are continually cited, with accuracy that is in marked contrast to vagueness about the birth of babies and about exactly what fast young men do that is so wicked. The precision, which shows her a child of the Oxford Movement, is of two types. There is the more conscious reference to matters which were occasions of theological controversy. The daily service, which the Tractarians were earnest to restore in accordance with the rubric, causes consternation to the conservative Sir Francis Willoughby in *The Castle Builders* and to the sporting junior curate of pious Julius Charnock in the much later *Three Brides*. By the time of *The Pillars of the House* there is sharp differentiation between the 'Low' late Communion and the 'High' early service, as well as the ritualistic choral Eucharist followed by sung Matins which Lance attends. In addition to these matters there is the round of steady devotion without marks of party, a round notable for the way in which it is taken for granted. Babies are christened on one Sunday in each month unless a special request for a private weekday service is made; the marriage service takes place after Matins.[41] It is accepted that these things must be rightly ordered, but without fuss.

A gift of the Oxford Movement was to restore confidence in visual imagery without fears of idolatry. The excesses of ultra-Puseyites grew from a general appeal to sensory experience in worship. The older Tractarians were far from ritualistic but there were, even in the thirties, bitter accusations about a cross on the black scarf or a pair of altar candles. Charlotte Yonge, impatient of extremes, was not afraid of symbols. The Cross as the emblem of salvation and the ground of faith was common parlance for Evangelicals and in the vaguely devout novel that claimed no party allegiance. Helen's ornamental cross in *Heartsease* is a real, tangible piece of jewellery, which is held and looked upon. Throughout the book, her posthumous influence seems to shine through it, bringing the new owner to comparable sanctity and the exercise of good to others. It is linked with the cross signed in baptism, a usage which the Church of England had kept against puritan opposition and which many Anglicans were not inclined to emphasize. Now the signing is a vital part of the sacrament:

I do not know whether it was from my hardly ever having been at a christening before, or whether it was the poor little fellow's distressing crying; but the signing him with the cross especially struck me, the token of suffering even to this lamb. The next moment I saw the fitness the cross given to him to turn the legacy of pain to the honour of partaking of the Passion – how much more for an innocent who has no penalty of his own to bear.[42]

This is specific, a contrast to the vague assertions of the age about inevitable suffering and the need for faith. The link is made between the child and the source of redemption, through the ecclesiastical symbol. Then, when the child is sick, he loves to play with the jewelled cross around his mother's neck. The domestic episodes of the novel can hold and personalize the life of disciplined faith. Charlotte's contribution in her humble way reflects the taut thinking and careful particularity of the Tractarian writers.

So too the sense of social duty, of visiting and almsgiving, become not vague axioms of good but part of the Anglican life in which the clergy oversee and the laity play their part. Charlotte herself was taking a Sunday School class at the age of seven; and her heroines are deeply engaged in similar works. No doubt many in life and in fiction can be seen, then as now, to be busy on behalf of their own needs rather than with full regard to others. The inadequacy of private charity in the growing complexity of Victorian society is clear to us; yet much was done by devoted individuals in areas which legislation had not reached and which would therefore have otherwise been left undone. There was still no substitute for the devoted spinster like Theresa Martindale or Charlotte Yonge.

The practical sense of Charlotte's heroines is notable. Where Mrs Pardiggle preaches to the family that is starving, Ethel May is earnest to supply food as well as good teaching. The aspiration for a new church in the neglected Cocksmoor district goes along with the need for a free school and the very practical problem of 'whether the National Society or Government, or something, would give them a grant, unless they had the land to build on'.[43] Never can good work be detached from right attitudes. The shared suffering of Lord St Erme and his workmen in the mine disaster brings him to a new sense of his responsibilities but also does the same for the miners. It 'has put an extinguisher on Chartism' despite the intransigence of a few 'determined village Hampdens'.[44]

While Charlotte Yonge is certainly not a novelist of social problems in the sense that the term could be used of Elizabeth Gaskell or Kingsley or Disraeli, study of her novels reveals that the developing social principles of the post-Tractarian Anglicans are reflected in them.[45] Such interdependence of the spiritual and the material was proper and indeed necessary for those who had absorbed the principles of sacramental life. Not nature only but the urban works of man could reflect the invisible world. If those who accused Pusey of caring only for ecclesiastical minutiae had listened to his sermons, they might have heard him say:

> Doubtless Dives encouraged the manufacturers of Tyre and Sidon, and the weavers of Palestine, while he bound not up the sores of Lazarus. . . . Miserable, transparent, flimsy hypocrisy. Were the employment of the poor our end, would they be less employed in manufacturing comforts for themselves than in weaving luxuries for us?[46]

Ultimately, however, the concern was with the shaping of individual character. From the right attitudes, all good would follow; but the cultivation of those attitudes is made more specific than the demands for 'change of heart' which characterize many mid-Victorian reforming novelists, from Dickens downwards. Charlotte Yonge is forward-looking in her realization that love is not only a Christian duty but the essential foundation of a balanced individual. Theodora Martindale suffers as a young woman from the lack of love in her childhood. Her condition agrees with modern psychology in its pride, alienation, inability to relate deeply. It is a harder lot than that of Guy Morville who suffers from the family temper; this he overcomes by willpower and faith, but Theodora needs to be offered and to accept love before she is made whole.

Charlotte's anxiety about the right formation of character was not confined to her creatures of fiction. At the age of twenty-seven she could produce a remarkable statement in her introduction to the first number of *The Monthly Packet*, a magazine for the young which she continued to edit for many years. The idea behind it was common enough, but its particular direction bears the hand of Keble:

It has been said that everyone forms their own character between the ages of fifteen and five-and-twenty, and this Magazine is meant to be in some degree a help to those who are thus forming; not as a guide, since that is the part of deeper and graver books, but as a companion in times of recreation, which may help you to perceive how to bring your religious principles to bear upon your daily life, may show you the examples, both good and evil, of historical persons, and may tell you of the workings of God's providence both here and in other lands.

A weakness in the Evangelical position, not indeed essential to it but too often followed, was the way in which assurance of final perseverance could lead to complacency. The Tractarian emphasis on the sacramental side of religion meant that the individual was kept continually on duty, but was offered an armour against temptation: 'how to bring your religious principles to bear upon your daily life.' The Evangelical would retort that reception of the sacraments could become mechanical, almost magical; everything rested on correct performance at a point of time and total commitment was set aside. One can understand this point of view when Arthur Martindale's child is hastily baptized lest it die soon after birth:

To his eye there was nothing at all like life in that tiny form. 'And yet how mavellous,' thought he, 'to think of its infinite gain by these few moments of unconscious existence.'[47]

The underlying doctrine had vexed theologians from St Augustine, had evolved the idea of Limbo and put the Anglican Prayer Book into a catechetical difficulty which the Oxford Movement brought into prominence.

Baptismal regeneration and the implications of infant baptism were focal points for theological trouble for many years. Pusey's three tracts on baptism (67, 68 and 69 of *Tracts for the Times*) had brought him firmly on the Tractarian side and had deepened the theological controversy of the movement. The Gorham decision of 1850, when Charlotte Yonge was at the start of her long career as a novelist, rested on the Anglican interpretation of what exactly was the effect of baptism. It is not surprising therefore to find her speaking firmly about the necessity of baptism for salvation, as a sacrament hindered neither by the unworthiness or insensibility of the recipient nor the status of the administrator. It must not be too long delayed; if a baby missed the special Sunday for public christenings, 'it could not be kept unbaptized for another month'.[48] 'I have to thank you for more than all the world besides,' Guy Morville exclaims to the old housekeeper when he learns that she had sent for the clergyman to christen him at home 'in that very china bowl – I have kept it choice ever since, and never let it be used for anything'.[49]

The sacrament of Confirmation was not quite so productive of controversy in public, but its new prominence in the minds of serious Anglicans was another result of the Oxford Movement. It had often been neglected, deferred, casually administered to an immense number of candidates who had had to wait for the infrequent episcopal visit. Thomas Arnold had thought it important and taken pains in preparing his boys for it, but had been content for it to be held every two years at Rugby and to lead to quarterly reception of Holy Communion.[50] As the Communion itself was increasingly seen as the central act of the Christian life, so preparation for it became more solemn. The aspirant had to be taught and tested by his parish priest or school chaplain, who would give him a 'ticket' when he was satisfactory in answering. The effect of the new seriousness – and infant baptism made this the first personal decision of the young Anglican – was liable to make the scrupulous delay confirmation as much as the careless. Or there might be subsequent fear of unworthy Communion: Samuel Wilberforce found many instances of 'unreasonable dread' which he tried to settle, with his well-known urbanity, by the assurance that confirmation made everything right. The same false scruples are shown as affecting Arthur Martindale in *Heartsease*: his selfishness and careless living have grown from his failure to obey the Church and receive the strengthening sacramental grace without which human nature will sin:

It had been grace missed and neglected, rather than wilfully abused. There had of course been opportunities, but there had been little culture or guidance in his early days; his confirmation had taken place as a matter of form, and he had never been a communi-

78

cant; withheld at once by ignorance and dread of strictness, as well as by a species of awe.[51]

Keble took great pains over the preparation for confirmation, seeking out the young people even in their own homes, and trying to get his instruction finished before harvest when they became elusive.[52] He taught his candidates every week, for six months to a year; and it was this kind of firm, loving discipline which did more than ritualism to win Tractarian victories in the parishes. Charlotte went to him twice a week, 'perhaps his first young lady scholar'. One hopes that he was more merciful on the village children than on her, with whom he compared different liturgies and studied Greek patristic authorities.[53] Still, she seems to have thrived; and one remembers Ethel May's voluntary use of the Greek Testament. His poem on Confirmation in *The Christian Year* states the view of his school, which often appears in Charlotte Yonge's novels, that it was a continual source of strength in later life:

> And oft as sin and sorrow tire,
>   The hallow'd hour do Thou renew,
> When beckon'd up the awful choir
>   By pastoral hands, toward Thee we drew;

> When trembling at the sacred rail
>   We hid our eyes and held our breath,
> Felt Thee how strong, our hearts how frail,
>   And long'd to own Thee to the death.

> For ever on our souls be trac'd
>   That blessing dear, that dove-like hand,
> A sheltering rock in Memory's waste,
>   O'ershadowing all the weary land.

Charlotte made her most explicit statement about confirmation, and about many things which the Oxford Movement was bringing into parish life, in *The Castle Builders*, with its unpromising sub-title *The Deferred Confirmation*. Published in volume form in 1854, it had been appearing in *The Monthly Packet* since 1851 and had therefore begun immediately after the Gorham judgement and the ensuing secessions. The story follows two sisters who have their 'tickets' but continually put off their confirmation – at first from a sense of unworthiness but later for more worldly reasons. They attend public worship and read *The Christian Year*, but their inner life suffers from lack of Communion discipline and grace:

> She was sorry that she had not been able to wind up her feelings to the point which she considered fit for receiving the sacred ordinance. She did not perceive how the grace therein received might have strengthened her on her entrance into the new sphere of trial and duty in which she had been placed. Emmeline and Kate did indeed know that life is a time of trial, but they did not so feel it; they were drifting quietly on the stream, without much thought of the course; and though they acknowledged the duty of attending to Church ordinances, these were to them duties in themselves, which stood alone, unconnected with practical life, and without influence over it. So, as confirmation was to come but once in their lives, why not at one time as well as another? And the thought of the Holy Communion made them still more inclined to defer it, since they would be afraid to stay away and yet dreaded to go without due preparation. They did not feel in their hearts, though in some degree they knew with their understandings, that prayers, Church services, Confirmation, Communions, were all steps to lead them on in the track of daily life, the waymarks set about their faith; nay, further, the wings which might bear onwards their steps.[54]

That paragraph contains a great deal about the Oxford Movement as it appeared to those who were trying to put its tenets into daily practice. The Romantic ability to 'feel in their hearts' would cut through the formality of fashionable religion and make the demands of the Prayer Book excitingly sufficient and valid. Understanding was not enough and emotion need not be undisciplined. For the Catholic life is personal, but under authority.

Failing to grasp these truths, Emmeline and Kate go from bad to worse. They become involved in parish work without proper authority and find that their dissenting colleagues are unwilling for children to be taught the catechism. This is too much, even for the unconfirmed: 'Committee, and children, and all shall see that we think the Catechism no badge of party, but the watchword of the English Church.' Nevertheless, their disobedience leads to lack of humility and disrespect to elders.

The road to salvation is found through the saintly cousin Frank, a devotee of early services, who gives up his wish for

ordination and agrees to enter the army because 'I've no business to hold out against my father' (a decision and reason at
variance with direct Gospel precept). When he is drowned and
the girls only narrowly escape, the memory of their promise to
him that they would be confirmed begins to strengthen them.
They are able to pass through a visit to London without the
sin of waltzes, though Emmeline is inveigled into a Roman
Catholic chapel for the sake of the music. Frederick Faber's
new Oratory in Brompton Road, which even Roman Catholics
of the old school were regarding as too Italianate, is probably
seen in the splendid building,

. . . in which Romanism is displayed with the greatest attraction to
educated and imaginative minds, keeping back as much as possible
all that is offensive, to a truly Catholic principle, and putting
foremost what is really true and beautiful, what it possesses as
being a Church, and hiding much of what belongs to Romanism *as
such.*[55]

The italics are Charlotte's, and no doubt Keble's too. At last
all is well and they forgo a trip to Paris so that confirmation
will not again be lost. In words reminiscent of Keble's poem
quoted above:

They kneel on the Altar step where they had never before
approached, the Apostolic hand is on their heads; the blessing is
spoken; that unspeakable gift imparted, that, unless they fall away,
will increase daily more and more, till they come to the everlasting
kingdom.[56]

No assurance of final perseverance, but the hope of a sanctified life leading to salvation through attention to Church ordinances. The importance of the sacraments was growing in the
years of arguments about authority and the recent restoration
of the Roman Catholic hierarchy. A year or two later, when
The Daisy Chain appeared, confirmation is seen as a major
event in the lives even of schoolboys. Norman May will not
defend himself against false accusations, not even if it means
the loss of a scholarship, unless he is in danger of losing his
ticket for confirmation. Young Harry is in misery and terror
lest his pranks result in his going away to sea unconfirmed.

Once again, Charlotte's religious discipline makes her more
concrete and specific as a novelist than those who were content

to depict vague remorse at sin. The scruples which afflict her characters are to be seen against the laxness which the Oxford Movement had tried to combat. A rediscovery of Catholic doctrine was bound to result in dread of losing or failing to honour the great gift. Fasting and self-denial were needed to control the will and make the body a fit vessel for the sacraments. After Pusey's Tract on fasting, there developed a pastoral attitude rather different from that of Members of Parliament in 1831, when the suggestion of a general fast during the cholera epidemic was met with cries of 'General *what*?[57] The abstinence need not be from food: 'one can do little secret things – not read story books on those days, or keep some sort of tiresome work for them.'[58] Keble could temper discipline with one of his rare flashes of humour: 'I can conceive cases where it would be more real self-denial to go to a party than to stay away from it.'[59]

All this was a long way from the world of the eighteenth-century parson who could conclude the day 'appointed to be observed as a publick Fast in these seditious times' with the comfort of 'Dinner to day rost Loin of Pork'.[60] Sometimes it fitted in only too well with the enormous guilt that afflicted the Victorians, faced by sweeping developments that seemed about to get out of control. The scruples of Guy de Morville which drive him to the painstaking correction of his story that a certain lady had smoked cigars, when in fact she had smoked only one, must be seen together with the way in which Charles Darwin came back into a room to correct an earlier statement about his travels.[61] For the Anglo-Catholic, this scrupulosity could become a religious duty, part of the serious attitude to all things which Keble had recommended in Tract 89 when he suggested that trifling and indifference in religion were worse than superstition. It could lead on to the trivial, fussy questions for self-examination which continue to appear in some devotional manuals.

That such attention to detail suggests a certain immaturity needs no stressing. To some extent it can be seen as part of the uncertainties both of the age and of a new movement. However, Charlotte Yonge's fiction bears more signs of failure to achieve maturity; despite her considerable talent, she never enters the first rank of Victorian novelists. She is at her best in the setting of the post-nursery but pre-adult world, the world of the young people in *The Heir of Redclyffe*, of the May family on their first appearance, of Emmeline, Kate and Frank in *The Castle Builders*. The problems of adolescence become vital: the entry into adult life is awaited with eagerness but some trepidation. It is so easy to go wrong, to make a bad start from which it will be difficult to recover. Therefore faults of character must be watched for and checked. Young men must work hard at their Latin and Greek in preparation for the university.

The adult world is a world of peril as well as opportunity. The threat to innocence was a common motif in Victorian fiction, notably in Dickens where the young person moves menaced but ultimately unscathed through the corruptions of the city. It lurks in *Alice*, where both dream-adventures bring encounters with threatening creatures who turn out to be only a pack of cards or a kitten: so, back to the nursery and safety. The fear of adult sexuality is plain, but its presence should not provide a narrow interpretation of what sex means. The achievement of full potency does not refer to a single type of act; and Christianity teaches that man can and should attain full power of life through grace.

Keble's *Lyra Innocentium* contains warnings about the threats to childhood innocence. Charlotte Yonge is conscious of the same fear, seen typically in the temptation and redemption of Norman May. The impetuous lad who will leave his pudding to find out a poor family in distress, the monitor who will suffer unjust accusations, develops into the Oxford undergraduate who reads books that shake his faith and causes terror to his father. But all ends well; he becomes a missionary in New Zealand. In *The Trial* we learn that his health has not allowed him to do anything spectacular there; but early training and good character allow him to accept a dull task with grace. The cynic may be tempted to murmur: 'It really was a kitten after all.' Cynicism is not the key to Charlotte Yonge, who needs to be taken on her own terms if she is to be understood.

Her terms include the absolute duty of devotion and obedience to parents. This too is less odd in the context of her times than it seems now. If we begin to yawn over the condemnation of Laura and Philip for concealing their 'understanding' from her parents, we must remember that parental consent to marriage was normally expected. The claims of parents come before lovers: John Martindale is condemned to wistful celibacy because his beloved Helen had to care for an imbecile grandfather. Emma Brandon's deception of her mother is censured as against 'the Catholic spirit'. 'It is not for us to question our father's judgements,' says pious Richard May. Charlotte herself was devoted to her father, and of course to Keble as her other father-figure. There is no bitterness in the sacrifices of her characters to parents. For, despite the demands for obedience, her fictional families are happy and playful – and above all, loving. The Mays and Edmonstones are a long way from the Fairchilds in one direction and the Pontifexes in another.

Charlotte kept more sanity and plain common sense about scruples and duties than many minor Anglican novelists. She avoids the danger, inherent in secular as well as religious puritanism, of valuing loss and suffering for their own sake. Her invalids – and they abound in her books – are not all saintly, and they are not made out to be more blessed than the fit. It is the attitude that counts, patient endurance in whatever way of life comes to one. There is wisdom, stern wisdom perhaps, in Mrs Edmonstone's advice to Guy:

'There is nothing,' said Mrs Edmonstone, 'that has no temptation in it; but I should think the rule was plain. If a duty such as that of living among us for the present, and making yourself moderately agreeable, involves temptations, they must be met and battled from within. In the same way, your position in society, with all its duties, could not be laid aside because it is full of trial. Those who do such things are faint-hearted, and fail in trust in Him who fixed their station, and finds room for them to deny themselves in the trivial round and common task. It is pleasure involving no duty that should be given up, if we find it liable to lead us astray.[62]

It was not wisdom alone, however palatable it might be to her readers, that made Charlotte so popular a writer. Shunning the excesses of Romanticism, sharing Keble's sorrow that wickedness could accompany poetic genius, she yet 'turned romanticism into a respectable church-going creed . . . no one before Charlotte had associated romance with everyday life'.[63]

84

The romance lay in making the decisions of life seem adventurous, fraught with consequences not to the choosing individual alone. It is a romance that looks back behind the Romantic Movement to the medievalism from which both the poets and the theologians had drawn some of their inspiration. Guy Morville is a Byronic figure, with his ancestral doom and his strange inheritance. But he is also a figure of Arthurian romance, with his choice of Galahad as the ideal to follow; and he and Amy, devout Anglicans, play out together the fantasy of *Sintram*.[64] He dies by saving one who had been his enemy; and he cannot die until a priest (Anglican, of course) has ministered to him. With such a mingling of romance and piety it is not surprising that the young Rossetti and Morris loved *The Heir of Redclyffe* and that it was 'the novel most demanded by the wounded officers in hospital' during the Crimean campaign.[65] The age needed some romanticizing of religion; the Evangelical temper was too opposed to sensory pleasure and therein nourished its own undoing. It was the gift of the Oxford Movement to give deep seriousness in faith without denying the imagination and the senses.

Charlotte Yonge's gifts as a novelist are seen to be largely those of other minor novelists of her age, if they are taken apart from the informing religious spirit. Her characters are rapidly identified and remain consistently recognizable throughout the action, without any obvious tricks of recurrent idiosyncrasies. The younger people are the more convincing; the older tend to be stereotypes of good advice, or bad example, or objects of charity. As the interest shifts more often to older people in her later books, so does her art decline.[66]

The creation of character, as well as the furtherance of plot, depends to a great extent on dialogue. Few novelists have so much conversation, and the result is that characters develop into the reader's consciousness with the same gradual unfolding that we experience in life. It means also that they mostly remain on a superficial level; few give any sense of shared growth in the imaginative world. Sometimes the dialogue runs on until the reader feels almost physically deafened by such a flow of feminine chatter.

Yet she is not inferior in description, particularly in setting the scene at the start of a novel or for an important episode.

She is best on domestic interiors and cultivated gardens, less certain with wild nature. But an exception to the last point must be made in her use of the sea and coastal scenery. The sea recurs time and again, an image of liberation and healing, or of menace and destruction. In *Heartsease* Violet and her baby recover in the Isle of Wight. For Guy Morville, 'everything looks so dull' away from the sea by which he grew up, but that same coast imperils his life and proves his manhood in the rescue from the wreck. Frank's death by drowning is a new birth of conscience for Emmeline and Kate, who have shared his peril. Ethel May, on her first sight of the sea, experiences new sensations:

At the edge of the water she stood – as all others stand there – watching the heaving from far away come nearer, nearer, curl over in its pride of green glassy beauty, fall into foam, and draw back.[67]

The sea is an image too common and too universal to admit of any single interpretation. We may see the Romantic wildness, the water of baptism, the archetypal source of destruction and renewal or the flow and ebb of sexual energy. We may see much more, or we may be content to observe the power of the sea in the destinies of Charlotte Yonge's characters as a linking theme.

She can be subtle and unexpected in her imagery. The accident of Philip with Amy's camelia at the beginning of *The Heir of Redclyffe* prefigures his blundering self-confidence which will end in her widowhood. After breaking her engagement with Fotheringham, Theodora Martindale is often haunted by a sudden vision of the green umbrella which he carried when they met. Harry May's Prayer Book which stops a bullet and saves his life is more convincing through contemporary eyes than it is today when such stories have been too often told.

It is a narrow world certainly, though it widens to include more public events such as the Crimea and the American Civil War, and the sensation of trial and prison in *The Trial*. By this time, Reade and Collins were publishing and restoring to the novel a sensational element within their cultivated realism. Even earlier, the Paris revolution of 1848 figures in *Dynevor Terrace*. She is never out of her age – even her historical novels bear the stamp of Victorian Anglican life – but she is not committed to it for standards of judgement. What was said above about taking her novels without the religious spirit offers an exercise of doubtful value. All works together when she writes. She transformed the 'church novel' from a fictionalized source of direct doctrinal teaching to a particular emphasis in the domestic novel. She was fortunate in her time, practising her art when the novel had strength and confidence to carry a message without being overwhelmed by direct propaganda (though many feeble novelists with messages still were overwhelmed). She was the best of those of whom a critic could write:

By degrees as these [Anglo-Catholic] doctrines became more and more clearly understood and acted on, the religious tale dropped its expository conversations and its preachments, and allowed the thread of the story to go on unbroken, trusting to the general tone of the whole to impress the reader with the great practical truths which hang upon and accompany the belief of doctrinal truth; faith is illustrated more by the life of the character described than by mere theological terms by which it may be expressed.[68]

The main limitation in Charlotte as a writer – and in Keble as a theologian – was a blank refusal to respect the opposition, the belief that doubt and resistance to the plain teaching of the Church were certainly sinful. Yet from him she gained that strong moral earnestness coupled with a regular devotional life which was a great gift of the Oxford Movement. Far away from the centres of controversy, she tried to show how doctrine could change not only worship but the whole tenor of life. The achievement of her best characters echoes what an old parishioner said of Keble: he was 'outside the Church what he professed to be inside it'.[69]

4

The Indignation of Charles Kingsley

In January 1864 *Macmillan's Magazine* was in its fifth year of growing reputation as a judicious literary review. Readers who worked their way assiduously through those ample review-articles which the leisurely journalism of the age produced came eventually to a notice of two new volumes of J.A. Froude's *History of England*. It was a friendly review, discursive, and intertwined with the reviewer's own opinions, among which was a diatribe against the Roman Catholicism of the sixteenth century. None of it was likely to flutter the fresh pages: Froude had gained a reputation with the earlier parts of his work, and if his anti-Catholicism was occasioned by a less purely Protestant spirit than the 'C.K.' who reviewed him, it was sufficiently acceptable to the majority of his readers. After accusing the Romanist authorities of various breaches of morality, C.K. continued:

So, again, of the virtue of truth. Truth, for its own sake, had never been a virtue with the Roman clergy. Father Newman informs us that it need not, and on the whole ought not to be; that cunning is the weapon which Heaven has given the saints wherewith to withstand the brute male force of the wicked world which marries and is given in marriage. Whether his notion be doctrinally correct or not, it is at least historically so.[1]

Thus began the greatest of all ¡the public controversies that developed out of the Oxford Movement, a quarrel in which both parties repudiated for different reasons the principles of Tractarianism from which it had all begun. It produced the most famous literary account of what that movement had been, contained in what is probably the greatest of English spiritual autobiographies. No one would have been surprised to learn that 'C.K.' the reviewer was Charles Kingsley, whose habit of provoking rows and finding himself at the centre of trouble was equalled by his detestation of all things Roman Catholic or Puseyite.

That review is a focal point in Kingsley's career, summing up much of his best and his worst even before the moment of truth in his long skirmish with Newman. He was reviewing the book of a man whom he had befriended and helped at a time when Froude was unemployed and disgraced after leaving his Oxford fellowship and publishing his sceptical novel *The Nemesis of Faith*. Kingsley had then sheltered him at the cost of opposition even from his own family, acting from one of the warm impulses that made his life as a Church of England clergyman such a patchwork of admiration and hatred. Froude married Kingsley's wife's sister and remained on close terms, though he could be exasperated by his volatile brother-in-law to the extent of complaining: 'his habit of thought and tone of feeling are so wholly uncongenial to me that I cannot even proximately estimate the worth of either.'[2]

The whole affair was typical of Kingsley's rushing into a fray without planning any campaign, and being surprised to find himself deeply involved after he had almost forgotten his words and taken up some new enthusiasm. There had been several such encounters, some carried through and others soon abandoned. Some had been concerned with the Oxford Movement and its results, into which his life had been drawn even more closely than was inevitable for any clerical thinker at the time. Kingsley could not let the Puseyites alone; he gave to them, and to those who had left them for Rome, a sparring-partner who drew and lost a fair amount of blood before the grand bout that ended in his decisive defeat.

Not that he ever really understood these opponents. He did not have the intellect of their best men, certainly not that of Newman whom he so disastrously underestimated. He could

89

never comprehend, and therefore could not respect as honest, their genuine sense of the development of belief through slow mental clarification of their position. When they developed, they appeared to him only to have changed – and to change in religion at that time seemed like treachery. Though he was critical of many features of his age and was eager for change, his basic optimism stopped him from understanding the Tractarian alienation, the backward vision that clung to an image of the Church as an Ark of Refuge in an evil time.

Now Kingsley was neither a moron nor a blunderer. He was not intellectually in Newman's class, but he had a lively intelligence with flashes of genius. When he seems in retrospect to have made a fool of himself, the fault is usually found to lie in his too-quick enthusiasm. He felt deeply, and thought deeply too; but his feelings often outran his thought. He was not a systematic thinker; but he had something which his own age valued and which both Roman and Anglo-Catholic opponents sometimes needed to save them from complacently ignoring crude, senseless attacks. He knew how to make articulate and coherent the religious attitude that was congenial to untheological minds. He could find true religion in a *via media* different from that of the Tractarians, avoiding both Catholic and Protestant extremes. For while it is his attack on the Catholic side that is mainly remembered, he was almost as much opposed to the Evangelicals as to the Puseyites and Romanists. The new movement and the older one alike housed objects of his scorn: 'undesirable coxcombs, who have not been bred by the High Church movement, but have taken refuge in its cracks, as they would have done forty years ago in those of the Evangelical.'[3]

For many of Kingsley's contemporaries, both clerical and lay, the distrust of extremes led to indifferentism and acquiescence in easy conformity – the attitude against which both Evangelicals and Tractarians had protested. For Kingsley himself, religion was a living force that should inform society as well as private life, demanding faith and also producing abundant works. Demanding charity too, for in spite of his frequent fulminations he was less ready than many more loose believers to make a total condemnation of all who differed from him. There was ready hospitality for the rebel Froude, generous admiration for the books of Charlotte M. Yonge which a young woman should read, 'becoming all the wiser thereby'.[4]

Kingsley cared about Christianity, and therefore he cared about what was going on around him. He had the temperament that could not stop from bursting out in praise or blame when he felt deeply. He shared with many in that age of individualism that belief that all would be well if each man could undergo a change of heart and live by the pure precepts of the Gospel. Though he supported plans and movements for reform, he remained at heart a visionary looking for special miracles. His ideal hero is the well-rounded man who learns to live at different social levels, probing and investigating until a final conversion adds the needed Christian grace. This is the course, though they start from different positions, of Lancelot Smith, Alton Locke and Tom Thurnall, in whom 'the old heart passed away . . . the heart of a little child' taking its place. Froude unaccepting but shrewd, noted Kingsley's absolute faith in the beneficial results of 'healthy animalism and God-made man'.[5]

Yet Kingsley was not less complex than other great Victorians, and he aroused varying reactions in his contemporaries. To some he seemed the epitome of all that was English, manly and honourable, like the Elizabethan adventurers that he and Froude popularized. He loved sports, particularly hunting and fishing, and described them in his novels with loving precision. He was once inhibited from preaching in London because he spoke up for the grievances of the poor, but he became a royal chaplain, tutored the Prince of Wales and held canonries at Chester and Westminster. For most of his working life he held a country rectory and was loved as a pastor who would rebuke his parishioners roundly but would nurse them in an epidemic. To a later and more critical generation he might seem rather a boor, to be coupled with Browning as an example of false optimism. Gerard Manley Hopkins who had theological as well as literary reasons for disliking him, could associate them together in 'the air and spirit of a man bouncing up from table with his mouth full of bread and cheese and saying that he meant to stand no blasted nonsense'.[6]

Yet there was something more than all these things, over-looked by most of his admirers and critics. Beneath the buc-caneering and the eulogies of outdoor life there was a darkness. Many Victorians shouted loudly to cover the deep uncertainty. Kingsley did this too, but he understood the dark night of the soul. Perhaps the inhibitions of the age made him guilty about his own strong sexuality; perhaps signs of homosexuality in his brother Henry made him fear the like in himself and pro-ject his fear in accusations of effeminacy against Puseyites and Romanists. Perhaps the anxiety was not sexual in the narrow sense but a deeper emotional longing risen from divided admiration for his father and love for the mother whom the father seemed to treat inconsiderately. Certainly there are moments when he looks forward to the generation of Hardy and Gissing, and on to the twentieth century. He could suffer with those who

> . . . have gone down into the bottomless pit, and *stato all' inferno* – as the children used truly to say of Dante; and there, out of the utter darkness, have asked the question of all questions – 'Is there a God? And if there be, what is He doing with me?'[7]

In the ecclesiastical divisions of the time Kingsley stood with the Broad Church, a follower of Frederick Denison Maurice in a line stemming partly from Coleridge, with ap-proval of matters on which the majority agreed stronger than condemnation for those on which they differed. The Broad Churchmen saw the Church neither as a narrow sect which must exclude all others nor as a fortress against secularism. It was to be comprehensive, freeing men from the bondage of 'one group or party right' and all the others wrong. They did not waive theology as of no account, but they wanted to examine dogma critically in the light of modern thought. Maurice had indeed been attracted to the Oxford Movement in its early years and had gained some Tractarian support for the possibility of a Chair at Oxford in 1836. It was the baptis-mal question as set out in Pusey's tracts on the subject which severed his sympathy.

Maurice was a greater thinker than most of his school. His theological writing caused more antagonism in his own time than did the usual run of Broad Church publications, and it has been much more influential in our own time. He always kept, however, his sympathy with seekers like Kingsley's Lancelot Smith among the warring sects:

[The High Church priest] told me to hear the Catholic Church. I asked him which Catholic Church? He said the English. I asked him whether it was to be the Church of the sixth century, or the thirteenth, or the seventeenth or the eighteenth? He told me the one and eternal Church which belonged as much to the nineteenth century as to the first. I begged to know whether, then, I was to hear the Church according to Simeon, or according to Newman, or according to St Paul, for they seemed to me a little at variance? He told me, austerely enough, that the mind of the Church was embodied in her liturgy and Articles. To which I answered, that the mind of the episcopal clergy might, perhaps, be; but, then, how happened it that they were always quarrelling and calling hard names about the sense of those very documents? And so I left him, assuring him that, living in the nineteenth century, I wanted to hear the Church of the nineteenth century, and no other; and should be most happy to listen to her, as soon as she had made up her mind what to say.[8]

With these insights into the weakness of sectarianism, coupled with the belief that enough good will could meet contemporary seekers' needs, it was inevitable that the Broad Churchmen should cross swords with the Puseyites. Willingness to compromise and make concessions seemed to the latter like a new manifestation of the hated Liberalism of 1833. One of the less creditable episodes in the story of the Puseyites is the witch-hunt for heresy which they pressed against some of the contributors to *Essays and Reviews*. When A.P. Stanley, Arnold's disciple and Kingsley's friend, was Dean of Westminster, Pusey refused to preach in the Abbey because Stanley had not condemned the views of Colenso; the boycott was shared by Keble, and Liddon would not occupy a pulpit from which Stanley and Maurice had spoken.[9]

At this distance of time, the separation of sincere Christians within the same Church seems tragi-comic when it is not simply foolish. The *odium theologicum* which had exploded at Oxford in the thirties was kept up by the Puseyites in their role as guardians of Catholic truth in the Church of England. From different premises, both they and the Broad Churchmen were able to look outwards and make the Anglican system less insular. Stanley's *Eastern Church* (1861) helped to foster understanding between Anglicans and Orthodox, as did Neale's writings in the Tractarian tradition. By the time that Charles Gore edited *Lux Mundi* in 1889, the heirs both of Pusey and of Maurice could draw together and find that they were working on common ground.

There might have been greater works if the understanding had come earlier. The likenesses were many, in detail as well as in the shared incarnational faith. In the Broad Church group, Kingsley occupied a position comparable to that of Keble among the Anglo-Catholics. Each of them was a devoted country rector; neither was the acknowledged head of his school, but each was the most famous within it as an imaginative writer. For each of them the needs of the parish were the primary claim on time and energy; they cared about the wretched conditions of the agricultural worker and the consequences of the prevailing system of poor relief.[10]

The Broad Churchmen were, for all their tolerance, all their desire to reconcile extremes, limited by the prevailing dislike and distrust of Roman Catholicism. They felt it as part of their staunch Church of England tradition, and they followed in a line of development which regarded that tradition as correct but did not intend to be fanatical about it; they have been called 'the true heirs of the Tudor settlement'.[11] Kingsley's antagonism to all forms of Catholicism was stronger than the Broad Church average. His curate in late years at Eversley recalled him as the most uncompromising opponent of Rome that he had ever known.[12] The slightest acquaintance with Kingsley's writing confirms this, and it goes some way to explain the considerable popularity which he enjoyed in his lifetime. He spoke for 'Protestant and common-sense England', challenging Papal claims in Carlylean terms: 'The only answer I give is John Bull's old dumb instinctive "Everlasting No!" which he will stand by, if need be, with sharp shot and cold steel.'[13]

If these attitudes from the work of Kingsley's maturity are unequivocal enough, they are comparatively mild against what is stated or implied in his historical novels – the baiting of monks and hermits in *Hereward the Wake* (1865) and the wild accusations of *Westward Ho!* (1855). This latter book owed much to Froude, whose historical views on the Reformation were well attuned to Kingsley's own, and who drew his attention to the story of John Oxenham in Hakluyt. The horrors of the Inquisition and the depravity of the priest trained Eustace are contrasted with the healthy activities and noble bearing which Protestant allegiance in the sixteenth century was understood to have carried with it. Kingsley's imagination was never slow to expand a few hints into a full-scale indictment of anything which he disliked. It was an uncontrolled richness which he shared with the greater Dickens and which was for both novelists a strength that occasionally led to artistic disaster. Kingsley's zeal in *Westward Ho!* was too much for even an Anglican reviewer, who found it an 'outburst of burly triumphant Protestantism and nationality'.[14]

All this rumbustious stuff was good for the popular market and, within the general reference of the time, might be seen as good clean fun and not given serious analysis. But Kingsley was too shrewd a man, and one who cared too deeply for individual choice, to be carried away on a wave of popular sentiment. He enjoyed putting fierce slogans into the mouths of his characters and he could feel sympathy with the real-life prototypes who said the same kind of thing. Yet he knew that Roman Catholicism could attract men not deficient in either intellect or character. He knew the conventual pull too well from the experiences of his wife and her sister. He knew too that Rome could draw a young man in moments of insecurity, for he had felt it while the black mood was on him as a Cambridge undergraduate. Then, in the despair of religious doubt and disturbance, he knew that there was a kind of certainty if the offer could be accepted. The release from warring sects that he later found in Broad Church syncretism could be in that monolithic and uncompromising claim.

What he feared most was not the fires of Smithfield or the seduction of nuns. He could laugh, wryly enough, at the fears of those like Lancelot Smith's uncle in *Yeast* who sees Jesuits behind all his misfortunes after his son has seceded. The old tales did well enough for popular propaganda, but the deeper dread was in greater comprehension. Good men could go over; therefore Rome had strength, even though her representatives might wield it unworthily. His appeal to his fellow-countrymen was not in essence for 'sharp shot and cold steel' but for awareness to combat the soporific claims of a Church that offered all the answers to Protestant divisions and insecurity. He enters the narrative in his own person to discuss recent conversions:

> If peace of mind be the *summum bonum*, and religion is mainly the science of self-satisfaction, they are right; and the wisest plan will be to follow them at once, or failing that, to apply to the next best substitute that can be discovered – alcohol and opium.[15]

To extend the hatred of Rome to hatred of Puseyites was commonplace, and Kingsley made the accusations of Romanizing which many others were making. Here again, he did more than express his opinion with clever invention and private fervour. Whether he was right or wrong in his judgements, he could see farther into Puseyism than the ritualistic externals. He could make fun of the follies of a girl who 'knelt and prayed at her velvet faldstool, among all those nick-nacks which nowadays make a luxury of devotion . . . for those who, as she thought, were fighting at Oxford the cause of universal truth and reverend antiquity', and who possessed 'several Popish books of devotion . . . on her table, which seemed to her to patch a gap or two in the Prayer-Book'. No, these things, and the new Anglican interest in religious sisterhoods, are only part of the 'rickety old windmill of sham Popery which you have taken for a real giant'.[16]

Then why all the fuss? What was the danger in this sham Popery that needed to be so stoutly combated? It was not primarily these points of ritual and ceremony; it was not even primarily theological. There was much in the Tractarian theology that could be enfolded in the ample wings of the Broad Church, and some things that Kingsley himself could actively approve.[17] He wished that there could be an Anglican doctrine of purgatory; it might remove some of the difficulties with the comminatory parts of the Athanasian Creed which troubled him. It would help to straighten out the problem of eternal punishment that had helped to drive Froude out of the Church and whose denial had cost Maurice a theological Chair. This was a doctrine that Kingsley saw as one of the worst features of Evangelicalism, compelling sorrow for the living in finality of judgement on the dead: 'Strange, is it not, that it was a duty to pray for all those poor things last night, and a sin to pray for them this morning?'[18]

There were other 'Popish' ideas which could receive a longing glance, even if a rosy Protestant blush soon followed. Private confession could be admired, taken as 'the thing itself which will do them good, without the red rag of an official name, which sends them cackling off like frightened turkeys' even if the 'true British bull-dog fashion' was to prefer a silent repentance 'too deep for all the confessionals, penances or acts of contrition'.[19] Even ceremonial, the chief popular complaint against the Puseyites, might hide a hopeful sign of the times in a revival of tradition tempered by Biblical Protestantism:

Look, again, at the healthy craving after religious art and ceremonial – the strong desire to preserve that which has stood the test of time; and on the other hand at the manful resolution of your middle class to stand or fall by the Bible alone – to admit no innovations in worship which are empty of instinctive meaning.[20]

Even an Anglo-Catholic clergyman might become a model pastor, loved by his flock despite his 'pomp and circumstance of worship' once he had proved himself manly in a crisis.[21]

So Puseyism could contain things which were good in so far as they were part of the English tradition, honestly rediscovered and subjected to scriptural proofs. Kingsley was not one of those who saw the revival as disloyal in its essence, to be utterly condemned. Accusations of secret Romanizing had been flung at the Tractarians ever since the Hampden affair, increasing with the publications of Froude's *Remains* and Ward's *Ideal* and rising to a crescendo with Newman's secession. The charge of having been a secret Papist, luring men to Rome while holding Anglican orders, was frequently made against Newman, and its sting was sharp until Kingsley unintentionally gave him the chance of dealing with it.

It was perhaps not surprising that the British public should have been driven near to panic by the appearance in parish churches of practices and doctrines which had always been regarded as Roman. The vestments and the many Catholic aids to devotion were known to the majority only from illustrations to Gothic novels about wicked monks, or the crude woodcuts of popular pamphlets.[22] It was too much for common sense to go on believing that every Puseyite clergyman was a Roman Catholic in disguise, dispensed by the Pope in order to make converts, whatever might be thought of the leaders. But it was widely held that the Puseyites were unwitting catspaws, that the Roman hierarchy under Wiseman was jubilant at their success and using it to further Papal incursions.[23]

Of course there were many things for which native honesty was obliged to admire the Puseyites. Their scholarship, their industry, their personal holiness and their devotion as pastors could be called in question only by the most extreme bigots. But British caution must assure itself with the maxims that there was no smoke without fire and more in the revival than met the eye. Where Protestant excesses were despised and satirized, Puseyites aroused fear as well as dislike: the popular reaction to them was similar in kind to that which was felt for Roman Catholics.

'Popery' became the word for all actions and emphases that seemed contrary to the basic Protestant settlement. It could be detached from declared allegiance to the Holy See, as Pusey discovered when he ventured to suggest to a Protestant clergyman in Ireland that Luther might not be a perfect spiritual guide. He was driven out of the room with a truly Irish blend of warmth and abuse: 'We are glad to see you here, Dr Pusey. We respect your learning and your character but we want no more Popery, Dr Pusey, no more Popery. We have enough of our own.'[24] Pusey's private use of the rosary was enough to raise accusations of Popery against him and was a factor in the inhibition from preaching that he suffered.

Lord John Russell, Newman's old aversion, was prepared to make the charge in correspondence with the Queen, who needed no encouragement to suspicion of extremes:

The matter to create national alarm is, as your Majesty says, the growth of Roman Catholic doctrine within the bosom of the Church. Dr Arnold said very truly. 'I look upon a Roman Catholic as an enemy in his uniform. I look upon a Tractarian as an enemy disguised, as a spy.'[25]

The novelists who joined in the controversy commonly showed the Puseyite clergy as foolish tools of the devil, or at least of the Jesuits, which came to much the same.[26] Even more tolerant and less credulous minds could find something dishonourable in the preaching of apparently Popish doctrines within the privileged fold of the Established Church. There was little appreciation of theological niceties at the popular level. A leading Quaker wrote in 1845: '*No one* disputes that Dr Pusey has a right to preach Puseyism, or any other ism, but can *any one* tell what right he has to preach it at the expense of the nation?'[27]

Charles Kingsley, a man quick to find enemies and generous in acknowledging the good in them, could not escape the tension over these matters. If he could tolerate and even partly admire some of the traditional features of the movement, his wild hatred of Romanism was aroused by those which seemed to be merely aping the latest Popish fashion. But this was not the only ground of contention; he found himself opposed to the Puseyites over many issues, and he was not the man to sit down and sort out his responses. He made himself a continual irritant to them, skirmishing and sometimes striking hard, until he was swatted by their lost leader. Their whole attitude to the nineteenth century was at variance with his, and with that of many great contemporaries. It was in these ways as much as in theology that they aroused opposition: yet they were giving society some correctives which its more optimistic members needed.

While they tended to seek in the past a refuge from a corrupt age and to deplore changes that exalted the power of the state over the authority of the Church, Kingsley was enthusiastic about the way things were going. Certainly he found much to annoy him in the society in which he lived, but it was the annoyance of a reformer who believed that things could be put right rather than the despair of a conservative. The Great Exhibition of 1851 moved him to wonder and admiration, not to disgust at its ugliness and materialism as it did William Morris. His chief social preoccupation for many years was public hygiene and sanitary reform, where Chadwick had shown how the dangers inherent in the present state of things might be removed. Kingsley, strengthened in resolve by his

experience at Eversley of a damp rectory and a village epidemic, was willing to go beyond all but the most enthusiastic
of his contemporaries. Each of the three novels set in his own
period depicts bad housing and insanitary conditions which
lead to disease. The question, important though it indeed was,
became almost an obsession with him. His response may have
owed something to an unconscious guilt about his own animal
vigour, which also fed his violence against celibacy.

Therefore he saw science not as the threat to faith which it
seemed to fundamentalists of both wings but as an agent of
new hopes for progress. He could deny Malthusian fears of
over-population in his address 'The Massacre of the Inno-
cents' to that symbol of several features of the age, the Ladies'
Sanitary Association.[28] Science would provide the means of
preserving lives that were saved; science was a stimulus to men
of faith, not a challenge. His own quick observation and love of
the natural scene fanned his enthusiasm. The awkward fossils
that troubled scientists of narrow faith like Philip Gosse, and
which Keble dealt with in a very unintellectual manner, roused him only to fresh wonder at the Creator's power.[29] As for
Colenso, it was a poor faith that could be destroyed by questioning a few texts:' . . . if all that Colenso says were proved to
be true, it would not take away from Scripture anything con-
cerning God, Christ or our own souls, which is of the least
importance to us.'[30] He even welcomed Darwin's theory as
posing a plain choice between a caring God and blind chance.

The implications of the new scientism were not confined to
the dating of the Earth or the mechanistic movements of the
stars. The passions which it aroused in religious matters went
into the whole view of human nature. Both the Evangelical
and the Anglo-Catholic had a belief in total human depravity,
to be redeemed only by a personal conviction of saving grace
or by the sacramental ministrations of the Church as the case
might be. Kingsley owed more in this respect to Rousseau and
Godwin. The Pelagian view that man can achieve positive
merit through his own efforts – one always attractive to the
British mind – appealed to him as he saw society slowly
improving and capable of further progress. He saw human
character less as a battleground between forces of spiritual
good and evil than as the product of environment, or at least as

strongly influenced by it. It seemed to him that this was in fact the prevailing view of the time, however the parties might pay lip-service to other ideas. His articulate young tailor sees it in both secular and Tractarian teaching:

So I began to look on man (and too many of us, I am afraid, are doing so) as the creature and puppet of circumstances – of the particular outward system, social or political, in which he happens to find himself. An abominable heresy, no doubt; but, somehow, it appears to me just the same as Benthamites, and economists, and high churchmen too, for that matter, have been preaching for the last twenty years, with great applause from their respective parties. One set informs the world that it is to be regenerated by cheap bread, free trade, and that peculiar form of the 'freedom of industry' which, in plain language, signifies 'the despotism of capital'; and which, whatever it means, is merely some outward system, circumstance or 'dodge', *about* man, and not *in* him. Another party's nostrum is more churches, more schools, more clergymen – excellent things in their way – better even than cheap bread, or free trade, providing only that they are excellent – that the churches, schools, clergymen, are good ones. But the party of whom I am speaking seem to us workmen to consider the quality quite a secondary consideration, compared with the quantity. They expect the world to be regenerated, not by becoming more a Church – none would gladlier help them in bringing that about than the Chartists themselves, paradoxical as it may seem – but by being dosed somewhat more with a certain 'Church system', circumstance, or 'dodge'. For my part, I seem to have learned that the only thing to regenerate the world is not more of any system, good or bad, but simply more of the Spirit of God.[31]

Kingsley was too much of an individualist, and too optimistic, to regard man as a 'puppet of circumstances'. Yet he was projecting on to the Tractarians an attitude prevalent in the Christian Socialist circles in which he moved. The Spirit of God was sometimes invoked as an afterthought, when a series of reforms had been canvassed to put right the sickness in the lives of the oppressed masses. The reference could be as vague as the change of heart which humanitarian novelists hoped to inspire; it was often far from the precise dogmatic formulations of the Tractarians and their successors. To say as much is not to impugn sincerity of either faith or goodwill in the Christian Socialists. They did not clearly think out the theological and the political areas of their protest, and they might have replied that they did not recognize any such distinction. It is a problem beyond present scope; but we may note that such blurring of boundaries was disliked by the men of the Oxford Movement and was the occasion of the first revolt in 1833.

Seeking political means to social reform, Kingsley and his fellows suffered some tension. He could admire the good in Chartism and could movingly state in *Alton Locke* (1850) the dilemma of the best workers who were driven into it by their articulate despair. As a boy at Clifton he had seen the Bristol riots in 1831, which moved him to both fear and compassion.[32] As he grew older, so did his respect for law and order increase and his old enthusiasm for Carlyle and radicalism wane.

Yet he never reneged on the question of basic human rights. The urban sufferings of *Alton Locke*, the rural ones of *Yeast*, always kept his sympathy. His heroes speak of Carlyle and Chadwick and Disraeli;[33] from the last he took more than a hint of Young England ideals, but their fulfilment was to be rather through the process of legislation and state power which was becoming the norm, though some still stigmatized it and called it socialism:

If man living in civilized society has one right which he can demand it is this, that the State which exists by his labour shall enable him to develop, or, at least, not hinder his developing, his whole faculties to their utmost, however lofty that may be.[34]

This was a long way from the fear of state encroachments which had united the Oxford reformers in the early days of the movement. The clash of politics and theology was inevitable: if the liberal Broad Church was the way of salvation, Christian Socialism was the way of amelioration. The extremists were therefore culpable for alienating the ordinary people of the land from their real hope and for blinding them with sectarian promises:

The masses ... seem ... to be losing most fearfully the living spirit of Christianity, and to be, for that very reason, clinging all the more convulsively – and who can blame them? – to the outward letter of it, whether High Church or Evangelical.[35]

Even the Crimean War produced theological differences between the supporters and opponents of the British action. Kingsley of course supported it – he was always liable to get chauvinistic when the sufferers were at a distance from him, and he accepted the doings of Brooke in Borneo and the bombardment of Canton. The war gave him a focal point for *Two Years Ago* (1857), where both the hero and the heroine go to take part in it and find their souls in loneliness and suffering. He was, like most thinking men of the time, critical of those mistakes in administration 'which have been but too notorious' and thus united for once in protest with Dickens and with Newman himself.

Basically, however, he had no doubt about the rightness of his country's cause. The war increased his suspicion that the Puseyites were not thoroughgoing Britons. He wrote to his fellow-socialist Tom Hughes:

I always knew that the Puseyites for superstitious feelings about 'The Crescent and the Cross' disliked the war . . . be sure that there is a strong Russian feeling among the Puseyites, just because they hanker after the Greek Church *faute de Rome*.[36]

The taint of disloyalty, growing from a genuine conflict of feeling, made the Puseyites more unpopular still in the country. Charlotte Yonge, years later, was anxious to repudiate the charge as far as Keble was concerned, while still expressing the difficulty which Kingsley had distorted in his own way:

He did indeed regret that justice required us to support an un-Christian power, but – not only on account of the personal friends engaged – his thoughts were greatly occupied with it.[37]

Another admirer of Keble's took a stronger Puseyite line on his behalf:

It grieved him sorely that England should have been compelled to league herself with a great Mahometan power against another Christian nation. He had a great love for the Greek Church, and could not bear that her sons should come into conflict with those of our own communion.[38]

It was typical of that age of religious ferment that feelings about the warring parties should have brought in theological questions. 'On moral grounds I sided with Turkey,' wrote

Francis Newman, a refugee from Anglican and other ortho-
doxies.[39] Even the devoted service of Florence Nightingale
aroused party feelings. She was a High Anglican, and willing
to include Roman Catholic nurses in her Crimean contingent;
some papers alleged that her leadership had been wrongly
preferred over the unquestionably Protestant Lady Maria
Forester.

Yet there were objections to all forms of Catholicism that
concerned Kingsley more deeply than any of these things. The
two main horrors, so far as he was concerned, were the exalta-
tion of celibacy and the bending of truth. Both appeared in the
unfortunate review in *Macmillan's*: the gibe about the 'brute
male force of the wicked world which marries and is given in
marriage' equally with the imputation of dishonesty.

Newman's personal conviction of being called to a celibate
life had come early. Hurrell Froude, with his love of the
medieval Church, had taught him a new ideal of dedicated
virginity which had spread to their younger followers when the
movement gained support. The Puseyites had been often
condemned for their attempts to revive sisterhoods; open
violence was directed against J.M.Neale for his religious order
at East Grinstead in Sussex. Kingsley's wife had been near to
entering the community set up under Pusey's aegis at Park
Village before he overcame her scruples and her family's
objections.

Thus once again personal experience played in with Kingsley's prejudices and with those of his age. His contemporaries
remarked on his animal vigour, his love of physical activity,
his enthusiasm for life – and these things are felt in his writing.
His marriage was happy, and passionate beyond what we have
come to believe of the Victorians and what they were prepared
to acknowledge about themselves. His enthusiasm for female
beauty was thought unbecoming in a parson; some of his
poetry was deemed sensuous to the point of impropriety and
he could draw nudes with a skill seldom associated with his
cloth. That he was a faithful husband and a priest fit to preach
morality is not seriously to be questioned. Yet there must have
been tensions for him in an age that laid so many restrictions
on the frank expression of sexual pleasure. Whether or not
his brother Henry was homosexual, the latter was certainly a

member of the misogynist Fez Club at Oxford – an association that Charles must have considered typical of the University which had nurtured Newman and Pusey.

Celibacy, and indeed any ascetic mortification of the flesh, was in his eyes no honour. Kingsley never missed an opportunity of taunting the celibate clergy with effeminacy. Although he never met Newman, he probably heard descriptions of the almost female delicacy which many people observed. In a letter written in 1851, which did not mention Newman by name but referred almost certainly to him and quite certainly to his disciples, he declared:

> In him and in all that school, there is an element of foppery – even in dress and manner; a fastidious, maundering die-away effeminacy, which is mistaken for purity and refinement; and I confess myself unable to cope with it, so alluring is it to the minds of an effeminate and luxurious aristocracy.[40]

The confession is perhaps as telling as the indictment; here as so often in dealing with Catholic practices Kingsley was out of his depth. It should be remarked too that 'effeminacy' in his time did not need to carry an imputation of sexual inversion. Here and elsewhere he was probably accusing his opponents of nothing more than a lack of the manly virtues which could produce a Hereward or an Amyas Leigh. The Roman and Puseyite clergy were being condemned not as pathics but as 'milksops'.

In *Yeast* Kingsley poured out his scorn as he fought again his struggle to win Charlotte Grenfell against family opposition and the pull of Anglo-Catholic conventual life. Lancelot Smith, who resembles the youthful Kingsley in some respects, including his stammer at moments of emotion, stands up to the machinations of the Puseyite vicar who is inveigling Argemone into entering a sisterhood. Lancelot takes on himself to explain how the celibate ideal had grown among the early Christians who saw marriage degraded in the corrupt pagan world and whose priests affected to despise the pleasures denied to them by canon law.[41] He stands for the ideal of chastity before marriage and faithfulness after: the false antithesis to celibacy is found in the 'liaisons' of Bracebridge, equally unnatural in practice and disastrous in consequences.

However, Kingsley succeeded in making both young men virile and hot-blooded enough for a High Church reviewer to miss or reject his main thesis:

> Above all, we are utterly at issue with him in an opinion that a certain amount of youthful profligacy does no real and permanent harm to the character: perhaps strengthens it for a useful and even religious life; and that the existence of the passions is a proof that they are to be gratified.[42]

Both his contemporaries and our own have tended, from opposite extremes of imbalance, to isolate the attack on sexual abnegation from Kingsley's broader objection to regarding the body as evil. Argemone is foolish and self-centred in her minor mortifications as well as in her dreams of celibate vows; Lancelot's Puseyite cousin Luke also finds unhealthy delight in asceticism. The sinister Vicar is shaken from what is left of his Protestant honesty and withholds the fatal letter from Lancelot because the temptation came to him on a Friday when he was fasting and 'his self-weakened will punished him, by yielding him up an easy prey to his own fancies'.

Kingsley rid himself of a good deal of rancour against Catholics of both obediences in *Yeast*.[43] In *Alton Locke* another Puseyite cousin of the hero appears but his level of churchmanship is seen less as the corruption of a good man than as the cynical affectation of an unpleasant youth. To make him an extreme Evangelical would have served as well, and made little difference to the main thesis of the novel. The attacks on Puseyism are incidental, as in the passage quoted above and the remarks of the country labourer on the new parsons:

> There's two or three nice young gentlemen come'd round here now, but they're all what's-'em-a-call-it? – some sort of papishes; leastwise, they has prayers in the church every day, and doesn't preach the Gospel, nohow.[44]

In *Two Years Ago* Frank, the young Puseyite clergyman, is mocked for his attachment to celibacy, but less savagely: 'convinced, with many good men of all ages and creeds, that a celibate life was the fittest one for a clergyman, he had fled . . . into the wilderness to avoid temptation'. But Frank is redeemed, for he behaves like a hero in the cholera epidemic and at last marries and settles down. In this book Kingsley shows himself more concerned with the positive ideal of marriage than with the negative attack on celibacy. He makes his couples come together after tribulation, and praises the pathetic loyalty of Lucia for the decadent poet Vavasour:

For to a true woman, the mere fact of a man's being her husband, put it on the lowest ground that you choose, is utterly sacred, divine, all-powerful; in the might of which she can conquer self in a way which is an every-day miracle; and the man who does not feel about the mere fact of a woman's having given herself utterly to him, just what she herself feels about it, ought to be utterly despised by all his fellows; were it not that, in that case, it would be necessary to despise more human beings than is safe for the soul of man.[45]

That tells us more of the real Kingsley than his outcry against monastic vows, and explains the scorn he felt for Newman's supposed attitude to 'the wicked world which marries and is given in marriage'. It also shows that an age that has been thought paralysed by sex taboos could state some truths as they should be stated.

Frank is allowed to find married happiness, for after all he does stick to the Church of England and also shows that he has a social conscience. He is not like Eustace Leigh in *Westward Ho!* who fails to make the Jesuit standard and is left to wander about 'trying to satisfy his conscience for rejecting "the higher calling" of the celibate'. The scorn for clerical celibacy outlived even the final quarrel with Newman. Kingsley's second lecture as Regius Professor of Modern History at Cambridge contained some digs at Salvian on celibacy and the theme crept into four sermons on David given as University Preacher in 1865. The virile King of Israel was used to launch attacks on monasticism, including the typically Kingsleyan comment that the monks had aimed at copying female virtues and succeeded only in attaining female vices. The chief fictional attack on the subject was made in *Hypatia* (1853); to this novel and its part in the great controversy we shall return in a later chapter.

Above all this, however, was the insult that principally aroused Newman to battle: Kingsley charged every sort of

Catholic, especially the clergy, with disregard for truth. Devotion to literal truth has always been dear to the English Protestant. It impelled the Quakers to keep the second person singular in discourse; it became part of the puritan objections to the theatre, which seemed to be a living lie; it often resulted in the condign punishment of children suspected of lying and the reprieve of those prepared to own up. The evasion of truth through casuistry and equivocation had been alleged against official Romanism from Macbeth's Porter onwards, and the new alarms about Catholic gains in Kingsley's time had strengthened this along with other hostilities. Even Tractarians believed that the Roman Church was not always to be trusted, especially in the methods of gaining converts. Keble referred sadly to 'their want of truth in dealing with people'.[46]

For Kingsley, and for most of his contemporaries, the Roman Catholics were considered worse in this respect than the Anglo-Catholics and the priesthood were worse than the laity. He reiterated in his controversy with Newman what he had already written in *Westward Ho!*, when Eustace Leigh was sent 'to be made a liar of at Rheims':

> In justice be it said, all this came upon Eustace, not because he was a Romanist, but because he was educated by the Jesuits. Had he been saved from them, he might have lived and died as honest a gentleman as his brothers, who turned out like true Englishmen (as did all the Romish laity) to face the great Armada . . . and as brave and loyal a soldier as those Roman Catholics whose noble blood has stained every Crimean battle-field; but his fate was appointed otherwise; and the Upas-shadow which has blighted the whole Romish Church, blighted him also.[47]

Yet the Puseyites seemed tainted by the same vice. Ever since the moderate Isaac Williams had written his Tract *On Reserve* the new movement had been associated in the popular mind with dishonesty, concealment and 'Jesuitry'. An Evangelical had publicly said of Tract 90 that he would be sorry to trust its author with his purse.[48] The question of honest dealing in religion is prominent in the later version of *Yeast*, where the machinations of the Romanists who win over Luke are only a little worse than those of the Puseyites who push him over the line.

Lancelot Smith seems to be speaking for Kingsley once again when he asserts that it is 'better to be inconsistent in truth than consistent in a mistake' – an axiom that sums up much of the author's strength and weakness. When Luke eventually secedes, Lancelot writes to him:

> Heathen as I am, I am still an Englishman; and there are certain old superstitions still lingering among us – whencesoever we may have got them first – about truth and common honesty – you understand me – Do not be angry. But there is a prejudice against the truthfulness of Romish priests and Romish converts.[49]

Luke soon runs into these Popish tricks, when his confessor tells him to conceal his conversion from his father, speaking in tones like those of which Kingsley was later to accuse Newman:

> I cannot sympathize with that superstitious reverence for mere verbal truth, which is so common among Protestants . . . It seems to me they throw away the spirit of truth, in their idolatry of the letter.[50]

When this advice is related to Lancelot it throws him into a paroxysm of rage and a belief that even Puseyites would not stoop so low – 'I shall believe henceforward that there is, after all, a thousand times greater moral gulf fixed between Popery and Tractarianism, than between Tractarianism and the extremest Protestantism'. Alas, the Puseyite Vicar soon shakes this faith; if he has not followed Newman all the way, he has 'considerable experience in that wisdom of the serpent whose combination with the innocence of the dove, in somewhat ultramontane proportions, is recommended by certain late leaders of his school'.

These dangers can creep even into art. Lancelot is counselled to admire the English naturalist painters with their faith in Nature as she really is; not in ideals that have been invented or abstracted but in 'actual and individual phenomena . . ., in these lies an honest development of the true idea of Protestantism', a marked contrast to the 'meagre eclecticism of the ancient religious schools, and of your modern Overbecks and Pugins'. What was coming to be called aestheticism and was at this time associated with the new Pre-Raphaelite Brotherhood, is seen as a moral temptation for the truth-loving Protestant:

The true hell of genius, where Art is regarded as an end and not as a means, and objects are interesting, not in as far as they form our spirits, but in proportion as they can be shaped into effective parts of some beautiful whole.[51]

To follow these alluring temptations is to seek the ruin which Lancelot sees in the distinguished clerical convert to Rome, clearly a portrait of Newman, of whom he thinks: 'What a man! . . . or rather the wreck of what a man! Oh, for such a heart, with the thews and sinews of a truly English brain!' Which thought, odd though its anatomical implications may be, sums up a good deal of Kingsley's opinion. The Oxford revival had misled some good men as well as some despicable ones, but it was no real challenge to the progress of commonsense faith. When a new edition of *Yeast* appeared in 1859, Kingsley felt able to deal more tolerantly with what seemed already to be moribund. His views at this time are worth quoting at length. The Puseyite scare was receding, though it would return with the persecution of ritualists in the years to come:

There is another cause for the improved tone of the Landlord class, and of the young men of what is commonly called the aristocracy; and that is, a growing moral earnestness; which is in great part owing (that justice may be done on all sides) to the Anglican movement. How much soever Neo-Anglicanism may have failed as an Ecclesiastical or Theological system; how much soever it may have proved itself, both by the national dislike of it, and by the defection of all its master-minds, to be radically un-English, it has at least awakened hundreds, perhaps thousands, of cultivated men and women to ask themselves whether God sent them into the world merely to eat, drink and be merry, and to have 'their souls saved' upon the Spurgeon method, after they die, and has taught them an answer to that question not unworthy of English Christians.

The Anglican movement, when it dies out, will leave behind at least a legacy of grand old authors disinterred, of art, of music; of churches too, schools, cottages and charitable institutions, which will form so many centres of future civilization, and will entitle it to the respect, if not the allegiance, of the future generation. And more than this; it has sown in the hearts of young gentlemen and young ladies seed which will not perish; which, though it may develop into forms little expected by those who sowed it, will develop at least into a virtue more stately and reverent, more chivalrous and self-sacrificing, more genial and human, than can be learnt from that religion of the Stock Exchange, which reigned triumphant – for a year and a day – in the popular pulpits.

I have said that Neo-Anglicanism has proved a failure, as seventeenth-century Anglicanism did. The causes of that failure this book has tried to point out; and not one word which is spoken therein, but has been drawn from personal and too-intimate experience. But now – peace to its ashes. Is it so great a sin, to have been dazzled by the splendour of an impossible ideal? Is it so great a sin, to have had courage and conduct enough to attempt the enforcing of that ideal, in the face of the prejudices of a whole nation? And if that idea was too narrow for the English nation, and for the modern needs of mankind, is that either so great a sin? Does Mr Spurgeon, then, take so much broader or nobler views of the capacities and destinies of his race, than that great genius, John Henry Newman?

This is a typically magnanimous response of the spirit which Kingsley so often shows, of respect for an old foe who is thought to have been defeated because the terrors which he first inspired have not been realized. The Oxford Movement seemed to have faded into history, and it was time to assess what its legacy would be. It had aroused new fervour, devotional and practical, in those unmoved by the conformist Establishment or by the Evangelicals. Where it had remained English, it had done much good; where it had flirted with Rome, its weaknesses had emerged. Its real leaders had gone over where they belonged, leaving only second-rate minds. So at least thought Kingsley and many of his contemporaries.

Why then did he in 1864 gratuitously insult Newman, whom so few years before he had praised? For one thing, Newman as the lost leader of a movement with noble potential was almost a different person from the distinguished Roman Catholic. Kingsley had long ago acknowledged Newman's quality, while attacking his new Church and complaining of the Catholic disregard for truth. In an article entitled 'Why should we fear the Romish Priests?' he had written:

One, indeed, we have lost first-rate in *talents* at least; but has not he by his later writings given the very strongest proof that to become a Romish priest is to lose, *ipso facto*, whatever moral or intellectual life he might previously have had? . . . Above all, in all their authors, converts or indigenous, is there not the same fearful *want of straightforward truth,* that 'Jesuitry', which the mob may dread as a subtle poison, but which the philosopher considers as the deepest and surest system of moribund weakness?[52]

The prejudice remained with him, never shaken off while other enemies came and went.

Now the reviewing of Froude's latest volumes had revived thoughts of Elizabethan Protestants against the Catholic villainies of Spain; and probably also of the fight to win their wives from Roman and Anglican sisterhoods. But more than all this, there is the simple fact that Kingsley did not always weigh his words or count their consequences. Puseyism was not so moribund as it had seemed even in 1859, for Kingsley had just suffered a defeat in Oxford itself where the offer of an honorary doctorate had been withdrawn largely on the urging of Pusey and his followers. Rome certainly was very much alive and one of her most brilliant apologists had been an irritant to Kingsley for many years. His review was occasional and quickly composed, unlike the reflective preface to a novel written some years earlier. Without much thought, he let fly the dart that was to call forth Newman's whole armoury.

It is unlikely that Newman would have seen the review of a secular history written by the infidel brother of his old friend, the Hurrell Froude whom he had loved years ago. Someone, probably anonymous and certainly not identified, sent him a copy of the magazine with the offending passage marked. Newman wrote to the publishers, disclaiming any desire for an apology or withdrawal and simply drawing attention to 'a grave and gratuitous slander'. This letter was seen by Kingsley, who wrote to Newman referring for his justification to 'many passages of your writings' but especially to a sermon on 'Wisdom and Innocence' preached in the Anglican days and later published. 'It was in consequence of that sermon,' Kingsley went on, 'that I finally shook off the strong influence which your writings exerted on me; and for much of which I still owe you a deep debt of gratitude.'

This was not unhandsome from so implacable a Protestant as Kingsley. The acknowledgement of gratitude squares well with earlier praise of Newman. That the sermon had stayed in Kingsley's mind is suggested by the passage in *Yeast*, quoted above, about the wisdom and innocence recommended by 'certain late leaders' of the Puseyites. Newman now replied with a stiff letter in which he remarked that the reference was to 'a Protestant sermon of mine' and expressed surprise at learning that Kingsley was the author of the review. Whether he was strictly truthful in the last assertion may be questioned. Would not his acute mind have spelt out 'C.K.' to read an inveterate opponent of Rome and an admirer of Froude?

Further correspondence followed, including a letter from an unknown person who tried to act as mediator. Despite his efforts, the exchange of letters became more heated. Newman, as we shall see, had suffered many tensions in recent years and he seems now to have suspected a plot to discredit him by publishing a guarded apology that would leave an innuendo of his dishonesty. Yet it is equally clear, in the light of what followed, that he was already preparing the ground for his great response.

Kingsley, who by now had had enough of this controversy, tried to bring it to a close by a letter in the next issue of *Macmillan's Magazine*:

In your last number I made certain allegations against the teaching of Dr John Henry Newman, which I thought were justified by a sermon of his. . . . Dr Newman has by letter expressed, in the strongest terms, his denial of the meaning which I have put upon his words. It only remains, therefore, for me to express my hearty regret at having so seriously mistaken him.

This was not good enough for Newman, who reduced the whole correspondence to a brilliantly sarcastic summary, including the comment: 'After all, it is not I, but it is Mr Kingsley who did not mean what he said.'

These two Victorian clergymen were now fairly embarked on a pamphleteering war more in keeping with the times of Martin Marprelate or the Augustan political polemicists than with their own. Kingsley brought out a pamphlet with the title *What, then, does Dr Newman mean?*, in which he raked over the arguments to date and added more fuel. He took exception to Newman's description of the quoted sermon as Protestant, and revived the old charge of concealed Papistry before secession:

All England stood round in those days, and saw that this would be the outcome of Dr Newman's teaching. How was I to know that he did not see it himself?

He dug from Newman's published work all that he could find about truth and concealment. He repeated his opinion, already made in *Westward Ho!* about the basically honest and loyal Catholic laity being misled by their clergy. He touched lightly on Tract 90, but almost lost control over the saints' lives which Newman had edited at Oxford. He may well have been briefed here by Froude, who had been persuaded to write one of them while he was still a Tractarian adherent. From this series – some items in which were certainly highly credulous – and from other gibes about relics and miracles, Kingsley made Newman seem to be blindly accepting even more than the majority of his co-religionists. Newman was said to have 'justified, formally and deliberately, some of the strongest accusations brought by the Exeter Hall Party against the Irish priests'. He had tried, 'by cunning sleight-of-hand logic', to suggest that the original accusation of dishonesty had shown bad faith on Kingsley's part.

In short, Kingsley produced the blend of invective, heavy humour, honest polemics and bad logic of which he had so often shown himself capable. He played directly into Newman's hands when he succumbed to conventional anti-Catholic sentiments. It showed up the prejudice that had inspired his first unprovoked attack. All that had seethed and often boiled over since his undergraduate days in the Tractarian decade now exploded once more. But in Newman too there was something seething and ready to erupt.

5

From Oxford to Rome

What had happened to Newman during nearly twenty years since he left Oxford for the last time? If he had passed from public attention, if he had fallen silent in speech or writing, the controversy following Kingsley's review would have aroused less interest than it did. His *Apologia* did not come as a voice from the dead; yet it was a return to the past not only in its evocation of earlier years but also in its reassertion of those charismatic gifts that had once held England breathlessly waiting for his decision.

Newman's conversion had meant the personal and social rupture that was inevitable in any movement to Roman Catholicism, more acute for a priest who for years had championed the Church of England against all opponents. Employment, position, respect, affection, friends – all had been sacrificed when he knelt before Father Dominic at Littlemore. To become a Roman Catholic in England at that time was to lay all past gains at the foot of the cross. Pusey came to take his leave; Keble sent a copy of *Lyra Innocentium* on its publication; but it was many years before the three Tractarian leaders met again. To the majority of his fellow-Englishmen Newman was as one gone into disgraceful exile, at best to be pitied for his delusion, at worst to be scorned as an unmasked traitor.

For those who had been closest to him there was compassion in the pain of loss. 'That place always reminds me of a great grief,' Keble said one day as he passed the spot where he had read Newman's letter of decision.[1] They grieved, but they could understand – if not with the comprehension that brings pardon, at least with the sense of inevitability that gave the deed a tragic power. The secession, and the personal sacrifices that went with it, seemed a logical end to his severity with himself and with others, his refusal to bend or compromise what he saw as truth. The man who submitted to Rome was the man who had once preached the need for a nation 'vastly more superstitious, more bigoted, more gloomy, more fierce in its religion'.[2] He had not sought the easy way: he had not encouraged his followers to seek it. Suffering was for him a necessary mark of the Christian life, and the reality of eternal punishment for failure in this world was a tenet of faith.

Some friends could have seen the coming decision: Newman's devotion to the authority of his diocesan bishop, overriding personal feelings about the man who held the office, foretold the ultimate acceptance of Papal power. His brother, who had disputed the question with him when they were both young, commented that 'it is strange that twenty years more had to pass before he learnt the place to which his doctrines belonged'.[3] J.A. Froude claimed similar hindsight after he too had left doctrinal conflict behind, though in a different direction. 'If there be any such thing as sin, in proportion to the depth with which men feel it, they will gravitate towards Rome . . . and sin with Newman was real.'[4] In the fictional character of Mornington, the priestly convert, Froude could recapture the spell of the lost leader. 'How often in old college years he had hung upon those lips, that voice so keen, so preternaturally sweet, whose very whisper used to thrill through crowded churches, where every breath was held to hear.'[5]

Now Oxford heard the voice no more and even the name of Newman was spoken in a whisper of malice or of sorrow. Perhaps neither those who triumphed in the parting nor those who mourned it understood how deeply he had been motivated by an increasing certainty that in Rome alone were the true marks of holiness, the glory as well as the power. More even than his respect for the seat of ancient authority, it was the desire for sanctity that led him on. The man who made his submission in 1845 had written four years previously: 'Where Almighty God stirs the heart, there His other gifts follow in time; sanctity is the great Note of the Church.'[6] He had never supposed that sanctity was to be purchased without cost: for him, the dark and suffering aspect of faith had been real. His chief hatred was the secular and ecclesiastical Liberalism which demanded privileges without accepting duties.

From his new position the tenets of Protestantism and humanism alike seemed vague and unheroic. Were the Pusey-ites more firmly based than his regrettable brother Francis? Seen from the Rock of Peter, they were almost clinging to one another in their instability:

Pusey says that to deny the Catholicity of the English Church, Frank, that to deny the acceptableness of such an unbeliever is (the ipsissima verba of each) 'blasphemy against the Holy Ghost'.[7]

Outsiders might see him as a man who had wilfully blocked his great intellect for the sake of peace. 'Newman falls down and worships *because* he does not know and knows he does not know,' Clough remarked two years after the secession,[8] and we have seen that Kingsley classed Roman obedience with opium and alcohol. For Newman himself, neither intellect nor any other gift was at his own disposal. He was certain of his part in a greater purpose, as certain as his fictional self-projection:

Charles's characteristic, perhaps above anything else, was an habitual sense of the Divine Presence; a sense which, of course, did not ensure uninterrupted conformity of thought and deed in itself, but still there it was – the pillar of the cloud before him and guiding him. He felt himself to be God's creature, and responsible to Him – God's possession, not his own.[9]

There was much in those first years to test his new allegiance. The distinguished convert found himself a mere postulant in a Church that was not disposed to make a fuss of those who, in her view, were receiving more than they brought. Although Wiseman had suggested that the expected converts from the Oxford Movement were to be given special consideration,[10] the reality for many of them was quite different. They 'began life anew, took their position as humble learners in the Roman Schools, and made the most absolute sacrifice of a whole lifetime that man can make'.[11] The clerical converts suffered most; if they were married, they could no longer exercise the priestly office; in any case they were considered as laymen who had to seek ordination. So Newman passed for a time into oblivion and disregard, left 'to stand at Dr Wiseman's door waiting for confession amid the Oscott boys'.[12]

He now could experience from the inside that deep bitterness, a compound of fear and ignorance, which the majority of his countrymen felt for his new Church. He had said and written some hard things about that Church, but he could never have begun to utter the kind of abuse in which he now had to share. In human terms, his position was tragic. We know how Kingsley looked upon converts, and he was an intelligent, warm-hearted man, whose opposition could in a moment turn to generosity. Newman's action was itself partly responsible for a more hysterical note in the volume of anti-Papal writing.

The cautionary tales against yielding to Roman blandishments came from divers hands which nothing less than the dread of a common enemy could have joined. The Anglican clergyman William Sewell was early in the field with horrific Jesuits in his novel *Hawkstone* (1845); his sister Elizabeth took a similar and only slightly more temperate line in *Margaret Perceval* (1847). The fact that the Jesuits were always particularly open to popular attack was a factor in the success of the English translation of Eugène Sue's *The Wandering Jew* (1844). Other fictional warnings against Popish machinations came from Frances Trollope with *Father Eustace* (1847) and Catherine Sinclair with *Beatrice* (1852). These and others like them were more typical of the age than the comparatively kindly portrait of Father Holt in Thackeray's *Henry Esmond* (1852).

Yet such novels were the more articulate and almost reasonable expressions of a feeling that ranged from the insensitive to the lunatic. Even forty years later a French resident in England could observe that 'No Popery' was still 'the cry of the English people . . . the hatred of Popery is pushed to the verge of absurdity'.[13] It was worse in the early years of Newman's conversion: he saw it, analysed it, tried to suffer it patiently:

Crowds do not assemble in Exeter Hall, mobs do not burn the Pope, from reverence to Lord Bacon, Locke, or Butler, or for anything those gifted men have recorded. I am treating of the unpopularity of Catholicism, now and here, as it exists in the year 1851 . . . and I say that this Tradition does not flow from the mouth of the half-dozen wise, or philosophic, or learned men who can be summoned in its support, but is a tradition of nursery stories, school stories, public-house stories, club-house stories, drawing-room stories, platform stories, pulpit stories; a tradition of newspapers, magazines, reviews, pamphlets, romances, novels, poems and light literature of all kinds, literature of the day.[14]

Among the 'literature of the day' there appeared the curious productions of Elizabeth Harris, who had been converted to Roman Catholicism in 1846 and had soon come to the conclusion that she was mistaken. Instead of trailing back as a Protestant penitent, however, she decided to stay where she was and try to warn others about the dangers of unthinking secession, hoping meanwhile to effect some kind of reconciliation between the English and Roman Churches. To these ends she wrote her novels *From Oxford to Rome* (1847) and *Rest in the Church* (1848).

By this time, the British public had a very garbled idea of what had been happening at Oxford over the past ten years, and writers like Elizabeth Harris did little to make the record straight. The popular impression in that loose tradition to which Newman referred was one of Popish plots which had seduced a number of young men, and a few seniors who ought to have set them a good example. The blend of such melodramatic sensation with the glamour that still clothed the name of Oxford was a gift to the popular novelist. The appetite for some very basic Protestant theology, with personal thrills and a glimpse of that high life so dear to the outworn but still vigorous 'silver fork' school of fiction, could all be fed in one story. At the same time, more thoughtful readers were genuinely anxious to discover why an Anglican priest, in the prime of his life and at the height of his influence, could sell his birthright for what was thought to be a mess of superstition.

Newman's attempt to give an answer was cast in the form of fiction. Apart from the challenge of *From Oxford to Rome*, which was certainly in his mind, the choice was less surprising than might appear. The novel had almost established itself as a reputable form of literature, despite the rearguard action of some of the older critical reviews. Novel-reading no longer seemed the wicked waste of time which had made the *Evangelical Magazine* set it on a 'spiritual barometer' lower than adultery and on a level with scepticism.[15] Its new status had come through a complexity of factors, social and economic as well as literary; among them was the willingness of the novelists to make concessions to the prevailing desires – not always mutually exclusive – for sermonizing and 'useful knowledge'. The novel had become a recognized platform for the promulgation of ideas in the confused social debate. Yet some could still be shocked to find a clergyman writing a novel. Frederick Faber informed Newman, perhaps not without some malice, that his former associates among the Puseyites thought that he had 'sunk below Dickens'.[16]

Newman was not intended by nature for the writing of fiction, in which neither the power of his intellect nor the quality of his prose style could find its fullest expression. Yet, since these aspects of his work have been critically examined many times, it is worth looking at his almost-neglected fiction. His first novel was by no means a disaster; it was taken seriously by contemporary readers, despite the prevailing distrust of Roman Catholicism and the hostility to his own secession. He published it anonymously, but the secret was not kept for long. 'There is a story book called Loss and Gain ascribed to Newman, truly or falsely as the case may be,' Arthur Clough noted soon after it had appeared.[17] It was true: Newman, now an Oratorian novice in Rome, had decided to tell his own story under the guise of fiction, so that others might begin to understand. It was the start of his long struggle to clear himself of accusations of apostasy and dishonest behaviour. In the preface he disclaimed any autobiographical intention, but those who knew the man could discern him behind the mask. Oakeley, also a recent convert, wrote to a friend:

Newman's new book *Loss and Gain, or the Story of a Convert*, will give you a great deal of pleasure. I am not certain whether he has ever written anything more showing the versatility of his genius and his knowledge of human nature. By those who did not know him it will be called 'satirical', however, it is Newman all over.[18]

It would be idle to claim that *Loss and Gain,* which was published early in 1848, occupies a high place in the roll of Victorian fiction. Yet though its intrinsic merits are not great, it is something more than an attempt to use the novel to set right misconceptions. It is a study of a man who acts along a line running contrary to the predispositions of birth and environment. Opponents might say of Charles Reding, as they said of his creator, that he was swept on blindly by emotion; but Newman shows that each step is conscious and, for him, logical. We are more than a generation away in spirit from the semi-determinism of George Eliot and the pessimistic conditioning of Hardy and Gissing. Where *Loss and Gain* stands above the apologetic and cautionary novels of the time is in its emphasis on the slow progress of a conversion and its avoidance of sensationalism in plot and episode.

Charles Reding does not speak for himself in the first person, but through the narrator who can see his story whole and comment on it with approved omniscience. Reding passes from sincere though not profound acceptance of his place in the Church of England to the final step of submission to Papal authority. He hears the views of men from all parties, contemporaries and seniors, Oxford dons and country parsons, at the university and in his home. We follow him through middle-class society in the years when the Tractarian controversy was at its height. We see almost nothing of the rest of the nation and its complex problems; nor was it necessary for Newman's purpose that we should. Kingsley enters areas in fiction where Newman never attempts to go; but Kingsley's heroes end with a looser and less convincing type of conversion. They owe more to others who guide them and to startling experience in the objective world, less to a quiet following of signalled truth.

Of course, Reding is not a simple cipher for Newman, who manages the story with remarkable detachment. The plot is not a parallel with Newman's life: Reding is still an undergraduate when the movement is in full development; he is converted to Rome soon after graduation, having led no party and published no tracts. Indeed, his youthful obscurity makes it hard for the reader to accept the supposed excitement which his conversion arouses. The feverish atmosphere at the end of the story owes more to Newman's last months as an Anglican than to those of a young neophyte. Reding is a clergyman's son, held by stronger ties than Newman to the Church of his childhood. He has three sisters but no brothers: no deep analysis is needed to see how willingly Newman would have done without the burden of his two wayward brothers.[19] Reding goes to Eton and thence into a more fashionable undergraduate life than Newman had known. He is rusticated by his college lest his Popish opinions should pervert younger men. He is hesitant about taking his degree because he cannot honestly accept the Articles.

Thus Reding passes in youth through some of the things that Newman suffered in maturity. The reflections of his author's personality, both trivial and important, are clear enough. He plays the violin; he is interested in the reading of character through handwriting; he comes from a family that is grieved by his change in religion. He feels himself called to celibacy, a vocation emphasized to that pathological extreme which infuriated men like Kingsley. When he sees a newly-married Anglican clergyman and his bride, Reding feels 'a faintish feeling come over him; somewhat such as might beset a man on hearing a call for pork-chops when he was sea-sick'.[20] The image succeeds only in inducing a Kingsleyan type of nausea in the reader; it does not rouse sympathy with the genuine celibate. Reding accepts his second class in the Schools with the stoicism that reflects Newman's attitude to a similar experience:

> As success had not been the first desire of his soul, so failure was not its greatest misery. He would much have preferred success; but in a day or two he found he could well endure the want of it.[21]

Deeper than these observable points of contact lies Newman's willing exposure of his own mind and soul. He wanted to show the world that a man in possession of all his faculties could accept Roman claims in free volition. 'You have a strong *will*,' Mary Reding says to her brother, assuring him that if he secedes it will be of his own accord and not because anyone has driven him to it. Reding passes through some of the phases that Newman had known: a growing sense of ambiguity in the Anglican formularies; the understanding that 'there is no creed given us in scripture' which Hawkins had explained; the fear of falling into the abyss of scepticism if no Church can give certainty; the realization that Roman claims allow only complete acceptance or complete rejection.[22] Above all – and Newman was writing only some two years after the stormy night of his own submission – both author and character experience the final sacrifice of family and friends, not for love of sacrifice itself but because 'I have put the subject from me again and again, and it has returned'.

Although the story is told continuously and chronologically, the voice of Newman's Roman present comments on his Anglican past. The convert Willis, at first an under-graduate with Reding, threads in and out of the book, urging a decision for one Church or the other; one cannot remain 'Anglo-Roman or Anglo-Catholic'.[23] Willis cannot be tripped by questions about relics and idolatry; he remains happy and serene in his new faith, accepting under obedience things which might have been offensive to his undisciplined reason. At last, as Father Aloysius the Passionist, he receives Reding's submission.

Willis often speaks for Newman who, both through him and as narrator, sets out to answer the question which above all others puzzled his more intelligent opponents. How could a man claim to have been converted through freely following his private judgement and then seem to suspend that judgement in submission to the dictates of his new Church? Newman compares private judgement to the lantern which lights a man on his way to a party but is not needed in the more brightly lit house when he arrives. 'There is no absurdity then or inconsistency in a person first using his private judgement and then denouncing its use: circumstances change duties.' This is a question-begging answer; the analogy is valid only if the conversion is accepted as a total breakthrough from error to truth – it justifies on its own terms.

Besides being a reflection of Newman's spiritual progress, *Loss and Gain* is an important document in the history of the Oxford Movement. In both respects it anticipates the great *Apologia* of 1864. It recaptures the earnest theological atmosphere of Oxford in the thirties, when men who had come up with passive acceptance of the Church of England found themselves plunged into a confusion of parties that set them arguing about both Roman and Protestant claims. There is satire based on the reality of those bitter years in the idea that the more committed Protestants spied on undergraduates and reported any Popish tendencies. So too in the newspaper rumour that the old law of Praemunire was to apply to seceders and the fines be devoted to a new Martyrs' Memorial at Cambridge. It is not a *roman à clef*, but *Loss and Gain* accommodates some leading figures. Pusey is praised by name as 'a very good man' but has no part in the action. There is a dig at Hampden in the latitudinarian university sermon of Dr Brownside; Emerson's voice is heard from the American Congregationalist Coventry who claims that Christianity is based on principles, not dogmas; Hawkins is reflected in the urbanely conservative Vincent.

Newman can make us understand how the Church of England appeared in those years to some of her more critical and serious members. There were aspects of her established position that could make them look more carefully at the claims of other communions, or could drive them into the exasperation that led to scepticism. The requirement of assent to the Articles starts Reding in one direction, as it started Froude and Clough in another. The definitions seemed unsatisfactory, based on the chances of a historical situation, uncertain in meaning:

> On his entrance he had been told that when he took his degree he would have to sign the Articles, not on faith as then, but on reason; yet they were unintelligible; and how could he prove what he could not construe?[24]

As for theology, the majority of those Anglicans who thought about their faith at all might seem to be holding a kind of Sabellian position.[25]

Nevertheless, the bruised and embattled Church of England could still inspire deep affection, could hold the loyalty and satisfy the spiritual needs of many. The love that still held Pusey, Keble, Williams and Marriott had once held Newman and did not entirely disappear when he found his new home. Respect, and some tenderness, remained for his Tractarian friends, 'the most exemplary men of that day, who doubtless are still, as clergymen or laymen, the strength of the Anglican

Church' – 'persons of great merit and high character'. He could still accept the sincerity of those like the 'sharp but not very wise' undergraduate White, who fully acknowledges the catholicity of Rome, agrees that much could be learned from it, but yet concludes: 'I have ever loved, and I hope I shall ever venerate, my own Mother, the Church of my baptism.'

While for White the Church of England was his mother, for Reding it was personified in his father, a clergyman of the best type within those limitations which the Tractarians were trying to enlarge. The character of Mr Reding shows how much of the Anglican tradition from the previous century was far from contemptible. It shows too that the distance between the better clergy of Addison's time and those of Newman's youth was less than the distance between the latter and the new generation. It reveals Newman at his most charitable and affectionate, though the criticism of the new Romanist for the old Protestant is only lightly veiled:

He was a most respectable clergyman of the old school; pious in his sentiments, a gentleman in his feelings, exemplary in his social relations. He was no reader, and never had been in the way to gain theological knowledge; he sincerely believed all that was in the Prayer-book, but his sermons were very rarely doctrinal. They were sensible, manly discourses on the moral duties. He administered holy communion at the three great festivals, saw his Bishop once or twice a year, was on good terms with the country gentlemen in his neighbourhood, was charitable to the poor, hospitable in his house-keeping, and was a staunch, though not a violent, supporter of the Tory interest in his county. He was incapable of anything harsh, or petty, or low, or uncourteous; and died esteemed by the great houses about him, and lamented by his parishioners.[26]

As strong as the pain of parting from a Church once loved, more hurtful because there was no similar compensation, was the parting from all that Oxford had meant to Reding as it had to Newman:

Whatever he was to gain by becoming a Catholic, this he had lost; whatever he was to gain higher and better, at least this and such as this he could never have again. He could not have another Oxford, he could not have the friends of his boyhood and youth in the choice of his manhood.[27]

So Reding gives his old tutor a copy of *The Christian Year* and speaks of his sadness at going among strangers. Years later Newman wrote his own postscript when he recorded in the *Apologia* that he had never since seen Oxford except its skyline from the train.

Judged as a novel, *Loss and Gain* leaves a number of criteria unsatisfied. With all allowance for changing fashion and for the requirements of fictional dialogue, it is hard to believe that undergraduates ever talked to each other like this:

'I am just going for a turn in the Meadow,' said Charles; 'this is to me the best time of the year; *nunc formosissimus annus*; everything is beautiful; the laburnums are out, and the may. There is a greater variety of trees there than in any place I know hereabouts; and the planes are so touching just now, with their small multitudinous green hands, half opened; and there are two or three such fine dark willows, stretching over the Cherwell; I think some Dryad inhabits them: and as you wind along, just over your right shoulder is the Long Walk, with the Oxford buildings seen between the elms.'[28]

It sounds as though a character out of Peacock had strayed into a botanical discourse by the father in *The Swiss Family Robinson*. The dialogue does in fact improve as the book progresses, but the characters develop little and remain foils for the hero's spiritual development. They are outlines, but recognizable outlines. Newman always denied that he had based any of them on real acquaintances and maintained that he had looked only to the lunatic fringe as far as the Tractarian characters were concerned. 'I knew none of them personally . . . persons whose religion lay in ritualism or architecture, and who "played at Popery" or at Anglicanism.'[29]

Accepted as types, the characters cover many aspects of the Tractarian world. There is Bateman, the advanced Anglo-Catholic with his ecclesiology and his restored chapel, who as a parish curate upsets his rector and churchwardens with talk of 'churches decorated as they should be, with candlesticks, ciboriums, faldstools, lecterns, antependium, piscinas, rood-lofts, and sedilia'. There are the Bolton sisters who make vestments but are uncertain about what to do with them, who believe that the Pope is infallible but wonder why he goes to confession. There is their mother who longs for 'good old

George the Third and the Protestant religion': Vincent who, at his gargantuan tutorial breakfast, advises Charles to shun living controversialists and stick to the Elizabethan and Caroline divines; Freeborn the Evangelical whose set is alien to Charles – 'another world'. All these serve their purpose in representing the wild confusion of nonsense and troubled sincerity which the Tractarians had evoked. They quicken our understanding but do not extend our experience. At the end, when Charles is bent on secession, he is visited by a number of dissuaders who are mere caricatures, types of temptation: Irvingites; a girl passing from Anglicanism through Connexion and Brethren to a new syncretism; a convert to Judaism, and others even stranger. They are not great fictional creations, but they do show that early Victorian religion was complex and not lacking in colour.

So at last Charles is received. As he wrote, Newman must have lived again his meeting with Father Dominic on that stormy autumn night:

He was still kneeling in the church of the Passionists before the Tabernacle, in the possession of a deep peace and serenity of mind, which he had not thought possible on earth. It was more like the stillness which almost sensibly affects the ears, when a bell which had long been tolling stops, or when a vessel, after much tossing at sea, finds itself in harbour. It was such as to throw him back in memory on his earliest years, as if he were really beginning life again. But there was more than the happiness of childhood in his heart; he seemed to feel a rock under his feet; it was the *soliditas Cathedrae Petri*. He went on kneeling, as if he were already in heaven, with the throne of God before him, and angels around; and as if to move were to lose his privilege . . . the new convert sought his temporary cell, so happy in the Present, that he had no thoughts either for the Past or the Future.[30]

In those last words was there some foreboding which the coming years were partly to fulfil? The peace had been gained through abnegation of many things; but there was no other way open. Newman was clear-sighted and honest enough to acknowledge the loss while rejoicing in the gain.

Despite the anecdotes that circulated in his lifetime and continued to do so after his death, there is no evidence that Newman ever seriously doubted the rightness of his decision.

Yet from the start it was assumed that he would soon be disillusioned. When he wrote *Loss and Gain* part of his declared purpose was to counter the assertion which Elizabeth Harris had based on her own experience. Her hero, an undergraduate at Oxford in the Tractarian days as is Charles Reding, is ordained and goes to a parish where his Anglo-Catholic ideas can be put into practice. Some are met with sympathy, others with repugnance. He and his strong-minded sister Augusta read Ward's *Ideal* together until his faith in the Elizabethan and Caroline Anglican authorities is shaken:

She had fallen, *he* was falling into the error, common to many of very strong Catholic desires, who have reflected much and with affection on the times of the undivided Church – of *mistaking* Romanism for Catholicism.[31]

Eustace's fall is completed by a holiday abroad when France and Italy confirm his drift to Romanism and Switzerland increases his distaste for Protestantism. After attending the Convocation where Ward is degraded, he and his sister are received; others follow, but all meet either a quick death or disillusionment.

To read Elizabeth Harris is to value Newman more highly as a novelist. Her characters are wooden, her dialogue stilted; and long passages of the short novel are given to descriptions of Anglo-Catholic and Roman practices, with reflections on the state of the two Churches and hope for the future. Anglicans can find true Catholicism in their own communion if they will be patient and let the beginnings of the Oxford Movement grow into acceptance. Her conclusion sums up the attitude to secession which Newman was trying to counter. The rapt joy of Charles Reding after his reception is like a direct reply to her gloomy censure on converts:

Soon they find that they have made a *great mistake*, that where God has permitted one branch of His Vine to be established, they may not with impunity sever themselves from it, and seek a self-chosen station with the excuse that they have no *sympathy*. 'No sympathy' will be the reiterated and bitter cry of their hearts for years after. Great unhappiness falls on them. A just correction.[32]

There were others who mingled no feeling of compassion

with their scorn. Within a few months of Newman's secession, an anonymous pamphlet which may have given him the title for his first novel was viewing the recent movements to Rome 'as a subject rather of congratulation than of regret, to sincere and enlightened members of our Church'.[33] The author warned the Roman Catholics, in terms reminiscent of Brabantio's farewell to Desdemona, that those who had dissembled as Anglicans might not prove any more trustworthy in their new faith. Elizabeth Harris had taken a better view of Newman's going: 'the deeper hearts of the sons and daughters of the Church of England were heavy with grief that day. A great light was dark.'

Newman wrote *Loss and Gain* not only to justify himself but also to defend and strengthen others who were on the same path. The tide of converts was continuing to flow strongly enough to unite Protestants and agnostics in anti-Papal alarm. Even those who had fled from the theological maelstrom, like Arthur Clough, could continue to deplore the secessions:

The perversion, as the Anglican people call it, seems to me a very sad thing – it is, according to all experience, so irrevocable a change. I have known one or two instances of a Return out of this Babylonish Captivity, but they seem rarely to happen.[34]

If he did not regret his decision or count it wrong, the subsequent career of Newman was to show many of the tensions and much of the tragedy inherent in such change. By challenging the concept of authority, by demanding personal decisions on matters which had hitherto been taken for granted, the Oxford Movement brought the tragic sense into an age that tended to see choices in melodramatic polarities of absolute good and evil. There were gains to literature, often losses to personal relations.

Newman's share in the tragedy helped to give the occasion for the *Apologia* and to order its composition. His life and work after 1845 have been studied, documented, evaluated. The bulk of his writing belongs to theology and philosophy, though it touches very many aspects of the Victorian world and of the abiding human situation. The present concern is with the two books which relate more directly the events of the first twelve Tractarian years. Between the anxious joy that ends *Loss and Gain* and the militant embarkation on the *Apologia* there are long years when Newman was constantly justifying his position by his speaking and writing as a Roman Catholic priest. The two works share more in common than the re-creation of Oxford experience.

On both occasions Newman was using a chosen excuse for his statement. Elizabeth Harris was not the first to suggest that the Oxford converts had made a terrible mistake; Kingsley was not the first to impugn Newman's honesty and that of his Church. When, each time, the choice was made, Newman's love of remembering the past gave strength to his defensive purpose. He was happy in the nostalgic summoning of events to recollection and in these books he could indulge his undying love for Oxford without disloyalty to that which had displaced it. Both in fiction and in autobiography he set out to show the consistency and honourable logic of the path from Oxford to Rome.

Without attempting to touch the deeper aspects or the detailed events of those intervening years, we may see in certain episodes why the Newman of 1864 had become as he was. The bitter reactions to his own conversion were repeated as more of his former friends and associates came over. Henry Wilberforce, son of the great liberator and leading Evangelical William Wilberforce, had been drawn to Newman at Oxford, so closely that his brother Samuel grumbled that he 'loses himself and his own mind'.[35] The affection between the two men endured through the early years of Newman's Roman priesthood until Henry followed the example of his secession. Samuel Wilberforce, now Bishop of Oxford, wrote of his action in terms which startle the modern reader who is confronted with the reaction of an educated, intelligent and devout man to such a change. Beneath the intolerance and lack of charity there is again the tragedy which the Oxford Movement often brought:

> I love dearest H. just as much as ever but I feel that our lives are parted in their purpose, aim and association. I heartily wish he might settle abroad; but having him here after this dreadful fall seems to me beyond measure miserable: and his broken vows and violated faith weigh heavily on my soul. May God forgive him.[36]

The recipient of this letter was another Wilberforce brother: Robert, who seceded in 1854 after a prolonged tug-of-war which would have had its comic moments were it not for the desperate seriousness of both sides. By correspondence and personal exhortation, Gladstone, Pusey, Keble and brother Samuel heaved to keep Robert from the grasp of Newman, Manning and brother Henry. The new convert to the Roman team, Henry Manning, was destined to do as much as any to win English respect for his Church. His progress thither had owed less to the direct influence of Oxford, though he had been associated with Marriott in the editing of extracts from the Fathers under the title *Catena Patrum*. He had gone down in 1830 and experienced his first conversion, through an Evangelical assurance of salvation, while working as a Government clerk in London. He moved on to a High Church position and to Anglican orders, but soon began to feel the same unease that was troubling Newman. For both men, the early feeling of election strove with a growing belief in apostolic and sacramental churchmanship. In 1839 Newman looked ahead for both of them when he wrote to Manning, who was having problems about a parishioner with leanings towards Rome:

Our blanket is too small for our bed. . . . We are raising longings and tastes which we are not allowed to supply – and till our bishops and others give scope to the development of Catholicism externally and wisely, we *do* tend to make impatient minds seek it where it ever has been, in Rome.[37]

The blanket provided less and less cover for Manning, who by 1846 was writing in his private journal: 'Though not Roman, I cease to be Anglican.'[38]

It was a feeling shared by others, some of whom seceded while some remained and accommodated their doubts. The Gorham Judgement of 1850 increased anxiety and hastened loss. Bishop Phillpotts of Exeter, alone among the English diocesan bishops, had shown real sympathy with the aims of the Oxford Movement, and had made himself unpopular in consequence. When he refused to license a clergyman named Gorham, who had failed to satisfy him on the question of baptismal regeneration, he started a trial of strength between Anglican extremes. As the novels of Charlotte Yonge often show, the nature of baptism had become a testing-point between Tractarians and Evangelicals.[39] Gorham's refusal to accept the authority of Phillpotts began a dreary and most unedifying process of litigation, appeal and counter-appeal. Finally, the Judicial Committee of the Privy Council upheld Gorham and ordered Phillpotts to institute him.

This was a severe blow to Anglo-Catholics. The State, whose interference in ecclesiastical affairs had occasioned the revival, now showed itself capable of the last word. A committee of lawyers could pronounce on doctrine and overrule a bishop in his own diocese. The successors of the Tractarians were being forced to be more militant, or to admit that their position was untenable. For Manning it was the sign he needed, though for a time he led Anglican resistance to the judgement. In 1851 he knelt for the last time to receive communion as an Anglican, rose and laid his hand on Gladstone who knelt beside him, and said simply, 'Come'. Gladstone did not follow, but was deeply hurt by what seemed a betrayal of all that they had worked for together. 'I stagger like a drunken man and am at my wit's end,' he wrote when Manning's reception as a Roman Catholic was announced.[40]

Manning found a warmer welcome than Newman and it was soon clear that he was being groomed for higher things. The six years since Newman had left Oxford had been eventful in his new communion and Manning came at a time which gave the right challenge to his talent and temperament. In 1850 the pressure of those English Roman Catholics who looked for closer links with the Vatican was successful. England could no longer be regarded as an infidel territory to be administered by Vicars Apostolic as in the old penal days. Nicholas Wiseman arrived as primate of a hierarchy of bishops with English territorial titles.

The ensuing uproar alarmed even the militant Romanists and terrified their timid brethren who had prophesied trouble. The legality of the titles was challenged, and Wiseman's own title of Archbishop of Westminster gave particular offence. He did nothing to conciliate the opposition by his aggressively triumphant pastoral letter, which made sure that his flock would not underestimate the importance of the change. Lord John Russell wrote an equally fervent manifesto which attacked Puseyites as well as Romanists; Wiseman and the Pope were burned in effigy; Protestant associations of the eighteenth-century type began to appear. Cries of 'Papal Aggression' were heard on all sides.

The first storm died down; Wiseman took his place without legal penalty or bodily violence, and began the task which Pius IX had laid on him. It was a triumph for the ultramontanes, almost as unwelcome to some of the old Roman Catholic families as to the Protestants. The direct ties with Rome were strengthened; the discipline and doctrine of the contemporary Church were more strongly enforced. Manning was delighted: Newman was not.

The man who had sought true Catholicism in the primitive Church found himself out of sympathy with the Counter-Reformation outlook and the Italian practices which Wiseman was introducing. To Newman many of the innovations seemed retrograde and unrealistic. His keen intellect which had carried him so far now revolted against official fears that there was danger in investigation and the idea of development. He found himself suspected of the liberalizing tendencies which he had opposed as an Anglican and censured by those whom he regarded as woefully mistaken.

Yet he kept obedience and made no protest. He was in the wilderness, his great talents only half extended, but he continued to speak and write on behalf of his Church. The publication in 1851 of his talks on *The Present Position of Catholics in England* made him the defendant in a libel action. Achilli, an unpleasant unfrocked Italian priest, had cashed in on the recent anti-Roman fever with some lurid revelations of the *Maria Monk* type. Newman accused him in one of his lectures of various offences involving sacrilege and sexual misconduct. It was due partly to the inevitable prejudice of an English jury at that time, partly to Wiseman's failure to support Newman with promised evidence, that Achilli won the case. Newman was fined a hundred pounds but his costs were high and had to be met by public subscription. The whole affair raised his standing in the country when the British sense of fair treatment reasserted itself. But for a man so sensitive it was a traumatic experience.

The years passed, bringing his appointment as first Rector

of the new Catholic university in Dublin, which shuttled him miserably to and fro between frustration in Ireland and procrastination in England but which also gave us *The Idea of a University* (1852). There were great achievements amid the disappointment and neglect; their tale is not told here, for our concern is with the Tractarian years and their direct results. Those years seemed now far off to Newman, not to be too often remembered, lest the loss should ever seem to outweigh the gain. Then Kingsley wrote his review of Froude in *Macmillan's Magazine*.

The book which we know as Newman's *Apologia pro Vita Sua* came before the world in weekly pamphlets. The central portion, which contains the history of his spiritual development up to 1845, was later issued in volume form. It was part of a controversy for which Newman was ready and perhaps eager; though the occasion was particular, he was replying to the slanders of twenty years. In 1862 he had given a sharp answer to a rumour that he might return to the Anglican fold:

I do hereby profess 'ex animo' with an absolute internal assent and consent that Protestantism is the dreariest of possible religions; that the thought of the Anglican service makes me shiver, and the thought of the Thirty-nine Articles makes me shudder. Return to the Church of England! No! 'The net is broken and we are delivered.' I should be a consummate fool (to use a mild term) if in my old age I left 'the land flowing with milk and honey' for the city of confusion and the house of bondage.[41]

He had not been so much out of the world as he sometimes affected to have been; he had read enough to know what people thought of him. Nor was he a gentle soul dragged into the limelight of controversy: he could be as rude about Canterbury as Kingsley was about Rome. At last his great moment came.

His first pamphlet replied to Kingsley's provocative question, 'What, then, does Dr Newman mean?' It showed up the falsity of Kingsley's arguments – it was hardly a fair contest as far as logic was concerned – and went on to accuse Kingsley of dishonesty where in fact he had been only clumsy. The fact that Kingsley had seemed to waive one charge and then brought up several others made him seem malicious. The fact

was that he would often hold to a controversy as if he would
never let go, only to drop it suddenly and then be amazed that
his antagonist wanted to continue. Newman's mastery of
words enabled him to make Kingsley's use of innuendo and
loaded language seem more offensive even than it was. He left
no doubt that he welcomed every chance to reply to the whole
series of past accusations: Kingsley's attack was only an
excuse for the greater defence:

> And now I am in a train of thought higher and more serene than
> any which slanders can disturb. Away with you, Mr Kingsley, and
> fly into space. Your name shall occur again as little as I can help, in
> the course of these pages. I shall henceforth occupy myself not with
> you, but with your charges.[42]

He turned next to the slanders which had not come from
Kingsley alone. 'For twenty years and more I have borne an
imputation, of which I am at least as sensitive, who am the
object of it, as they can be, who are only the judges.' The
ageing controversialist had lost none of his skill in those twenty
years of calumny. The sneers of Protestants, the coldness of
former friends, the Achilli case, the disappointment over
Dublin and the tensions with Wiseman and Manning, all
found release in the controlled power of his reply. He went on
to defend himself against accusations of dishonesty, especially
those of being a concealed Papist while still at Oxford:

> It is the impression of large classes of men; the impression twenty
> years ago and the impression now. There has been a general feeling
> that I was for years where I had no right to be; that I was a 'Roman-
> ist' in Protestant livery and service; that I was doing the work of a
> hostile Church in the bosom of the English Establishment, and knew
> it, or ought to have known it.[43]

To refute this charge, by showing the honourable progression
of faith that had led him from one communion to another, was
the main purpose of his brief autobiography.

The *Apologia* is a depressing rather than an invigorating
work. It enshrines the basic pessimism with a corrupt age
which had set off the Oxford Movement and was shared by
many who remained outside. But it is a work of aggression as
well as defence. Newman's delight in conflict revived as he
wrote; intellectual demonstration that his successive positions

had each been reasonably held and openly abandoned when untenable did not exclude emotion. The friends and allies of those days are recalled, to be treated with courtesy and even affection, although the partings had been sorrowful. As he paused for a while in the long hours of writing that he imposed on himself, he may have pondered the irony that had occasioned his definitive defence through the work of Hurrell Froude's apostate brother, once his own disciple.

The issues of those distant years were brought before a society bemused by 'Puseyism' and 'Papal Aggression' until it had forgotten how the situation had appeared to many churchmen in the thirties. The immediate controversy was submerged beneath the passionate avowal of former necessities, but was not lost altogether. Newman returned at last to Kingsley, answering him in general and in detail, enumerating a long list of 'blots' in his misrepresentations. If the affair is judged as a debate, with no bias about the theological positions of the antagonists, there is really very little left of Kingsley; he suffered the fate of a pugnacious man who brought a hasty charge and then refused to withdraw. Andrew Lang affectionately wrote his epitaph in this affair:

He threw his cap into the ring, he took his coat off, he fought, he got a terrible scientific drubbing. It was like a sixth-form boy matching himself against the champion.[44]

Although Newman was scrupulously fair in telling the story of the Oxford Movement, he naturally told it from the position of one who had found in it only a path to Rome. This needs to be remembered, since probably more people have taken their information about that movement from the *Apologia* than from any other source. It is not, and was not intended to be, a history of the Tractarian revival: it is the history of one man's search for truth. The detailed account of that search did much to refute the accusations of dishonesty. In the final pamphlets Newman quoted extensively from Romanist and Anglican opinions about the value of telling the exact truth, and made it clear that he did not accept even such allowance for equivocation as some divines of his own Church had made. His justification is greatest, however, in the plain recital of how he had progressed.

Whatever anyone thought of Newman after reading his defence, none could have continued to suspect him of Italianate tendencies:

Still more confident am I of such eventual acquittal, seeing that my judges are my own countrymen. I think, indeed, Englishmen the most suspicious and touchy of mankind; I think them unreasonable and unjust in their seasons of excitement; but I had rather be an Englishman (as in fact I am) than belong to any other race under heaven. They are as generous, as they are hasty and burly; and their repentance for their injustice is greater than their sin.[45]

It was an approach that the Victorian reader could not resist, and it beat Kingsley on his own ground. Newman could still charm men, as he had once charmed them from the pulpit of St Mary's. Even those who hated his ideas had to warm to his sincerity – and Kingsley too had acknowledged a debt of former admiration. Was it with a justifiable sense of accomplishment in the *Apologia* that he later chose as his Cardinal's motto '*cor ad cor loquitur*'?

His brother Francis once said that Newman always tells the reader who taught him what, but not why, he changed.[46] The accusation is not viable if one realizes that the search which passed him from one authority to another sprang from his deepest nature. He could not be contented by anything less than perfection, and he found perfection only in one Church. He found it not as one blind to all blemishes, but in the belief that other sources of good were all imperfect in more serious ways. The *Apologia* shows that he had never been in full sympathy with the Evangelicals, any more than with the liberalist logic that he had imbibed from Whately. He found that Evangelicalism 'had no intellectual basis; no internal idea, no principle of unity, no theology'. As for Whately – 'I owe him a great deal . . . [but] his mind was too different from mine for us to remain long on one line'.

The debt to Whately, and to Copleston too, was indeed great. The power of exposition and logical argument first learned in the common room at Oriel now served him well, perhaps better than ever before. The deep feelings evoked by his writing the *Apologia* could have been verbalized as the expression of introspection only. The stringency with which he had learned to present argumentation saved him now from the personalism that had prevented his being a first-rate novelist. Yet some of that personalism helped him to share with basically unsympathetic readers the reasons for his development. To read Newman and be admitted into his world of insight is to believe that we too are being insightful. 'No other prose writer of his century has invaded the world of subjective things with senses as alert as his nor more completely realized in his own work his conception of the power and dignity of literature.'[47]

The *Apologia* stands for ever high in the ranks of great English prose. It is not hard to see why Newman was being used as a model for schoolboys' composition at Harrow a few years later.[48] His achievement here is deceptive in its clarity and directness – deceptive because its effects were produced by a man who had learned, in the pulpit and on paper, how to make the language behave as he wished. The mental discipline of his scholarly and priestly training had gained much and lost nothing through the pastoral discipline of ministry in two communions. The speaking voice is never far from what is written. The reliving of Oxford days brought back the manner of those university sermons which friends and critics alike had praised. The style is simpler and more direct than much that he had written since his secession. He had tended to become more rhetorical, though no less vivid. He had handled longer sentences – handled them brilliantly with a secure sense of total structure, but inevitably drawing away some little distance from the reader's normal communication. Now he wrote again as men would like to believe that they speak when the occasion demands both persuasion and clarity. If we are not totally deceived, it is because we know how hard and long he laboured at writing which seems easy.[49]

Newman shares with some of the greatest English writers in all centuries the ability to mingle passages of classical grandeur with direct simile, homely allusion, even colloquial phrases. The transition and return seem effortless, but a lesser writer who makes the attempt will often produce only disharmony and lack of decorum. Newman could address his fellow-countrymen in those familiar terms which in themselves seemed to absolve him from any suspicion of deceit – 'One man's meat was another man's poison', 'I saw the hitch in the Anglican argument', 'like a swarm of flies', 'in the same boat', 'a flight of undergraduates', 'be large-minded enough', 'only try your hand', 'let me off'. It was a consummately skilful way of meeting the suspicions of the aggressively English Englishman who would rally naturally to Kingsley's side.

When the defence of his faith moved him, he could exploit the fullest resources of the language, building up sentence after sentence to the climax when the reader almost suspects some trick but cannot be sure how it has been done. For example, his defence of the infallible definition of dogma:

I do not see how any question about the narrowness of theology comes into our question, which simply is, whether the belief in an Infallible authority destroys the independence of the mind; and I consider that the whole history of the Church, and especially the history of the theological schools, gives a negative to the accusation. There never was a time when the intellect of the educated class was more active, or rather more restless, than in the Middle Ages. And then again all through Church history from the first, how slow is authority in interfering! Perhaps a local teacher, or a doctor in some local school, hazards a proposition, and a controversy ensues. It smoulders or burns in one place, no one interposing; Rome simply let it alone. Then it comes before a Bishop; or some priest, or some professor in some other seat of learning takes it up; and then there is a second stage of it. Then it comes before a University, and it may be condemned by the theological faculty. So the controversy proceeds year after year, and Rome is still silent. An appeal perhaps is next made to a seat of authority inferior to Rome; and then at last after a long while it comes before the supreme power. Meanwhile, the question has been ventilated and turned over again and again, and viewed on every side of it, and authority is called upon to pronounce a decision, which has already been arrived at by reason.[50]

Newman himself was not infallible but he was almost irresistible when he wrote like this. The passage is typical of his method, in exposition as in his own life. With Newman, more than with most writers, one feels that the style is indeed the man himself. The general question to be considered is posed, provisionally answered and then approached through a culminative series of particularities until the definitive conclusion is reached. 'Authority is called upon to pronounce a decision which has already been arrived at by reason.' That had been his own path from Oxford to Rome.

The *Apologia* is the work of one who had declared a few years previously: 'Literature is the personal use or exercise of language.'[51] Kingsley had accused him of not dealing honestly in his use of words and provoked a reply which remains a model of clarity. Its immediate effect was almost entirely beneficial to Newman; the recalling of Oxford years brought him greater esteem than he had enjoyed since those years ended. Most of the leading periodicals, even such notoriously astringent ones as the *Quarterly* and the *Saturday*, gave favourable notice to the *Apologia*. There was less enthusiasm in the *Athenaeum*, which commented: 'how briskly we gather round a brace of reverend gentlemen when the prize for which they contend is which of the two shall be considered as the father of lies!'[52] George Eliot 'found it impossible to forsake the book until I had finished it', and found in it the revelation of a life, 'how different in form from one's own, yet with how close a fellowship in its needs and burthens – I mean spiritual needs and burthens'.[53]

The controversy with Kingsley seemed to exorcise some of the frustrations which had followed Newman for many years. Things went more easily with him, and more gently. In the following year he had a brief reunion at Hursley with Pusey and Keble. He said a mass for Kingsley's soul when the latter died in 1875. He became a cardinal, without the normal obligation of living in Rome. When he died in 1890, nearly ninety years old, there passed from this earth the greatest of the Tractarians, the most honoured and the most reviled, a man whose place as an English writer is secure beyond polemics. Yet in the end there remains the misfortune of one who desired submission and certainty, who was dragged by circumstances and by his own great gifts into a position of leadership. When it came to a fight he was tenacious, but every time the hurt was deep. There was something in him which made even his opponents generous. Matthew Arnold, the son of his old enemy and himself far from sympathetic with his beliefs, remembered him in terms of which greatness might be proud:

From Oxford to Rome

Forty years ago he was in the prime of life; he was close at hand to us at Oxford; he was preaching in St Mary's pulpit every Sunday; he seemed about to transform and renew what was for us the most national and natural institution in the world, the Church of England. Who could resist the charm of that spiritual apparition, gliding in the dim afternoon light through the aisles of St Mary's, rising into the pulpit, and then, in the most entrancing of voices, breaking the silence with words which were a religious music – subtle, sweet, mournful? . . . Or, if we followed him back to his seclusion at Littlemore, that dreary village by the London road, and to the house of retreat and the church which he built there – a mean house such as Paul might have lived in when he was tent-making at Ephesus, a church plain and thinly sown with worshippers – who could resist him there either, welcoming back to the severe joys of church-fellowship, and of daily worship and prayer, the firstlings of a generation which had well-nigh forgotten them?[54]

6

The Appeal to Antiquity

'I do not think that we have any right in the nineteenth century to contest an opinion which the father of the Church gave in the fourth.'[1] Kingsley had little sympathy with his fictional character; Lord Vieuxbois, who gave that opinion, was conceived as a satirical portrait of the backward-looking tendencies of the Oxford Movement. One of the achievements of that movement was to make Anglicans see their Church as part of a historical continuity. Instead of complacently accepting it as a contemporary institution, they were forced to look back not only to the Reformation but far beyond it. The backward view was of course neither confined to that movement nor initiated by it. Apart from the common human desire to dwell on past glories, there were pressures in the age which made reformers look to the past for justification, while the timid sought there for escape. The appetite for historical novels from Scott's time on through Lytton, Ainsworth, G.P.R. James, Reade and further in the century, had its causes in the present.

Some of the Tractarians, and more of their successors, got as far as the long and amorphous Middle Ages in their quest for authority. For a time there was common ground in the idealized medieval view between the Oxford Movement and the Young England group in the Tory party. They soon drew apart, and Disraeli became a bitter enemy of Anglo-Catholicism. Hurrell Froude, alone among the first Tractarians, found his ideal in the medieval Church and made it his basis for attacking the Reformers and urging his fellow-churchmen to repudiate most of what had been done in the sixteenth century. The others were concerned rather to judge both Roman and Reformed Churches against the purity of much earlier times, when even the schism between East and West had not taken place. When the Church was undivided, surely her position was closer to the Will of God. 'Our appeal was to antiquity – to the doctrine which the Fathers and Councils and Church universal had taught from the creeds,' wrote one who became critical of the later developments in the revival.[2]

The part actually played in the Oxford Movement by the appeal to antiquity is important but not exclusive. Keble, loving the Latin tongue and living on terms of easy familiarity with the classical poets, found his main security in the more recent Anglican traditions which his High Church upbringing had taught him to love. The continuity of the Church of England with the Catholic Church back to apostolic times was for him an undoubted and joyous truth rather than a matter for polemical argument. Pusey, an even better classical scholar, was more inclined to look inward than outward when matters of faith were to be asserted; the guide of conscience and numinous feeling could be relied on more than formulated 'evidences'. He would use the Fathers to illuminate theological opinions, not to provide his credentials for holding them.

Nevertheless, the appeal to antiquity came to be one of the badges of particularity associated with the Tractarians. A service to theological scholarship grew out of the desire to find justification for Anglican claims in the doctrines and organization of the early Church. In 1838 Keble, Pusey and Newman as joint editors initiated *The Library of the Fathers of the Holy Catholic Church*, a series which continued to appear until 1885, when it contained forty-eight volumes. About the same time, at Cambridge, Richard Trench was surprised to find 'how seldom an original and independent collection of materials has been made by commentators'.[3] Before caution supervened, Samuel Wilberforce was willing to recognize the validity of appealing not only to the Caroline divines but also to 'the Primitive Church of the first three centuries'.[4] Thomas Arnold, however, would have none of it.

I never have thought that what people call the Primitive Church, and much less the Ante-Nicene Church more generally, was any better *authority* per se, than the Church of Rome, or the Greek Church.[5]

It was Newman who, as usual, looked farther and more deeply than his contemporaries. A youthful reading of Joseph Milner's *History of the Church of Christ* had brought him to awareness of the patristic writers who were still generally neglected even in Church circles. He brought the primitive Church into the centre of the Tractarian controversy. He loved Hurrell Froude, but the latter's medievalism became distasteful to him. The authority of very early Christianity, which had hovered in the background of the kind of High Churchmanship professed by Froude and Keble, became a major question. The first Tracts were concerned with the Apostolic Succession and the assertion that Anglican clergy stood in that unbroken tradition. Where then should they appeal if not to the days of the Apostles and those who had immediately succeeded them?

Even at the time of the Hadleigh Conference the name 'Apostolical' was being assumed by those who looked for a new assertion of Church rights. The direct appeal of Tract 1 for support of the Bishops as successors of the Apostles seized the imagination of supporters as surely as it alarmed and alienated opponents. It passed beyond the Oxford circle and in 1835 Manning, then an Anglican, could take this High view of the Church of England ministry.

The Roman fever that gripped some of the younger enthusiasts of the movement around 1840 brought new problems. Most of these were little concerned about the early Church, which seemed irrelevant to the splendour that they were discovering in contemporary Roman Catholicism. W. G. Ward found his ideal in a visible entity: 'the study of primitive times was uncongenial to his unhistoric mind.'[6] Nevertheless, that study was coming to be vital both to those who wanted to check the secessions and those on the Roman side who wanted to hasten and increase them. After Newman went in 1845, it was to the early Church that both sides turned for their justification. The movement which had begun as a vindication of the High doctrine of the Church as against the subjection of the Church to the State had taken on a new dimension. Puseyites wanted to prove that they were true Catholics without acknowledging the Pope as supreme; Roman Catholic apologists claimed that their Church was the sole repository and guardian of Catholicism.

Primitive evidence was the more important because it had played so large a part in Newman's conversion. A slight expansion of what has already been related about that event may illuminate the fiction which he and others derived from the world of early Christianity. His reading had slowly led him to see Rome as the abiding source of Christian truth. The Anglicanism that he had been defending came to appear like certain heresies: Romanism stood firm, then and now, unshakeably orthodox. He never forgot what the Tractarians had done to revive the understanding of Apostolic Succession when 'a few good old men were its sole remaining possessors in the Church'.[7] Yet, the more he followed that lead, the more he found that the Anglican position was untenable.

For one thing, it rested on discrete and chosen aspects of early Christianity, whereas Rome could point to an unbroken and total development from the beginning. Still he did not believe that all was lost; if Rome was not the evil thing that he had once believed her to be, at least her strength need not undermine that of his own Church. By 1840 he was ready to concede: 'Rome is the only representative of the Primitive Church besides ourselves.'[8] Yet was antiquity the same as catholicity? His description of the change in his own thinking is important in relation to the disputes about authority in the succeeding years:

The Anglican disputant took his stand upon Antiquity or Apostolicity, the Roman upon Catholicity. The Anglican said to the Roman: 'There is but One Faith, the Ancient, and you have not kept to it': the Roman retorted: 'There is but One Church, the Catholic, and you are out of it.' The Anglican urged: 'Your special beliefs, practices, modes of action, are nowhere in Antiquity'; the Roman objected: 'You do not communicate with any one Church besides your own and its offshoots, and you have discarded principles, doctrines, sacraments, and usages, which are and ever have been received in the East and the West.'[9]

145

The logic of his investigations drove him on. Did the Anglican claim depend too much on antiquity and succession, while dismissing the seriousness of the present isolation and separation from the largest undoubtedly Catholic body? To be in direct line from the Apostles might not be enough. The idea of development, which became increasingly important in his thinking after 1838, led him in a new and unwelcome direction. What if the distinctively Roman doctrines were not innovations but were in fact rooted in the same ancient Church from which Anglicans claimed their authority? Then, surely, Anglicans were in schism, at best in partial possession of what Rome had preserved wholly.

So he came to believe; and the acceptance that brought him to secession is summed up by Charles Reding when he says that he finds Rome to have all the marks of Catholicity which the Anglican divines have severally demanded. 'And *seeing* it to be *like* the apostolic Church, I believe it to be the same.' He adds, characteristically both of himself and of his creator: 'Reason has gone first, faith is to follow.'[10] The matter was settled for Newman, but the arguments on both sides grew sharper as both Churches tried to prove that their Catholicity was total as well as ancient. There was a crop of polemical writing of the type which Newman satirized in the scene when the young Anglo-Catholic clergyman is asking his wife which book she wants: 'Is it "The Catholic Parsonage" . . . or "Lays of the Apostles" or "The English Church older than the Roman" or "Anglicanism of the Early Martyrs"?'[11]

Most subjects of debate in the Victorian period got an airing in the novels of the time as well as in more direct forms of exposition. Too often both methods got confused, to produce books that were ostensibly fiction but occupied a great many of their pages in overt presentation of arguments and supporting facts. Disraeli included long sections of political theory in his novels, and lesser writers were worse offenders. By the late forties the novel was well on the way to becoming the 'loose, baggy monster' which Henry James deplored. Novels about the early Church were among those written to prove a case; the type remained popular down to the end of the century, but there are a few written during the main period of controversy which claim particular attention.

The popularity which novels of this type enjoyed cannot, however, be ascribed solely to religious interest even in that religiously tormented age. It was not only those learned in Church history who felt themselves close to the ancient world. There was a common bond in antiquity between those who had received anything more than minimal education, and the interest had percolated into popular culture as well. The limitation of the grammar schools to their founders' intentions that Greek and Latin should dominate the curriculum was enforced by Eldon's judgement in 1805 and continued until the Grammar Schools Act of 1840. It is true that the novels of the early Church were, inevitably, later in period than the major classics, but there was still an easy familiarity of reference in this world of procurators and decurions, slaves and freedmen. It seemed less exotic than contemporary foreign cultures: yet, in Europe at least, educated men could find common ground and even a common tongue in what remained of their schoolboy memories.

Those memories contained more than an objective reference to the past: there was the sense of a present ideal. From Tudor times, Englishmen had found themselves mirrored in the classical culture that stretched from heroes of Greek mythology to those of Roman Imperial power. Decades after the Tractarians, John Morley urged the value of that tradition:

All through the ages, men tossed in the beating waves of circumstance have found more abundantly in the essays and letters of Seneca than in any other secular writer words of good counsel and comfort. And let this fact not pass, without notice of the light that it sheds on the fact of the unity of literature, and of the absurdity of setting a wide gulf between ancient or classical literature and modern, as if under all dialects the partakers in Graeco-Roman civilization, whether in Athens, Rome, Paris, Weimar, Edinburgh, London, Dublin, were not the heirs of a great common stock of thought as well as speech.[12]

The Victorian turn of mind – and it is a human failing not confined to one century – made it possible to ignore the more uncomfortable aspects of classical analogues, such as the Jacobin cult of Roman liberators that apotheosized Scaevola and Brutus. So too, in those pre-Freudian days, the classical myth could be tamed and made a source of good examples. Though

Kingsley laughed at the historicism of Lord Vieuxbois, he could produce *The Heroes* and conclude his preface with the assertion that the meaning of these stories was 'true, and true for ever, and that is – Do right, and God will help you'.

It was not only Broad Church optimists who could make the cheery adoption of the classics into the Christian system. Keble had no reticence about making classical allusions in *The Christian Year*. Andromache speaks words of comfort and divine hope; the country streams have their nymphs; the amaranth wreath is a heavenly reward.[13] He loved an inscription in Latin, since it was 'the language more nearly of the Universal Church, and no doubt feeling the more perfect expression and allusiveness'.[14] The tensions that could exist in such synthesis seemed to trouble very few. J.A. Froude, recalling through fiction his boyhood, expressed the more sceptical view. 'I remember thinking it odd that I should be taught to admire Hector, and Aeneas, and Ulysses, and so many of them, when all they were idolators too.'[15]

Theology, secular attraction, underlying tensions, all played their part in the production and success of the Early Church novel. The fact that some of these books were written by men already famous in religious controversy, either by early association with the Tractarians, or drawn in as the conflict sharpened, helped to increase the appeal. There were excursions into fiction by those who would not otherwise have been tempted to such writing, as well as attempts at the early Christian background by writers already established.

Nicholas Wiseman had the distinction not only of being the first English Cardinal to reside in this country since the Reformation, but also of being the first one ever to write a novel. No doubt his enemies as well as his friends would have reasoned that a man who could successfully ride out the storms surrounding the restoration of the Roman Catholic hierarchy was capable of anything. Those enemies were not confined to the militant Protestants; the dispensation which he inaugurated was not welcomed by all the English Roman Catholics, many of whom wanted only to practise their faith in security but without public sensation. Wiseman came to Westminster from being Rector of the English College in Rome, a supporter of the ultramontanes and full of enthusiasm for the Italian modes of worship. Add to that his abundant energy and the ebullience of his Irish ancestry, and his novel seems almost inevitable.

Wiseman's *Fabiola* (1854) took its part in the controversy about religious authority. It presents the early Church as already distinctively Roman, centred in the Imperial capital and owing allegiance to the Bishop of Rome as Pontiff. Wiseman was writing of the city which he had only recently left, where the ruins of former days stood to remind the nineteenth century of what had once been. From his intimate knowledge of the present he could reconstruct the past, dwelling imaginatively upon the ruined structures where he had often walked with reflections considerably different from those of Gibbon in the previous century.

A man like this, occupied as he was with business and controversy, could now reasonably produce a novel. Lingering Romantic notions of the artist in solitude, far removed from the madding world, were fast disappearing as every hurrying polemicist found time to put his ideas into fiction. The novel of the fifties could be written

. . . at all sorts of times and in all sorts of places; early and later, when no duty urged, in scraps and fragments of time, when the body was too fatigued or the mind too worn for heavier occupation; in the roadside inn, in the halt of travel, in strange houses, in every variety of situation and circumstances – sometimes trying ones. It has thus been composed bit by bit, in portions varying from ten lines to half-a-dozen pages at most, and generally with few books or resources at hand.[16]

Such an attitude comments on the prolific number and length of Victorian novels, the sense of urgency and the weaknesses of structure which are common in minor works and infect sometimes even the masters.

Fabiola was written to inaugurate a 'Popular Catholic Library'; its sub-title, *The Church of the Catacombs*, suggested a series of novels each dealing with a period of significance in the development of the Church. It is unquestionably the work of a priest writing for the faithful – and a priest who had spent a lot of time in contemporary Rome. Plot and episodes are based on saints' legends and the hints of the Roman breviary: all treated as firmly as the facts of recorded history which give the external framework of the story. It is a novel not only for Roman Catholics, but for Victorians. Although the novel had gained both popularity and status, it was a form still bearing a touch of boldness and even impropriety for the puritanical of all allegiances. Not Evangelicals alone might be anxious about admitting a novel into the home. It was only a few years since Newman's enemies had been able to attack *Loss and Gain* not only for its ideas but also for being in the form of fiction. Wiseman, enthroned primate though he was, thought it necessary to reassure his potential readers that he would neither corrupt their morals nor waste their time.

It was necessary to introduce some view of the morals and opinions of the pagan world, as a contrast to those of Christians. But their worst aspect has been carefully suppressed, as nothing could be admitted here which the most sensitive Catholic eye would shrink from contemplating. It is, indeed, earnestly desired that this little work, written solely for recreation, be read also as a relaxation from graver pursuits; but that, at the same time, the reader may rise from its perusal with a feeling that his time has not been lost, nor his mind occupied with frivolous ideas.[17]

He need have had no fears; *Fabiola* was widely read, not by Roman Catholics alone. It ran through several printings in the first year and was translated into ten European languages including no fewer than seven translations into Italian.[18]

For the setting, Wiseman took the period of persecution under Diocletian at the beginning of the fourth century. He collected into the story an assemblage of such famous martyrs as Sebastian, Agnes and Cecilia – well known to his readers through painting and poetry. The story itself is woven round the eponymous heroine, a haughty but high-souled young rich woman who is converted from her attachment to pagan philosophy and becomes a Christian. There is also a properly Victorian allowance of villains, to be either spectacularly converted or despatched in painful retribution for their misdeeds at the end. The progress of the plot is frequently halted by passages of archaeological detail relevant to the catacombs, and other aspects of early Christian practice.

These digressions seem less irritating if the reader relates them to the didacticism that is common enough in minor novels of the time. The catacombs may seem less relevant

than the factories, both to modern ideas and to the main preoccupations of the Victorian age, but Wiseman was following
his own purpose as other writers of fiction followed theirs.
He declared indeed that he was not trying to be erudite and
'fill half of each page with notes and references' However, the
proportion of footnotes that might be thin in a scholarly treatise can seem all too substantial in a novel. The sections dealing with the social life of Imperial Rome are inappropriate
from a writer who admits to taking considerable liberties with
chronology and who seems to give credence to legendary
material. One feels, perhaps unfairly, that learning is being
used to give verisimilitude to more doubtful things.

Yet an unsympathetic approach produces only awareness of
the weaknesses which are readily apparent. An imaginative
effort to read through the eyes of those for whom the book was
first written can arouse interest and even some excitement. The
archaeological passages would be fascinating to readers who
felt both theological and secular respect for Roman antiquities
but were not well versed in them – and this at a time when
excavations and research were continually bringing new knowledge. Wiseman was a learned man who shared the gift of
many greater Victorian novelists: he could tell a good story.
He shared too, in stronger measure, the zest for action and
experience that animated even the pessimists among his contemporaries. He could describe adventure, excitement, cruelty, with such personal involvement that it was hard not to
become a participant.

Within the carefully presented ancient setting, *Fabiola* deals
with a major problem of Wiseman's own time. Conversion,
apostasy, the challenge to Christianity itself, were questions of
the day. Wiseman not only urges the claims of Christianity:
he asserts that those claims are valid only in the name of the
Roman Catholic Church. He wrote when the stream of conversions to his faith was still flowing strongly, while at the
same time Puseyite writers were setting out the claims of the
Church of England to be as Catholic as Rome. The under-
ground Church of the novel gives allegiance to the Bishop of
Rome, who is referred to on numerous occasions as Pope.
When the Pope sends a letter of command, 'to hear was to
obey'. The idea that Romanism shows a continuity of doctrine

and practice from the earliest times to the present is continually urged. Newman had been drawn to secession partly by his belief that contemporary Roman Catholic features were traceable back to the primitive Church, there to be found either in substance or in embryo. Wiseman, the lifelong Romanist, makes the same claim.

Thus the evidence of an epitaph in the catacombs informs us that 'the belief in the real presence of Our Lord's Body in the Blessed Eucharist was the same then as now' (p. 225). Development is shown by a comparison of ancient and modern baptismal rites: 'any one perusing the present rite of baptism in the Catholic Church, especially that of adults, will see condensed into one office what used to be anciently distributed through a variety of functions' (p. 305). Auricular confession was practised, especially by converts before baptism (p. 321). As for ordination in the Apostolic line which the Tractarians claimed anew for their clergy, the true descent could be found from those early bishops who acknowledged the primacy of the Pope: the latter's own acts of ordination are the archetype for later ages.[19]

It is not only the proud claims for Roman supremacy that make *Fabiola* distinctively a novel of the fifties, of the early years of the restored hierarchy and the running fight with both Protestants and Puseyites. Wiseman shows himself very much aware of his own times; his enthusiasm for antiquity does not stop him enjoying those times and sharing in their prejudices. There are references to the Great Exhibition of 1851, where his readers might have seen reconstructions of Roman buildings. The horror of the prisons to which the early Christians were sent is contrasted with the model Victorian gaols 'to which a poor man might court committal, hoping there to enjoy better fare and lodging than he did at home'.[20] The records of the Christian martyrs are much more edifying than the contemporary fiction for which Wiseman felt some disapproval even as he wrote:

If the reader would compare the morbid sensibility, and the overstrained excitement, endeavoured to be produced by a modern French writer, in the imaginary journal of a culprit condemned to death, down to the immediate approach of execution, with the unaffected pathos and charming truthfulness which persuades the corresponding narrative of Vivia Perpetua, a delicate lady of twenty-one years of age, he would not hesitate in concluding, how much more natural, graceful and interesting are the simple recitals of Christianity, than the boldest fictions of romance.[21]

Which suggests that Wiseman had not given much thought to the art of fiction but was prepared to share Evangelical feelings about truth and lies. The power of imagination found no Romantic shrine in him.

He did, however, show some awareness of the less happy features of the novel – particularly that of the years shortly before. There is a distinct intrusion of the 'silver fork' school in the account of the house of Fabius:

> Besides possessing many treasures of Eastern art, it abounded with the rarest productions of the East. Carpets from Persia were laid on the ground, silks from China, many-coloured stuffs from Babylon and gold embroidery from India and Phrygia covered the furniture while curious works in ivory and in metals, scattered about, were attributed to the inhabitants of islands beyond the Indian Ocean, of monstrous form and fabulous descent.[22]

The florid method of many contemporary novelists was too strong a temptation for the florid tendency in Wiseman himself. His elaborate, adjectival style is an unhappy contrast to the dignified simplicity of Newman.

Teacher, apologist, man of his age – Wiseman reveals himself as all these. More, he writes as a Roman Catholic in a nation where his Church, though permitted and gaining in strength, was yet bitterly unpopular with the majority. The active persecution of Diocletian reflects the less official hostility of Victorian England. What the early Christians suffered should be an encouragement to modern Roman Catholics in their slighter but still uncomfortable disability. Fabiola's father, the rich Fabius, is the comfortable latitudinarian who despises as bigotry all manifestations of strong religious feeling. Apostates like Torquatus may turn traitor and harm the Church – the case of Achilli was fresh in Wiseman's mind. Not only the pagans but the 'heretics' are already using the noble name of Catholic as a term of abuse. 'Heretics ridiculed Catholics' for using *Deo gratias* as a greeting but 'Catholics employed it because consecrated by pious usage'.[23] The Christian scriptures, especially the Old Testament, were being used as sources of attack by enemies who could find them unedifying and corrupt: the frequency of this attack in Wiseman's time needs no emphasis.

While Wiseman was writing in the short bursts of production that his archepiscopal work allowed, an equally ebullient and polemical clergyman was giving his own views in fiction about the early Church. Charles Kingsley's novel *Hypatia* appeared in serial form in *Fraser's Magazine* in 1852–3 before being issued as a volume in the latter year. It has its special place in Kingsley's own development and in the fight with Newman which culminated in the *Apologia* in 1864. Kingsley had no intention of supporting Puseyite claims to catholicity, but he was drawn into the controversy about authority and the development from antiquity. It was another instance of the way in which the aftermath of the Oxford Movement kept interfering with his peace of mind. The hares which were started at Oxford between 1833 and 1845 ran across a lot of unexpected and indirect paths in the following years.

When we read *Hypatia* with the gift of later knowledge, we can see it as a defiance to the whole way of thinking that characterized Newman and other defenders of both his first and his second Church. It is set in Alexandria, not in Rome, and at a later date than that of *Fabiola*. The story is in the time of St Cyril, when Christianity was fully tolerated throughout the Empire after the Edict of Constantine. The reaction attempted by Julian the Apostate has passed away and the Church is growing in strength. Yet ecclesiastical power is not willingly accepted by many citizens, who despise the teaching and resent the intrusion of the hierarchy into matters of secular as well as spiritual obedience. As the Church gains power, she becomes more corrupt and more tyrannical. In short, the Church occupies the place that the Roman Catholic Church occupied in Kingsley's forebodings. Emancipated in 1829, proudly furnished with a new hierarchy in 1850, she was a threat to the nation that accommodated her. Cyril, the Bishop of Alexandria, is almost certainly based on Wiseman. He is not by any means seen as wholly bad; Kingsley, as we know by now, was an honourable and not a scurrilous opponent. Cyril is praised for his boldness and his energy (better, no doubt, than the 'effeminate' Newman and his fellow-converts). Unfortunately, he does not always show a pure Protestant regard for the strict truth. He will plot to gain his own ends, and go half-way to accept evil for what he believes to be a good outcome. And he is badly counselled by his more fanatical supporters. 'Truth, for its own sake, had never been a virtue with the Roman clergy.'

The plot of *Hypatia*, though hardly subtle, becomes unnecessarily complicated. Hypatia, founded on a historical figure, is a beautiful and high-minded teacher of the old philosophy. Although she sees the pagan gods only as symbols of the deeper truth, she secretly longs to restore the former cult and take away the power of Christianity over the minds of men. She is proud and aloof until she finds her womanhood through a surge of physical love. She finds also her allegiance to the new faith which she had condemned, only to be martyred not by the pagans but by the monks and their attendant mob.

Hypatia's power falls on Philammon, a young monk out of the desert who comes to Alexandria, finds his suppressed virility through attraction to the philosopher whom he goes to convert, and falls into hatred of monkish ways. Yet he returns to the devoted life, his perceptions heightened and his insight increased by contact with the active world. Meanwhile the young Jew Raphael ben Ezra, another of Hypatia's admirers, goes out of Alexandria for his own taste of reality. After many adventures he finds true love and also true faith – yet another of Kingsley's heroes to be brought to Christianity by a good woman.

Within the story too are the Goths who befriend Philammon. It is not important that they are Arians and that Christian tenets rest very lightly on their old culture: they are virile, they hate monks, and they knock down people who annoy them. Pelagia, Philammon's lost sister, is the mistress of their leader until she is rescued from this fallen state and carried off to a life of holiness in the desert. There is also Raphael's mother Miriam, an evil, lapsed nun who practises witchcraft. And, of course, a whole crowd of monks who are a very bad lot, led by a villain called Peter the Reader. Any relationship to the name of the first Bishop of Rome according to

Papal claims is probably wholly intentional. In short, the whole thing is full of Kingsley's enthusiasms and prejudices.

Yet he did not write only from the heart. He did a good deal of research for the book until he could be accurate in his account of the city and its life. He was a much better novelist than Wiseman and avoided the distraction of footnotes and long didactic passages. As a story of action and adventure, with some good fights and a lot of shouting, *Hypatia* is still worth the reading. Yet it does not require very thoughtful study to find a worryingly negative quality in it. Kingsley had a splendid hate-session, until it is by no means clear of whom he approves and which system he wants to succeed. The comparison with *Fabiola* is instructive: Wiseman's book, for all its artistic faults, is direct and positive in its urging of Roman claims. Kingsley speaks not only for himself but, as usual, for many of his contemporaries. If what he says turns out to be muddled and indeterminate, the cause is not only in the untidiness of his own mind. The Catholic revival had aroused reactions which, except for the most acute thinkers, were often constrained by anxiety to be ill-defined.

There is the usual hatred of monks, whose celibacy denies proper masculine virility and fulfilment. Kingsley had dealt with this theme previously in the world of his novels, and would return to it. His own personal struggle is relived once again when Raphael has to win his bride from her father's intention of putting her into a convent. The account of how the desert monks fear sex and regard women as dangerous and evil is perhaps not merely anti-Catholic but a veiled protest against the whole set of taboos which society was then imposing. However, the monks are not only celibate but they do not bathe and thereby they offend Kingsley's sanitary code. The pagans do rather better in this, as in other respects. Physical beauty is a divine gift, to be denied at peril of losing understanding as well as virility:

The righteous instinct which bids us welcome and honour beauty, whether in man or woman, as something of real worth – divine, heavenly, ay, though we know not how, in a most deep sense eternal.[24]

More still of the essential Kingsley emerges in the warning

to those who 'begin by lying for the cause of truth; and setting off upon that evil road, arrive surely, with the Scribes and Pharisees of old, sooner or later at their own place'.[25] Admittedly he prefaces the warning with an application to all, 'whether orthodox or unorthodox, Papist or Protestant'. For there is good as well as bad in all men; even the wicked monks are devoted in their own way. Philammon ends his days in a truly Broad Church view of the possibility of finding the good and bringing any man to the truth. Kingsley speaks both from Christian Socialist convictions and from his own experience when he sees dangers in a Church grown fashionable and successful, so that preachers who are too outspoken about social conditions can suffer inhibition.[26] A further link with his own experience is the probable prototype of Raphael ben Ezra in Alfred Hyman Louis, to whom he had administered baptism in the church at Eversley. The continual mingling of personalism with stern warnings to society of the need for reform is typical of Kingsley's method.

Never guilty of excessive subtlety, Kingsley underlined the contemporary reference of *Hypatia* by its sub-title 'New Foes with an Old Face',[27] and made the point even more explicit in the last paragraph of the book:

And now, readers, farewell. I have shown you New Foes under an Old Face – your own likenesses in toga and tunic, instead of coat and bonnet. One word before we part. The same devil who tempted these old Egyptians tempts you. The same God who would have saved these old Egyptians if they had willed, will save you, if you will. Their sins are yours, their errors yours, their doom yours, their deliverance yours. There is nothing new under the sun. The thing which has been, it is that which shall be. Let him that is without sin among you cast the first stone, whether at Hypatia or Pelagia, Miriam or Raphael, Cyril or Philammon.

Despite this charitable close, *Hypatia* suffers from the fact that it contains a large didactic element which gives many more examples of what to avoid than what to imitate. It is not clear if anyone is right, except possibly Synesius, the Bishop of Cyrene, who is often referred to and finally makes his entry. He appears to be the good Broad Church all-rounder, hearty but not fanatical, vigorous but kindly: the image of the author if he had been projected back into the ancient world, been given his deserved place and left with his faculty of self-analysis:

The Bishop of Cyrene, to judge from the charming private letters which he has left, was one of those many-sided, volatile, restless men, who taste joy and sorrow, if not deeply or permanently, yet abundantly and passionately. He lived . . . in a whirlwind of good deeds, meddling and toiling for the mere pleasure of action; and as soon as there was nothing to be done, which, till lately, had happened seldom enough with him, paid the penalty for past excitement in fits of melancholy. A man of magniloquent and flowery style, not without a vein of self-conceit; yet withal of overflowing kindliness, racy humour, and unflinching courage, both physical and moral, with a very clear practical faculty, and a very muddy speculative one – though, of course, like the rest of the world, he was especially proud of his own weakest side, and professed the most passionate affection for philosophic meditation; while his detractors hinted, not without a show of reason, that he was far more of an adept in soldiering and dog-breaking than in the mysteries of the unseen world.[28]

Of course, one could not write such a book at that time without receiving a great deal of hostile criticism. As usual, Kingsley was surprised to find himself being blamed for his good intentions. His attack on monasticism and his praise of a pagan philosopher seemed to be attacks on Christianity itself. His enthusiasm for physical beauty and his comparative freedom in describing sexual attraction – mild and reticent though it may seem today – could be regarded as incitements to immorality. Critics were not slow to suggest that a clerical author was particularly culpable if he went too far in such matters:

We must take the liberty of saying, with all deference, that a clergyman of the Church of England might occupy his leisure more usefully than by writing books of this kind . . . there are many parts and passages of history which, out of respect for public morals, had much better be left unexplained.[29]

Poor Kingsley, suffering from the puritanical taboos of the age on the one hand, and from the anti-clericalism which the Oxford Movement had helped to aggravate on the other! Yet he honestly believed that he was showing the Church what path she should follow. What matter if the Goths were violent, sensual, drunken, heretical? All was pardonable since they

brought new, virile blood to the effete Roman Empire repressed by monkish asceticism. He thought that he was strengthening his case by relating his Goths to the Germanic drive to the
west, with Hengist and Horsa landing in Kent and the English
nation beginning 'its world-wide life'.

Not all the criticism was hostile, for Kingsley had once more
shown himself to be the spokesman for a substantial section
of the population. There were many then – and the breed is
not yet extinct – who thought that any attack on Roman
Catholicism was a stout blow for Protestantism. It was a short
step to the idea that any who came into conflict with Rome
were really Protestants at heart, even if the clash came long
before the concept. It was the apparent sensuality of parts of
the book which caused worse offence, disturbed those who
were in agreement with the anti-monastic theme, and gave
ammunition to those who were out to squash the author on any
pretext. In *Hypatia*, the power of physical attraction overcomes the resistance of the clerical celibate and also of the
philosophical scholar; and these were two figures very dear to
the Tractarians and their sympathizers. Kingsley's opponents
took their time in finding revenge. The review which led to
the correspondence with Newman, and ultimately to the
Apologia, appears in deeper perspective as part of revived hate
against all types of Catholicism if we recall what had happened
in the previous year.

Kingsley was sponsored for an honorary doctorate at Oxford by no less a patron than the Prince of Wales, to whom he
had at one time been a tutor. An Anglican clergyman with such
support would normally have been accepted readily. The years
that had passed since the parting of the first Tractarian leaders
had confirmed Pusey both as head of the Anglo-Catholic party
and also as a man of influence at Oxford where he had held
the Chair of Hebrew for a long period. A few months previously, Pusey had shown his strength by leading a movement
to refuse Jowett his salary as Professor of Greek on the
grounds that his contribution to *Essays and Reviews* had contained heresy. The enmity towards Jowett dated from his
published Broad Church views, and similarly the dislike of
Kingsley had a long antecedence. Pusey, devout and holy in
his personal life, could harbour a grudge and act spitefully

when he thought that his principles were concerned; he carried on that *odium theologicum* which had been an unpleasant feature of Tractarianism from the start and in which Hurrell Froude had excelled.

The opposition of the Puseyites was strong enough to overcome the princely recommendation. The attack was swift, openly declared and successful. *The Times* reported:

Dr Pusey has found another opportunity for gratifying his rabid theological tastes ... [Kingsley's] name has been withdrawn, on account of the determined opposition offered in the Hebdomadal Board by Dr Pusey, Dr Mansel, and others of the bigoted section. Their ground for opposition was, it is said, the heretical and immoral character of Mr Kingsley's works, more especially of *Hypatia* – a work which, though it necessarily describes the external aspect of a slowly rotting society, is in tone and object the highest of all Mr Kingsley's writings.[30]

Attack and defence lay still in the future. An immediate action was Newman's second incursion into the novel, taking up Kingsley's challenge in a manner which foreshadowed the more open conflict of 1864. He had been working on the idea of a novel about the primitive Church as early as 1848, but the idea was laid aside until 1855 when, with the speed that always seized him when he was excited by a fresh controversy, he turned his notes into a complete novel. There can be no doubt that Newman's *Callista* was inversely influenced by *Hypatia*: it is probable that the publication of *Fabiola* also impelled him to imitation – and perhaps oliquely to criticism – of his Archbishop.

The setting of *Callista* is again North Africa; the period is earlier than that of either *Hypatia* or *Fabiola*. The events are supposed to take place in the third century, before the Diocletian persecutions and the edict of Constantine. Newman thus shows a Christian Church – and for him this meant a Church already acknowledging Roman supremacy – contemptuously tolerated in a society that was still ready to break out in violence against it, to believe any calumny and to make it a scapegoat for any misfortune. In fact, he depicted the Church as he believed his own Church to be in the England of his time: he had already examined that position factually in his lectures on *The Present Position of Catholics in England*. For

'Christian' read 'Roman Catholic' for 'pagan' read 'Protestant', and there is clear comment in passages like this:

Whatever jealousy might be still cherished against the Christian name, nevertheless, individual Christians were treated with civility, and recognized as citizens; though among the populace there would be occasions, at the time of the more solemn pagan feasts, when accidental outbursts might be expected of the antipathy latent in the community.[31]

The relationships between *Callista* and *Hypatia* are remarkable, in point both of likeness and difference. Where Kingsley sees a Church growing daily more powerful, arrogant and ready to persecute, Newman sees only the peril of indifferent tolerance which lightly overlays hatred. In both books a pagan girl is converted and martyred and is wooed by an ardent Christian youth. Newman's heroine is a Greek artist, a maker of images, who is mistakenly arrested as a Christian and then finds herself unable to do the required sacrifice to the old gods. After a struggle in which her old friends try to persuade her, she dies as a convinced Christian. Her bereaved lover Agellius, a Christian by upbringing, survives to become a bishop and suffer martyrdom in the persecution of Diocletian which was Wiseman's theme in *Fabiola*.[32]

Naturally, almost every bias and implication in the two novels is diametrically different. Newman starts from a point of absolute regard for the Roman Church as pure and totally Catholic, persecuted not persecuting. Instead of the worldly Cyril, her typical bishop is the holy Cyprian. She looks to the Pope as her spiritual head, and that title is firmly attached to the Bishop of Rome. The point is made explicit more than once. St Fabian's martyrdom is given special significance:

It did not become a pope of that primitive time to die upon his bed, and he was reserved at length to inaugurate in his own person, as chief pastor of the Church, a fresh company of martyrs.[33]

The question of ultimate authority which was vexing so many of Newman's contemporaries is solved for Agellius when he is fully instructed in the faith which he had imperfectly understood:

He now too had a consciousness of the size and populousness of the Church, of her diffusion, of the promises made to her, of the essential necessity of what seemed to be misfortune, of the episcopal regimen, and of the power and solidarity of the see of Peter afar off in Rome, all of which knowledge had made him quite another being.[34]

Thus Agellius, thus Charles Reding, and thus Newman himself in November 1845.

It is not only dogmatic theology, however, that sunders Kingsley and Newman in these books and all through their lives. The idea of female beauty in *Callista* is cold, almost clinical as compared with that in *Hypatia*. Kingsley's heroine remains beautiful in her martyrdom, 'naked, snow-white against the dusky mass around'. Callista's beauty is destroyed by her suffering in prison and she dies marred but chastely covered. The first physical descriptions of the two girls point the contrast between their authors; it is significant too that we get no visual image of Callista until over half-way through the story, while Hypatia is described near the start. Hypatia is flawed only by 'too much self-restraint in those sharp curved lips ... but the glorious grace and beauty of every line of figure and face would have excused, even hidden those defects'. In Callista there is 'the calm of Greek sculpture; it imaged a soul nourished upon the visions of genius, and subdued and attuned by the power of a strong will'. In one, coldness is a fault which love will overcome; in the other, it is a virtue which opens the way to the sanctified chastity of the Christian martyr.

For Newman sex is a troublesome force which only the power of faith can tame. Strabo, the father of Agellius, gets a kind of fringe benefit from his Christianity when he finds that he is not compelled to continue living with his pagan wife. Admittedly she is an unpleasant woman, but there is the relief also of the natural celibate who finds that 'the Church did not oblige him to continue or renew a tie which bound him to so much misery, and that he might end his days in a tranquillity which his past life required, and his wife's presence would have precluded'.[35] For Kingsley, marriage is the only proper state for a healthy Christian. The Church which exalts celibacy shows thereby her own departure from truth. Raphael taunts Synesius in words which precisely anticipate Kingsley's taunting of Newman in the Froude review:

I had a dream one night, on my way, which made me question whether I were wise in troubling a Christian bishop with any thoughts or questions which relate merely to poor human beings like myself, who marry and are given in marriage.[36]

The antagonism between the two authors appears in minor ways as well as in these major emphases. Newman sees the Goths not as stout, admirable fellows, but as barbarian menaces who, in the words of a character, 'will give us trouble'. The Britons are even worse, lacking any conception of civilization; far from anticipating the glories of the British Empire, the typical Briton was 'painting himself with woad' or 'hiding himself to the chin in the fens'.[37] The Egyptian monks of the desert are not the scared, life-denying creatures of Kingsley's imagination but saints 'living in the practice of mortification and prayer so singular, and had combats with the powers of darkness and visitations from above so special, as to open quite a new era in the spiritual history of the Church'.[38] An even more direct hit at *Hypatia* comes in the satirical attack on Greek philosophy made by Arnobius, which is thrust in gratuitously and rather awkwardly in the story.

Callista is a better novel than *Loss and Gain*; although it does not suggest that Newman's priesthood was a great loss to Victorian fiction, it does show that he gained in skill whenever he developed a new line of activity. The characters come to warmer reality, despite the more distant and exotic setting. As in the earlier novel we have little visual description, but the speech idiom is more confident and less artificial. The opponents of Christianity are more now than simply morality types: Jucundus the uncle of Agellius is a convincing figure, almost Dickensian in his prejudices, his bursts of temper and generosity. Juba, the evil brother, manages to hold conviction even in his spectacular madness and his equally spectacular final conversion. If direct description of people is thin, Newman's power of observation and verbal depiction comes out triumphantly in the long account of the locust swarm which precedes and occasions the persecution of the Christians.

Newman as a novelist lacks the warm ebullience which sustains interest in both Kingsley and Wiseman, different though those two are in other respects. *Callista* is a novel in a minor key, exploring a more tentative situation. Frederick Rogers noted how Wiseman described the metropolitan scene, with families already established in the Christian tradition, while Newman went to the outskirts of the Empire and to Christians either recently converted like Cyprian or imperfectly instructed like Agellius.[39] Where he gains in interest today is in the obvious personalism of his story.

A little of Newman appears in Agellius, whose Christianity has to be made perfect through learning and sorrow. A great deal appears in Callista herself; she passes through the struggle which Newman had experienced between 1841 and 1845. Her friends and family try to dissuade her, as contemporaries had wrestled with Newman himself. 'After all, what did she know of Christianity? – at best she was leaving the known for the unknown: she was sure to be embracing certain evil for contingent good.' Again, for 'Christianity' read 'Roman Catholicism'. 'She is neither one thing nor the other. She won't say she's a Christian, and she won't sacrifice!' So Newman had been charged with crypto-Papism. And the account of Callista's inner struggle reveals Newman living again the years of questioning at Littlemore:

> She was neither a Christian, nor was she not. She was in the midway region of inquiry, which as surely takes time to pass over, except there be some almost miraculous interference, as it takes time to walk from place to place. You see a person coming towards you, and you say, impatiently, 'Why don't you come faster? Why are you not here already?' why? – because it takes time. To see that heathenism is false – to see that Christianity is true – are two acts, and involve two processes.[40]

For here, as in *Loss and Gain*, Newman was bent on showing how a person can pursue and find truth despite the barriers set up by family, training, social climate and personal inclination.

The differences shown by these three novels are interesting, though not more significant than might be deduced from our objective knowledge of their authors. More interesting is the common ground, the debate within which three well-known clergymen could set out to prove contentions about the nature and authority of their Churches. Does it matter whether or not any branch of the Church can prove continuity with the Church of the early centuries? Some today would say that it does matter: many more would have said it a hundred years ago. If the preoccupations of the Victorians were often different from our own, that does not make them contemptible; we too have our anxieties and desires, which can often be made more comprehensible by consideration of those which our precursors revealed in different guises.

Each of the books has an eponymous heroine. The female image expresses the Victorian cult of idealized but suppressed womanhood. The heroine in each case is proud, aloof, clever and sophisticated; but in the end the power of conversion breaks down all the things in which she had trusted and shows her utter dependence. So did Victorian Christianity often provide a taming influence, an outlet in devotions and limited charity, for those who might be cherishing ideas of emancipation. It is not surprising to find an Olive Schreiner or an Annie Besant repudiating orthodox Christianity in the struggle for greater recognition of true female power.

Another Victorian fear that all the authors introduce is the dread of a mob out of control, a mob burning, looting and destroying. Writing as they did only a few years after Chartism had channelled the smouldering violence of a large section of the population, they put in a past setting the present fear which Dickens had similarly distanced in *Barnaby Rudge* and *A Tale of Two Cities*. Behind them lay the tradition of the French Revolution which continued to haunt Victorian dreams and to detect in social reformers 'the violence of a French Jacobin'.[41] The fear was real enough then and later; but it should also be remembered that it made good material for an episode when the novelist felt inclined to show off his descriptive skill.

The literary influence of the early Church novel continued throughout the century. The idea of authority was overshadowed by interest in the quest itself and the possibility of change in personality through increased knowledge. When Walter Pater wrote *Marius the Epicurean* (1885) he used the antique setting for the progress of a postulant who is male,

eclectic and less surely directed towards the Christian conclusion. Into Marius he put something of himself, as Newman
had in Callista, and something of his friend the Anglo-Catholic
clergyman Richard Jackson. Pater's course was steered far
away from Newman's, but he too had been for a time drawn
into the wake of the Oxford Movement and he took his own
lesson from the 'lovely, pure and noble' Callista.[42] The
influence on J.H.Shorthouse has still to be considered.

The appeal to antiquity did not confine itself to the con-
firming or refuting of Roman claims directly. Ever since the
late sixteenth century, Anglican theologians had been interested in the Orthodox Church with its longer schism from
Rome and its undoubted continuity of episcopal government.
Contacts had mostly been occasional and brief until the Tractarians revived the question of whence true catholicity was
derived and where it was to be found. The first serious move
towards a better understanding that might lead to reunion was
made by William Palmer of Magdalen College[43] who visited
Russia in 1840 to discuss the position of the Anglican Church
with the Orthodox bishops. In 1846 he published his *Harmony
of Anglican Doctrine with the Doctrine of the Eastern Church*,
but the effect of his labours was tarnished by his conversion to
Roman Catholicism nine years later. The work was carried on
by George Williams, a Cambridge man who had been chaplain to the first Bishop of Jerusalem and who founded the
Eastern Church Association in 1864 to foster better understanding between the churches.

The most interesting of those who concerned themselves
with the Eastern Church, and one of the most attractive followers of the Tractarians, was John Mason Neale. He too was
a Cambridge man and had been prominent in founding the
Camden Society there. Much of his ministry was spent at East
Grinstead in Sussex where he suffered episcopal censure and
popular obloquy for his attempts to restore the conventual life.
His story has yet to be written in detail, but his work for reunion with the Orthodox has come to be admired by many
who would not follow him in other ways. He wrote a long
history of the Eastern Church, which was completed by
George Williams after his death, and translated Greek hymns
which have passed into the regular use of the Church of

England.[44] He found time too for stories and novels of which *Ayton Priory* (1843) is of some interest in dealing with the problems of conscience of those whose wealth was derived from sequestered monastic lands. We have seen how Charlotte Yonge looked at the question in *Heartsease*; Neale's hero hands his estate to the foundation of an Anglo-Catholic monastery – a solution which is in good Tractarian orthodoxy but begs a number of questions.

One at least of Neale's novels, formerly admired but now almost forgotten, should not be allowed to fade entirely. *Theodora Phranza* came out in serial form in 1848 and as a novel in 1857. It tells the story of the siege and fall of Constantinople in 1453, with the intention of promoting English interest in the Greek Church and in the possibility of reunion. Neale's symbolism is lively but not subtle. Richard Burstow, the son of an English father and a Smyrniot mother, leads his men on a series of daring adventures against the Turks; his exhortations and their responses owe more to the early-Victorian view of military glory than anything that came out of the Byzantine Empire. Burstow is under the command of Sir Edward de Rushton, the English head of the Imperial bodyguard, who woos Theodora Phranza, the daughter of a court official and finally escapes with her from the sack of the city.

The book is an exciting piece of work for those who can read it with the right suspension of disbelief. Neale combined a scholar's knowledge with the ability to tell an eventful and fast-moving story. His archaeological details are incorporated into the narrative without any need for the footnotes to which Wiseman had resorted. His dialogue is less convincing. 'Nay, then, if you will cross my way, have at you in St George's name!' shouts Sir Edward as he charges into battle.[45]

Although the background is medieval, the relation of *Theodora Phranza* to the novels of antiquity and the quest for authority is clear. The possibility of uniting the Western and Eastern Churches – towards which an attempt was made at the time of the historical siege – runs along with the story. Fanatics like the monk Cennadius work up popular feeling against reunion by exaggerating the differences between the Churches. Some traitors will even collaborate with the infidels in order to avoid contact with Rome – a situation which had its own parallel in Neale's time. On the other hand, Latins and Greeks find common faith in adversity and learn to pray together: the Cardinal and the Patriarch together absolve the hostages before execution. Every attempt is made to show the 'Catholic' practices of the Greeks, although Neale's learning and honesty make him show the differences too. There is once again the eponymous heroine who, though she does not find faith out of paganism, provides the unifying link and symbolizes the author's desire when she escapes to England and a son is born to her and Sir Edward. The latter has already vowed to give:

... a chantry to the church at Rushton, with two acres of pasture land, and bread, wine, and lights, if I ever bring Theodora Phranza to my own country as my own bride.[46]

The publication of the total work soon after the end of the Crimean War raised some questions about alliance with Turkey against Russia. Neale boldly grasped the issue; referring to a prophecy that Turkish rule over the Byzantine Empire would last for four hundred years, he continues:

That the late war has to a certain extent fulfilled it, no one can doubt who, like myself, is convinced that, let whatever dynasty succeed to the possession of the Byzantine Empire, the sands of the Turkish domination are now very fast running out.[47]

(Preface to first edn).

The interest in the Orthodox Church was not confined to Puseyites. A.P.Stanley, a Broad Church disciple of Thomas Arnold and a strong opponent of Anglo-Catholicism, also wrote a history of the Eastern Christians in which he declared: 'If there is any Church which may be expected to learn congenial and useful lessons from the study of Eastern Christendom, it is our own.'[48] He went on to warn against making too much of 'the possible connection of the ancient British Church with Eastern missionaries before the arrival of Augustine'. There were some, however, to whom the connection was a real answer to Roman claims. 'What's Rome to us? We come from the old British Church; we don't meddle with Rome, and we wish Rome not to meddle with us, but she will.'[49] Not all went so far as the eccentric Cornish priest who wore 'a pink brimless hat, after the Eastern type'.[50] Isaac Williams urged the claims of the old British Church in his poems published as *The Cathedral* (1838). Noble and loving priest though he was, it cannot really be claimed that his efforts in this direction added much either to theology or to poetry.

From the moment when the Tractarians came to realize that the Roman Church was not Anti Christ but a serious challenge to Anglican claims to catholicity, the attempt to establish authority through the appeal to history had to be made. The attempt embodied wider contemporary aspirations towards certainty and security. Roman and Anglo-Catholic apologists were often derided, but they were envied too because, whether or not they found the answers, they knew where they were looking.

7
Uphill all the Way

For human reasons, which she herself would have thought in-adequate as explanations of spiritual progress, Christina Rossetti was a natural recruit to Anglo-Catholicism. 'Her poetry is full of tensions,' concludes one of her most sympathetic critics;[1] so it is, and so was the Oxford Movement. The men of that movement were trying to restore Catholic doctrine and practice to a society which was aggressively opposed to any savour of Popery. The alienation which they felt within their own age was the experience also of the best poet whom they directly inspired.

Christina Rossetti was the product of a mixed family, more Italian than English in descent but of the Victorian middle class by environment. Her maternal grandmother had dealt with the religious division by having her sons brought up as Roman Catholics and her daughters as Anglicans. Her early childhood had passed, like that of many of her contemporaries, under Evangelical influence. As she was entering on the impressionable years of puberty her mother and aunts were caught up in the new ideas which were reaching London from Oxford. Ideas previously excluded as Romanist were now heard freely in pulpit teaching and home discussion. Theology joined politics in the house where her father's visitors discussed in Italian the latest events in that land from which he was exiled by political beliefs.

Add to all this the anxieties of an intelligent woman in an

170

age that offered little fulfilment for women whose sense of duty held them to the socially acceptable paths of marriage or domestic spinsterhood. The sensuous hunger of her southern temperament warred with a growing sense that her lot was to be renunciation. If her religion was a release of tensions which it partly created, there is no derogation of that faith or of the writing which it influenced. Her sister Maria made the total renunciation and entered conventual life, an act which itself was sometimes a declaration of independence for Victorian women.[2] The wrath aroused by the spread of both Roman and Anglican convents had more behind it than was overtly stated. For Christina, renunciation kept her in the world and was no easier.

There was personal suffering too: her own ill-health which was probably connected with emotional strain; the death of the beloved and dedicated sister; the slow disintegration of the brilliant brother Dante Gabriel. There was unhappy love, with two engagements broken off by her on the grounds of religious difference. There is the strong possibility of a long and hopeless love for a married man.[3] It is enough, one might say, to give a convincing table of occasions and explanations for her poems.

Yet the solution is not so simple and the association of her work with biographical events is difficult. Down to the age of thirty-six the dating is possible because dated manuscripts have survived. Beyond that, and including the greater part of her devotional poetry, the chronology is uncertain. The editorial work of her brother William did little to elucidate the problem; he was often uncertain, or perhaps deliberately vague for reasons of family piety. When she wrote a particular piece, why, and to whom it was addressed – or indeed whether it was addressed to anyone – must often remain undetermined. The certainties, however, do not depend on particularity. There was strong passion, consciously suppressed and offered in the course of faith. There was a dedication of the self which was verbalized in terms of personal attachment to the Saviour, within the disciplines of contemporary Anglo-Catholicism. The Oxford Movement captured the scholars, the antiquarians, the discontented, the seekers after sensation. It spoke also to the lonely, the dissociated, the sincerely questioning, and therein lay much of its strength and the proof of its goodness.

The Church gave to Christina Rossetti what it gave to many, but she made the gift particularly her own. She was never, for all her orthodoxy, a mouthpiece for Anglican teaching as such. Ideas which others could formulate in more precise theological terms passed through an acute and creative mind. What Charlotte Yonge heard from Keble appeared in her novels, made dynamic by imaginative creation but not transformed in scope or application. What Christina Rossetti learned was felt deeply and then verbalized in terms less limited by particularities of situation. The submission of both women to circumstances was outwardly complete but Charlotte did not find in herself or her situation anything warranting a lot of fuss. Christina had to achieve by hard discipline the dedication of her discontent.

The involvement too was different, in a physical environment far from the rural peace of Hursley. Her mother and her aunts were drawn to the new type of worship, perhaps at first by the aesthetic appeal of ceremonial which conformist Anglicanism had sternly refused. The dedication soon became deeper and by 1843 they were attending Christ Church in Albany Street. Less notorious in record than the scenes of riots like St Barnabas, Pimlico and St George in the East, Christ Church had considerable importance in the development of fashionable Tractarian ideas in London. Pusey had been closely associated with its dedication in 1837 and with the appointment of William Dodsworth as incumbent. The preaching there was soon famous. Dodsworth himself was eloquent and prophetic;[4] Manning and Hook were among the visiting preachers. It must be remembered that one of the gifts of the Tractarians to the Church was their preaching; although they emphasized the sacramental and sacerdotal aspect of religion they also attached great importance to the sermon as a mode of teaching. Newman's sermons at St Mary's were recalled in detail years later by his critics as well as by his abiding admirers. Christina Rossetti received the impact of this kind of preaching at an early age. She was introduced to Tractarian ideas by men who were themselves close to the authors of the Tracts.

She entered into the new atmosphere with enthusiasm. At the age of twenty she wrote a story in which the heroine reproduces her own situation of poor health and Anglican piety.[5] This young woman is oppressed by guilt and feels herself unworthy to receive Communion. Critics have sought for some hidden secret of Christina's life or dismissed the narrative as immaturely lacking in motivation. As we shall see, neither answer need be the true one. Certainly Christina had a great deal of spare affection and admiration to lavish on the clergy, and it must be said that she was discriminating in her regard. There was W.J.E.Bennett, driven out of London by opposition to his advanced Puseyism, who was at Frome when Christina and her mother set up a school there for a time in 1853. He was a signatory of a protest against the Bath Judgement, with Keble, Pusey, Neale and Williams.[6]

Then there was Burrows, who succeeded Dodsworth at Christ Church in 1850 and taught Christina the practice of auricular confession. This office, which the early Tractarians had used sparingly if at all, was becoming one of the distinctive features of advanced Puseyism – zealously advocated and bitterly opposed. Novelists and pamphleteers told horrific stories of how unscrupulous priests abused the confessional to gain power over their penitents, even to win the allegiance of women away from their husbands. In her quiet, unspectacular way. Christina became a regular user of the confessional. When Dante Gabriel was suffering from deep depression and distress she wrote to him:

I want to assure you that, however harassed by memory or by anxiety you may be, I have (more or less) heretofore gone through the same ordeal. I have borne myself till I became unbearable by myself, and then I have found help in confession and absolution and spiritual counsel, and relief inexpressible. Twice in my life I tried to suffice myself with measures short of this, but nothing would do; the first time was of course in my youth before my general confession, the second time was when circumstances had led me (rightly or wrongly) to break off the practice. But now for years past I have resumed the habit, and I hope not to continue it profitlessly.

      'Tis like frail man to love to walk on high
        But to be lowly is to be like God'
is a couplet (Isaac Williams) I thoroughly assent to.[7]

She came to ask Burrows for approval of what she wrote, as Charlotte Yonge did with Keble, and at the age of thirty-six was hoping for 'the revision and sanction' which he might give to her devotional work *Called to be Saints*.[8] There was the influence also of R.F.Littledale,[9] who played a part in helping her through some of the hardest years:

> And when he marked me downcast utterly
> Where foul I saw and faint,
> Then more than ever Christ-like kindled he,
> And welcomed me as I had been a saint,
> Tenderly stooping low to comfort me.
>
> 'Embertide'

Littledale, whose Irish sense of humour endured through the trials of his vocation and his own struggle with bad health, was able to give her something that other priests often lacked. He could foster her own ability to laugh at herself and her situation:

> 'Tis but too true, dear Miss Christina,
> What publishers to you reply,
> A time like this has always been a
> Time when the frighted Muses fly;
> *Inter arma silent leges*
> ('Twas Marcus Cicero who said it),
> And all but newspapers are tedious
> When Dizzy wants his vote of credit.
> The public likes a *Prince's Progress*,
> But only in the *Morning Post*,
> And makes a *Goblin Market* ogress
> Of Russia's or of Turkey's host.[10]

Christina was close to men who were themselves associated with the early heroes of the Oxford Movement, but who were also engaged in the struggle for wider acceptance which followed the ending of the Tracts and the secession of Newman. She found release, and something much more positive, not only in the directly devotional side of Puseyism but also in the conflicts over particularities. Burrows, like most Puseyite clergymen, wanted to abolish pew-rents in his church. Christina described, with delighted satire, the outrage of the leading parishioners:

We have borne with chants, with a surpliced choir, with daily services, but we will not bear to see all our rights trampled under foot, and all our time-hallowed usages set at nought. The tendency of the day is to level social distinctions and to elevate unduly the lower orders. In this parish at least let us combine to keep up wise barriers between class and class, and to maintain that fundamental principle practically bowed to all over our happy England, that what you can pay for you can purchase.[11]

One of the gifts of the Oxford Movement to women was the opportunity for social protest without the taint of being socialistic or unladylike.

The movement itself was becoming more assertive, more inclined to innovate than to correct imbalance. In matters of ritual, as over the question of confession, the Tractarians themselves had been cautious and had regarded underlying principles as more important than outward signs. 'We had a further distinct fear with regard to ritual,' Pusey recollected, 'and we privately discouraged it, lest the whole movement should become superficial.'[12] Soon, however, ritual became a more positive feature and the lack of it could be stigmatized as a lack of due reverence for the sacraments. Particularly in urban surroundings, the aesthetic appeal to the senses could be a release from the squalor of the slums or the oppressive drabness of middle-class streets. In this respect too the worship at Hursley was very different from the worship at Christ Church, or at All Saints in Margaret Street to whose associated sisterhood Maria Rossetti was admitted.

Yet for all her love of sensuous beauty – or perhaps because she thought that this too must be disciplined and restrained in the name of religion – Christina gives little place in her poetry to the outward appeal of Catholic worship. She would have been happier perhaps in the comparatively austere practice at Littlemore. She was absorbed by the personal sense of devotion engendered by the sacramental emphasis. The sonnet 'After Communion' does not dwell on colour or music or architecture; its symbols are plain, unelaborated, and they serve not to distance but to intensify the immediate access to divinity:

> Why should I call Thee Lord, Who art my God?
> Why should I call Thee Friend, Who art my Love?
> Or King, Who art my very Spouse above?
> Or call Thy sceptre on my heart Thy rod?
> Lo now Thy banner over me is love,
> All heaven flies open to me at Thy nod:
> For Thou hast lit Thy flame in me a clod,
> Made me a nest for dwelling of Thy Dove.
> What wilt Thou call me in our home above,
>   Who now hast called me friend? how will it be
> When Thou for good wine settest forth the best?
> Now Thou dost bid me come and sup with Thee,
>   Now Thou dost make me lean upon Thy breast:
>   How will it be with me in time of love?

The sense of close personal encounter with God, which can appear to be a distinctively Evangelical emphasis, was an abiding element in her faith and in that of the Oxford Movement. She and several of the Tractarians shared that Evangelical upbringing which was not easily thrown off. Nor was there any reason to eschew it, since immediacy could be found equally in a Catholic view of the Church and her offices. William Rossetti, not sharing her faith, had enough brotherly love and understanding to see how basically simple that faith remained. Her poems, he explained, were 'passionate communings of the believing and loving soul, with the God believed in and loved, and also feared'.[13] For Christina, like George Herbert, knew the God who demands not less than all:

> 'Give Me thy youth.' – ' I yield it to Thy rod,
> As Thou didst yield Thy prime of youth for me.' –
> 'Give me thy life.' – 'I give it breath by breath;
> As Thou didst give Thy life so give I Thee.' –
> 'Give me thy love.' – 'So be it, my God, my God,
> As Thou hast loved me even to bitter death.'
>
>   ('Not Yours But You')

'God beholds thee individually, whoever thou art,' Newman had declared in a sermon of his Anglican days.[14] The idea of conversion and personal commitment remained strong in Tractarian and Puseyite teaching. The Anglo-Catholic iconography of Holman Hunt's painting 'The Light of the World' had its exegesis in the search of Christ for the individual soul buried in sin, and was consequently acceptable to those non-conformist households which generally abhorred the notion of religious pictures.

What personal choice might involve for the Puseyite, however, was greatly different from Evangelical ideas. The revival of religious communities, first for women and later for men, brought a new possibility of the ultimate in commitment. Public hostility was strong, based partly on the dislike of declared celibacy which so upset Kingsley, and aggravated by the fact that the rules and devotions of the new communities were inevitably taken from Roman Catholicism. Maria Rossetti translated the Breviary for use in the community to which she was professed in 1873.

The existence of Anglican religious houses, and the decision that Maria made in entering the All Saints sisterhood, were important influences on Christina. Her affection for Maria was very great, from those childhood days when the elder sister could gently soothe the younger's passionate tempers. Maria was a source of strength in Christina's spiritual development and perhaps regarded as something of a protector. Her identification with the Lizzie of 'Goblin Market' who redresses the trouble which Laura brings by her folly is less popular than it once was. However, William Rossetti stated that the poem was closely connected with Maria and even drew attention to 'a more than normal amount of melancholy and self-reproach' in the poems which immediately preceded it in date.[15] Was Christina in fact saved by Maria's wisdom from some folly like elopement? The legend that Maria slept on the doormat to prevent it is unconvincing, to put it mildly.[16] Yet there is the interesting ambivalence of the self-sacrificing Lizzie and the maliciously interfering sister of the poems written soon afterwards – of 'Noble Sisters' and 'Sister Maude', 'who lurked to spy and peer'.

Whatever happened in those early years, Christina was personally grieved and also spiritually moved by Maria's death in 1876. She wrote to Dante Gabriel of how the Mother Superior of the order described Maria's readiness for death 'as such that it would need an act of resignation on her part to resign herself to life. . . . Surely through the darkness God compasses her around.'[17] She felt more perhaps even than sisterly love – a sense of identification with the dying nun. The attraction of the conventual life as a solution to some at least of her problems had been with her for many years. The first Anglican sisterhood to grow out of the Oxford Movement had started under Pusey's direction at Park Village, in close proximity to Christ Church.

This event caused stir and opposition even in that Tractarian parish. It seized Christina's imagination and brought the figure of the nun out of the realm of sensational historical fiction and into reality. The theme of religious vows, usually taken in deliberate and penitent renunciation of earthly love, became a feature of her poetry. 'The Convent Threshold' written in 1858 is a striking example; its opening stanza is a passionate statement of the two loves:

> There's blood between us, love, my love,
> There's father's blood, there's brother's blood;
> And blood's a bar I cannot pass.
> I choose the stairs that mount above,
> Stair after golden sky-ward stair,
> To city and to sea of glass.
> My lily feet are soiled with mud,
> With scarlet mud which tells a tale
> Of hope that was, of guilt that was,
> Of love that shall not yet avail;
> Alas, my heart, if I could bare
> My heart, this selfsame stain is there:
> I seek the sea of glass and fire
> To wash the spot, to burn the snare;
> Lo, stairs are meant to lift us higher:
> Mount with me, mount the kindled stair.

The theme is heard again in 'Soeur Louise de la Miséricorde':

> I have desired, and I have been desired:
> But now the days are over of desire,
> Now dust and dying embers mock my fire:
> Where is the hire for which my life was hired?
> Oh vanity of vanities, desire!

In herself, Christina felt the contrast between the nun and the fallen woman. Her association with the St Mary Magdalene Home in Highgate for the reclamation of prostitutes was the practical manifestation of a deep sense of the sorrows of illicit love and illegitimacy. The treatment of the subject in the narrative poem 'The Iniquity of the Fathers upon the Children', written in 1865, has truly been described as 'decades ahead of the mid-century Victorian novelists on the same subject'.[18] Compassion for the unmarried mother was rare but growing: compassion and understanding for the child was unhappily even rarer. In 'Cousin Kate', Christina even allows the mother to feel joy in 'My fair-haired son, my shame, my pride' and to boast of him against her married but childless cousin. The more desolate lot of the outcast woman is movingly told in the sonnet 'From Sunset to Star Rise'.

These tensions, deeply felt and expressed more frankly than was usual at the time, were for a long time associated by her critics with the broken engagements to Collinson and Cayley: the former was rejected for veering between the Anglican and Roman communions, the latter for being of questionable orthodoxy. More recently, the supposed affair with Scott has been called in as explanation. William Rossetti acknowledged in her poetry 'a noticeable combination of the outspoken and the self-repressing', and continued: 'She had nothing to hide away, but much to keep down under the control of a strong and resolute will.'[19]

There could be unsolved mysteries here or perhaps the mystery is within her. Certainly she made an early acceptance of the belief that normal fulfilment in love was not for her: it appears in such poems of her adolescence as 'The Novice', 'The Dream' and 'Love Attacked'. The idea persists, and at the time of her engagement to Collinson she was writing premature dirges for herself in 'When I am Dead' and 'Remember Me'. This period was seemingly her time of conversion; she did not remain in mere acquiescence in the probability of spinsterhood but made a more conscious dedication of herself to God. Poor Collinson did not have much chance with the girl who was writing 'A Testimony', 'One Certainty' and 'Three Stages', with its tale of movement from hope to the wakening of despair:

> I must pull down my palace that I built,
> Dig up the pleasure-gardens of my soul,
> Must change my laughter to sad tears for guilt,
> My freedom to control.

It is impossible to say how much the conflict of personality and religious allegiance entered into the renunciation. It may be that another man could have won her from dedication to wifehood. Or it may be that any lover would have had the experience of the narrator in Graham Greene's novel *The End of the Affair*, who believes that his mistress is in love with another man, only to discover that her outpouring of passion in writing was addressed to God. With Christina, it is certain that the possibility of human love faded away more and more into the desire for divine love. That there was protest and rebellion is clear from 'An Apple Gathering' and the playful but intense 'Winter: my Secret'. Yet by 1857 she was offering the pain of renunciation as totally as a solemn vow of religion could have made it:

> My life is like a broken bowl,
> A broken bowl that cannot hold
> One drop of water for my soul
> Or cordial in the searching cold.
> Cast in the fire the perished thing;
> Melt and remould it, till it be
> A royal cup for Him, my King:
> O Jesus, drink of me.
>
> ('A Better Resurrection')

She found her vocation in the world, but the desire to give all to the all-demanding God was there. From the time when Hurrell Froude had taught Newman to make a conscious discipline from his personal feeling for celibacy, the Tractarian teaching had been giving a high place to dedicated virginity. Pusey had made use of his great scholarship in encouraging the growth of religious communities: he had the authority of the Fathers and the approval of Anglican divines like Andrewes and Taylor.

That Christina felt the call to dedicated chastity and regarded her engagements as lapses into worldly temptation is more likely than the idea that disappointment in love turned her more and more towards God. If Collinson had little chance, Cayley had less. She felt a quiet, sisterly affection for him, a regard which outlasted their period of engagement and recognized that his feeling had been stronger than hers:

I am at least unselfish enough altogether to deprecate seeing C.B.C. [Cayley] continually (with nothing but mere feeling to offer) to his hamper and discomfort: but, if he likes to see me, God knows I like to see him, and any kindness you will show him will only be additional kindness loaded on me.[20]

These are not the sentiments of a woman who has been in love. The Cayley episode was not a decider but rather a catalyst in her sense of vocation. After 1866 she wrote the greater part of her devotional poetry and seldom referred again to the possibility of marriage for herself.

Like all vocations, it was not achieved without cost. Her ill health may have been largely the result of emotional tensions. We still know too little of the relations between mind and body; one day the phrase 'psychosomatic illness' may become a tautology. For her the suffering was real enough, whether it came from repressed desire, from some unknown guilt – or from purely physical causes. The tension certainly showed itself in fairly conventional ways, such as her hostility towards her brothers' wives. When she moved herself and her mother away from William's household, all was done smoothly enough. But she made it clear that it was her deliberate choice and was able to express her disapproval of the disputes which had made it necessary. Even here, the trouble did not lie entirely in that jealousy of a spinster towards a fertile sister-in-law which might give an easy explanation. William and Lucy were agnostics and did not have their children baptized. Christina herself performed the office for one of them who was dying. The lack continued to worry her, and she wrote to Lucy about it in terms which reveal not only her criticism but also her own deeply-felt and other-worldly religious position:

We were talking about your 'happy' children. And so I think them in the daily home-matters. But I cannot pointedly use that word *happy* without meaning something beyond the present life. And baptism (where attainable) is the sole door I know of whereby entrance is promised into the happiness which eye hath not seen nor ear heard neither hath heart of man conceived. I now live so much in the other world – or at least I ought to do so, having my chief Treasure there – that please do not take offence at what I say.[21]

The tension between human and divine love was not fully solved – few can ever solve it – and the effect on her poetry was not always good. There is a certain ambivalence from time to time, a leap from the passionate to the ascetic which can seem in reading like an anticlimax or a failure of nerve. She did not always handle it so well as in the 'Monna Innominata' sonnets, which are some of her highest poetic achievements. Here she recognizes and admits the problem; the ninth sonnet tells that she can still stumble on the path which she believes to be her way to heaven:

> For woe is me who walk so apt to fall,
> So apt to shrink afraid, so apt to flee,
> Apt to lie down and die (ah woe is me!)
> Faithless and hopeless turning to the wall.
> But yet not hopeless quite nor faithless quite,
> Because not loveless; love may toil all night,
> But take at morning; wrestle till the break
> Of day, but then wield power with God and man.

In growing certainty of divine love, she grew in command of herself. Faith becomes deeper and also more personalized as her life and work ran on. She eschewed the grand manner and the prophetic tone of more conventional Victorian poetry, as surely as did Clough for his own very different reasons. The challenges which the Oxford Movement threw down could bring the desire for self-revelation in which both the confessional motive and the desire to enlighten others played their part. So it was with Newman when he wrote the *Apologia* and with J.A.Froude when he wrote *The Nemesis of Faith*. Such was the ground of Pusey's veneration for St Augustine.

The desire for self-fulfilment through self-revelation was not, of course, confined to literary Puseyites but was common to many of the generation which had imbibed Romantic ideas. The Brontës had it, linked to more awareness of contemporary society than their critics once supposed. Christina Rossetti too did not live out of this world in living beyond it. She could be alert over questions of copyright and royalties. Her personal charities were many but clear-sighted and she learned to recognize a rogue. She read Layard's archaeological account of Nineveh at an early age, and she could make intelligent suggestions about where to buy a glass case for mummified specimens.[22] At the time of the Franco-Prussian war she wrote two poems in support of France.

Yet all these signs of her ability to live efficiently in reality serve only to emphasize the nature of her true commitment. She turned inwards more and more, writing about the things of faith after they had been absorbed fully into her own experience. She had known what conversion meant; and now came the long years in which she must persevere and win through to salvation, for those taught the principles of the Oxford Movement could not rest on assurance of salvation. Personal experience and the individual encounter were no less important, but thereafter came the daily living in hope, with the strength of the Church to supply what the individual could not. She had been taught in the way that Charlotte Yonge was taught by Keble. Charlotte too sought for certainty and peace; and she makes one of her clerical characters warn the girls whom he prepares for confirmation against the dangers of emotional conversion that does not last:

We must try to have root in ourselves, stability of character, and that was one great help in the Church rites. Besides the grace, which is the great thing, the associations will always be revived.[23]

For Christina Rossetti the struggle was in some ways grimmer, against bad health, family troubles and a more passionate nature. Anglo-Catholic discipline made her outstandingly the poet of sacrifice and abnegation. The struggle was not only against temptations which a less dedicated mind would consider permissible pleasures. It contained also the desire for submergence, almost for annihilation save that the Christian conception of human and divine personality gives no possibility of Nirvana. Call it blessed humility or call it psychic maladjustment, the desire remains:

> Give me the lowest place; not that I dare
>   Ask for that lowest place, but Thou hast died
> That I might live and share
>   Thy glory by Thy side.
> Give me the lowest place: or if for me
>   That lowest place too high, make one more low
> Where I may sit and see
>   My God and love Thee so.

('The Lowest Place')

183

It can be verbalized in the extreme of pietistic imagery:

> I am sick for home, the home of love indeed –
> I am sick for Love, that dearest name for Thee:
> Thou who hast bled, see how my heart doth bleed:
> Open Thy bleeding Side and let me in:
> Oh hide me in Thy Heart from doubt and sin,
> Oh take me to Thyself and comfort me.

('Zion Said')

In her last illness she could rejoice in the sense of Christian unanimism and the anonymity of intercession. She wrote to her sister-in-law:

> Various kind souls will remember me in prayer, and each one who joins the praying band confers on me a favour beyond money and beyond price. I have asked the prayers of the congregation at my Church, but without my name being given out, as I deprecate getting into 'paragraphs' and these are so in vogue nowadays.[24]

The sense of numinous awe which the Oxford Movement had restored to matter-of-fact Christianity was bound to result in a strong feeling of unworthiness and a striving for self-effacement. It was particularly developed in the devotions of religious communities such as the one which Maria joined and with which Christina felt affinity. Christina's abnegation of worldly things springs from this other-worldly awe rather than a Puritan retreat with refusal to see good in anything material. It was not easy for her to accept the lowest place; she knew her quality even as she strove to conceal it. In 1856, the year of 'The Lowest Place', she dealt with the problem in a prose story 'The Lost Titian' which was later included in *Commonplace*. Her renunciation was of the only kind that is valuable – of things good in themselves and felt to be so. It was the Lenten sacrifice that goes beyond the daily battle against sin.[25]

The minor sacrifices and mortifications can become trivial and productive of their own kind of pride. This happened too often in an imperfect acceptance of Anglo-Catholic discipline as the novels of Charlotte Yonge occasionally show. Christina Rossetti took the path which leads from particular acts of will to the total obedience. The ideal of obedience to God in all things, not as a counsel of perfection but as an essential of salvation, was preached by the Tractarian leaders with all the urgency which they believed the national situation to demand. At the time of Christina's first serious theological thinking, Pusey was exhorting from the pulpit:

Obey *now* His voice or ask *now* for grace to obey it; purpose *now* in utter mistrust of self, yet trembling trust in Him, to break off some besetting sin, to cherish some neglected grace.[26]

It was little wonder that those who came under Tractarian influence were so often driven to total acceptance or total rejection. For Christina, the tremendous sense of awe as a creature of a commanding God who offered eternal communion as the reward of obedience inevitably led to a rejection of worldly values. 'Vanity of vanities' became a favourite text and a recurring poetic theme. The strain of melancholy in the Rossetti family was given purpose. But sometimes purpose was not so clear; the often anthologized 'One Certainty' has no note of Christian hope to relieve an almost Hardyesque pessimism that was always near the surface. Housman might have written the last stanza of 'A Testimony':

> A King dwelt in Jerusalem;
> He was the wisest man on earth;
> He had all riches from his birth,
> And pleasures till he tired of them;
> Then, having tested all things, he
> Witnessed that all are vanity.

More often, however, and increasingly as the years passed, the feeling of the world's vanity brought aspirations to heaven. At a time when the opponents of Christianity were more and more accusing religious people of neglecting this world for the sake of future salvation, the Tractarian theology was bringing a sense of heavenly reality closer to daily living. The notion of the Church Triumphant was out of fashion among Anglicans until they were forcefully reminded that they were part of a great communion, seen and unseen, living and departed. The neglect meant that imagery and language had not developed; much of what was said and written came in terms that seem distasteful to the modern sense, though we have not competently solved the problem of how to improve on it. Pusey

G

could preach on the idea of total union with Christ, so that the believer might join,

The white-robed army of the redeemed, which ever followeth Him, drawn up by the Sun of Righteousness, away from the damp of this earth, gathering around Him, and glorified by his light, and reflecting it.[27]

Such visions could lead Christina to her less happy poetical moments:

I think of the saints I have known, and lift up mine eyes
To the far-off home of beautiful Paradise,
Where the song of saints gives voice to an undividing sea
On whose plain their feet stand firm while they keep their jubilee.
As the sound of waters their voice, as the sound of thunderings,
While they all at once rejoice, while all sing and while each one sings.

('So Great a Cloud of Witnesses')

For all the sincerity of her feeling, she was least herself as a poet in her attempts to depict the joys of heaven where Biblical apocalyptic imagery was too much in control. She did better in the plain desire for peace and assurance, without attempting to give a visual picture, as in the pair of sonnets 'There Remaineth Therefore a Rest for the People of God'.

The tension between this world and the next was one of the prevailing difficulties of the age, and it did not resolve itself so neatly as the opponents of Christianity liked to claim. It is true that social reform was not a lively concern of the early Tractarians, though Hurrell Froude could number it among his preoccupations. It was strong with W. G. Ward and became a feature of later Puseyism with men like Gore, Stanton and Headlam. The kind of work which Christina Rossetti did at the St Mary Magdalen Home may have left much to be desired in terms of modern social casework, but it shows that the heavenward raising of her sight was not that of the Pharisee. She had hopes of joining Florence Nightingale in the Crimea but was not accepted; once again it is too easy to argue about the mixed motives of service and escapism – Kingsley cleverly fictionalized them with the Crimean work of Grace in *Two Years Ago*. She could entertain the idea of total sacrifice to redress the wrongs of the poor. The narrator of 'A

Royal Princess' learns as a revelation about those who toil to serve her father,

> That these too are men and women, human flesh and blood;
> Men with hearts and men with souls, though trodden down like mud.

and is prepared to make a Christ-like act towards them:

> They shall take all to buy them bread, take all I have to give;
> I, if I perish, perish; they to-day shall eat and live
> I, if I perish, perish – that's the goal I half conceive,
> Once to speak before the world, rend bare my heart, and show
> The lesson I have learned, which is death, is life, to know.
> I, if I perish, perish: in the name of God I go.

It may be thought that Christina's later development shows a decline, both ethically and poetically. There was no diminution in deeds of kindness, but a lack of assurance, a distrust of self-will which could mean some inhibiting of activity. The poetry too has often a less certain control over shared experience. She distrusted more and more the attractions of the world. The images of hardness, sterility, sacrifice, become more frequent; they had been there from early days, in the cold of 'In the bleak mid-winter' and the self-abasement of 'A Better Resurrection'. Yet the hardness must be broken; Tractarian piety taught that mere contemplation of the Passion was unavailing; there must be willingness to enter into the suffering:

> Am I a stone, and not a sheep,
> That I can stand, O Christ, beneath Thy cross,
> To number drop by drop Thy Blood's slow loss,
> And yet not weep?
>
> Yet give not o'er,
> But seek Thy sheep, true Shepherd of the flock;
> Greater than Moses, turn and look once more
> And smite a rock.
>
> ('Good Friday')

As self-certainty waned, so there grew the desire for a religious life of system and discipline. One of the great achievements of the Oxford Movement was the restoration of precision and pattern to those who felt lost in the less defined terms of Evangelical assurance. It was also one of its most dangerous features for those who were content to leave all to the fulfilment of certain duties. Yet the possibility of growth in holiness was real and attractive. Anglican divines like Taylor and Law had already given some spiritual guidance. Butler had taught that right action was important in the development of Christian character and this became a major tenet of the Tractarians. Good deeds are good just because they are part of the great drive towards holiness. They are none the less important for this pragmatic approach: there is no understanding of God without doing the divine Will.[28]

The great stress laid on right actions could lead to scruples of the kind which today can make some of Charlotte Yonge's characters seem unconvincing. Philip Morville's refusal to join in social pastimes, however, is of a kind with Christina's decision to give up playing chess because she was so anxious to win. She, like many contemporaries, was almost morbidly afraid of stumbling by exaggeration or false emphasis and could find it necessary to write to her own brother:

> I want to correct a mis-statement I made some time ago. Something you said led me to answer in a general way that morning prayer took me (about?) half an hour – but it did not and does not take me so long. This has justly worried me, as the inaccuracy told in my own favour.[29]

On another occasion she was unwilling to have some of her poems set to music by a man who was alleged to have some scandal connected with him; she withdrew her consent and then got worried about his protestations of innocence. Such anxieties were not at variance with the earnestness of Tractarian teaching. It was hardly possible to be too strict. Isaac Williams, her admiration for whom has been quoted, was by no means the most severe of preachers but could say:

> Every duty is a denial of self, and therefore a bearing of the Cross, and as the Image of Christ Crucified passes into all things that are His – like the Sun in the Heavens infinitely multiplying itself in all things, even the smallest of daily occurrence. If painful – yet because they are painful, are they all the more connected with peace and hope.[30]

Minor scruples then are healthy as signs of a desire to sacrifice one's own will. There would have been substantial agreement on this among Tractarians and Evangelicals and many who shunned orthodox dogmas of any kind. There was a further problem which particularly afflicted Anglo-Catholics – the great load of guilt within the Christian life. Evangelicals saw in guilt the way to repentance and acceptance of the saving act of Christ. Thereafter all should be well, though some of the noblest among them could feel guilt at the apparent ease with which salvation was gained. For those who followed Tractarian teaching there were greater difficulties. The Church gave the means of salvation, but there was still a load on the individual who had to steer a right course. It must be confessed that there is a certain ambiguity, one might even say muddle, in Tractarian thought here. Its Evangelical emphasis on the Cross alone is strong – as strong in Pusey himself as any – but the sacraments of the Church are elevated to unique and incomparable channels of grace. Augustine and Pelagius are not easily reconciled.

As so often, the question of baptism becomes important. The Puseyites were strong for the idea of baptismal regeneration and in being so they tended to take a position of dubious orthodoxy in the mainstream of Catholic tradition, though it was found in the early Church for which they had so much regard.[31] Through baptism alone was the saving grace of Christ given for total remission of sin. Any falling-away after baptism was particularly grievous; it could be dealt with by penance, but only as a second-best for those who could not keep their baptismal state in purity. It was to that state that faith must cling:

> If most of us have too probably tarnished our baptismal purity . . . yet to all is something left. If we have not the original purity of our white robes, we may wash their spots with our tears, and He will cleanse them with His Precious Blood.[32]

Now we have to make an imaginative effort to understand the effects of this kind of piety, these aspirations and scruples. The sense of guilt, of temptation fought and sometimes not overcome, is pervasive in Christina Rossetti's poetry. There need be no deep mystery in her biography to explain it, no dreadful actual sin. For those who aspire to perfection, ordinary living will seem full of guilt. The girl in *Maude* who feels unworthy to communicate need not have done anything sensational; we met her fellows in the fiction and the reality of Charlotte Yonge's ambience. That Christina felt the attractions of youth for youth need hardly be questioned; that her load of guilt was caused by anything more than her chosen sense of dedication imperfectly realized is improbable. The temptation, fall and salvation in 'Goblin Market' is a generalized Christian parable. Those with holiness in their hearts have the deepest horror of sin, and the greatest sensitivity to the presence of evil in the world: 'Amor Mundi' and 'The World' are wrung out of the understanding that there is a perpetual battle in human life. For them too is the worst self-loathing; no man, it has been wisely said, knows anyone as bad as himself. The torments revealed by Hurrell Froude in his journals, the anguish of Hopkins in the dark night, are akin to what Christina sets out in poems like 'Who Shall Deliver Me?' with the lines

> God strengthen me to bear myself;
> That heaviest weight of all to bear,
> Inalienable weight of care.

The staid Victorian spinster must be seen in the same light that illuminated the medieval visionaries. Whether we judge them pathological or divinely favoured, we must judge her the same.

> Wearied of sinning, wearied of repentance,
> Wearied of self, I turn, my God, to Thee;
> To Thee, my Judge, on Whose all-righteous sentence
> Hangs mine eternity:
> I turn to Thee, I plead Thyself with Thee,
> Be pitiful to me.
>
> Wearied I loathe myself, I loathe my sinning,
> My stains, my festering sores, my misery:
> Thou, the Beginining, Thou ere my beginning
> Didst see and didst foresee
> Me miserable, me sinful, ruined me,
> I plead Thyself with Thee.
>
> I plead Thyself with Thee Who art my Maker,
> Regard Thy handiwork that cries to Thee;

I plead Thyself with Thee Who wast partaker
  Of mine infirmity;
Love made Thee what Thou art, the love of me,
  I plead Thyself with Thee.

('For Thine Own Sake, O My God')

In the opinion of some critics her poetry shows a decline
as the devotional element becomes dominant and more intense.
It would be true to say that she shared and did not fully overcome the difficulties of the age with regard to religious poetry;
also that she brought unique gifts to the problem. With the
revival of intense religious feeling linked with ecclesiastical
discipline, poetry was simply lacking the language that was
needed. Religious statements outside the work of trained theologians had become imprecise and relating to vague principles.
Where poetry took a religious theme, it generally borrowed
the prevailing diction or gave a metrical cast to the language
of the Bible in its Authorized Version and of the Book of
Common Prayer. Such was the form of *Lyra Apostolica*
and *The Christian Year*, and the work of Isaac Williams:
poems by men well-acquainted with Anglican prose and
romantic poetry.

Christina Rossetti joined the revolt against this tradition,
including the flight from the way in which Tennyson was
giving it a new direction. She was, after all, the sister of one of
the founders of the Pre-Raphaelite Brotherhood, whose members were not disposed to regard *Idylls of the King* as the mode
for contemporary poetry. The departure from smooth, even
lines and circumscribed vocabulary found its first real success
with the publication of 'Goblin Market' in 1862. Some contemporary critics indeed were offended by its colloquial tone
and found it harshly prosaic. Today we can more readily
recognize a new departure – or rather a rediscovery of what
Wordsworth had taught and sometimes practised – in lines
like this:

She ran and ran
As if she feared some goblin man
Dogged her with gibe or curse
Or something worse:
But not one goblin skurried after,
Nor was she pricked by fear;

191

The kind heart made her windy-paced
That urged her home quite out of breath with haste
And inward laughter.

If Christina had always managed her diction with this controlled freedom, she would perhaps not be accused of poetic
decline as the devotionalism in her poetry grew.

Regrettably the Biblical strain too often dominates what she
wants to say. Patmore and Hopkins broke through to a new
linguistic dimension in religious poetry but Christina's language too often falls short of her intense feeling. She needs to be
read with acceptance of the current convention – not yet
extinct – that there was something particularly reverential
about Jacobean English. Even her admiring brother William
had to be rather defensive about it:

> The reader of Christina Rossetti's poems will be apt to say that
> there is an unceasing use of biblical diction. This is a fact; and to
> some minds it may appear to detract seriously from her claims to
> originality, or to personal merit of execution. Without pre-judging
> this question, I will only remark that the Bible was so much her rule
> of life and of faith that it had almost become a part of herself, and she
> uttered herself accordingly.[33]

That is the truth; she could not verbalize religious experience
without keeping close to the Bible. In common with most
believers of her own time, she would not have thought the
attempt to get away from traditional language a worthy
one.

She did not solve the linguistic problem, and to this extent
her religious poetry falls short of greatness. The simplicity of
vocabulary and the tone of the speaking voice are not so frequent as in some of her earlier work, but they are not altogether absent. She can still use her technical skill in prosodic
variations and in the controlled repetition of key words and
phrases which gives an incantatory effect. She has not the
equipment, perhaps not the nerve, to achieve the startling
contrasts of the seventeenth-century religious poets whom she
loved. The diction which was contemporary for them was
archaic for her; the conceits that were part of their poetic sensibility became fussy and mannered. There are occasions,

especially in the years of earlier devotion, when she reaches something even more remote in style but takes it out of temporal fashion:

> Enough for Him, whom cherubim
> Worship night and day,
> A breastful of milk
> And a mangerful of hay;
> Enough for Him, whom angels
> Fall down before,
> The ox and ass and camel
> Which adore.
>
> Angels and archangels
> May have gathered there,
> Cherubim and seraphim
> Thronged the air;
> But only His mother
> In her maiden bliss
> Worshipped the Beloved
> With a kiss.
>
> What can I give Him,
> Poor as I am?
> If I were a shepherd
> I would bring a lamb,
> If I were a Wise Man
> I would do my part,
> Yet what I can I give Him,
> Give my heart.
>
> ('In the Bleak Mid-Winter')

The naturalism here of stable animals in supranatural moment gains its confidence from something more than the traditional iconography of the Nativity. For Christina Rossetti the natural world is a complex symbol of the spiritual world which increasingly became her reality. In her notes on the Commandments, *Letter and Spirit* (1883), she wrote in Platonic terms of the visible world as a shadow of invisible verities. The idea of earthly mirrors of the divine had appeared a few years before in the poem 'Mirrors of Life and Death'. Here, in a series of traditional images, she develops the theme:

The mystery of Life, the mystery
Of Death, I see
Darkly, as in a glass;
Their shadows pass,
And talk with me.

Platonic and Pauline, the idea is not new or startling in a
Christian writer. There are, however, reasons for looking at it
in a little more depth as it concerns her poetry. Her delight in
the animal world was developed early and did not fail her: the
ox and ass of the Nativity, the eagle and the dove of more
mystical symbolism, are introduced as actual creatures that
she would have loved to see and have near her. Her pleasure
in queer, odd creatures was shared with such diverse fellow-
Victorians as Charles Kingsley, Lewis Carroll, Beatrix Potter –
and her brother Dante Gabriel. In all of them perhaps there
was a concealed protest against conformism and conventional
notions of what was accepted as beautiful. Certainly all of
them would have understood the pleasure of a twenty-eight-
year old woman who could report:

We have revisited the Z[oological] Gardens. Lizards are in strong
force, tortoises active, alligators looking up. The weasel-headed
armadillo as usual evaded us. A tree-frog came to light, the exact
image of a tin toy to follow a magnet in a slop-basin. The blind
wombat and neighbouring porcupine broke forth into short-lived
hostilities, but apparently without permanent results.[34]

The direct issue of these observations included the erotic
crocodile of 'My Dream' and the creatures of 'Goblin Market'.

There was more than fascinated delight. There was a
Coleridgean sense of the mystic union of all creatures, a belief
that love must manifest itself not in human relations alone. Her
passionate hatred of 'that horror of horrors, Vivisection'[35] was
a simple and practical result of a more comprehensive commitment. Her new Anglican piety had taught her that the visible
and invisible worlds were not sharply separated. Here again
Butler had exercised his influence on the development of
Newman and Keble. The motive power of the feelings, so
important in producing the good actions that led to holiness,
were affected by natural surroundings. The moral sense, given
by divine grace, was the harmonizing factor not only of human

senses but of all the universe. This plus Wordsworth was the progenitor of *The Christian Year*. This plus a more advanced sacramental doctrine passed into Tractarian teaching:

> To those who live by faith, every thing they see speaks of that future world; the very glories of nature, the sun, moon and stars, and the richness of the beauty of the earth are as types and figures. witnessing and teaching the invisible things of God.[36]

Such doctrines as these were received joyfully by Christina. Her delight in nature was something that could be sanctified – this at least need not be renounced and denied. She would acquiesce in the Christian Platonism that now took a deeper meaning. In her commentary on the *Benedicite*, that great canticle of praise from all creation, she wrote:

> Wise were those ancients who felt that all forms of beauty could be but partial expressions of beauty's very self: and who by clue of what they saw groped after Him they saw not. Beauty essential is the archetype of imparted beauty; life essential of imparted goodness; but such objects, good, living, beatific as we now behold, are not that very Goodness, Life, Beauty, which (please God) we shall contemplate in beatific vision.[37]

The beatific vision sometimes came to her; with such imaging of divinity in all around her, the sacrament was a special concentration of living experience. It is not surprising that she left little poetic expression of the aesthetic side of worship.

The unity of all things did not always give her comfort. The three sonnets collectively titled *The Thread of Life* relate her failure to find empathy with the delight and apparent rejoicing of the natural scene, and conclude with the existential reflection:

> I am not what I have nor what I do;
> But what I was I am, I am even I.
>
> Therefore myself is that one only thing
> I hold to use or waste, to keep or give;
> My sole possession every day I live,
> And still mine own despite Time's winnowing.

In the long poem 'An Old-World Thicket' she faces the same terror when nature emphasizes isolation and insecurity:

Surely the ripe fruits tremble on their bough,
They cling and linger trembling till they drop:
I, trembling, cling to dying life; for how
Face the perpetual Now?

Here, however, sunset and a flock of sheep bring peaceful assurance in the Wordsworth tradition.

The closeness of human life to nature, in its tragedy and despair as well as its delight, connects with her Incarnational faith. The personal encounter is with God who has shared the worldly experience and triumphed over it as she desires to triumph. The images of cutting, pruning, moulding, are frequent. Commonplace observation brings her to the heart of mystery:

Thou who didst hang upon a barren tree,
My God, for me;
Though I till now be barren, now at length,
Lord, give me strength
To bring forth fruit to Thee.

('Long Barren')

My vineyard that is mine I have to keep,
Pruning for fruit the pleasant twigs and leaves.
Tend thou thy cornfield: one day thou shalt reap
In joy thy ripened sheaves.

Or, if thine be an orchard, graft and prop
Food-bearing trees each watered in its place:
Or, if a garden, let it yield for crop
Sweet herbs and herb of grace.

('Yea I Have a Goodly Heritage')

Thus she early parted company with the Pre-Raphaelites, for whom nature was an escape rather than a seal of commitment. She embraced with joy the Puseyism of which they were sometimes suspected for their medievalism and ecclesiastical subjects. Her brother painted her as the Blessed Virgin, but he changed the title of his picture from 'Ecce Ancilla Domini' to 'The Annunciation', lest he be accused of Mariolatry and all that it meant to Protestant society. Some of Dante Gabriel's poetry is a good corrective to the idea that Christina's religious language is purely derivative and conventional. See, for

instance, the technical skill but lack of involvement in faith
shown in 'The Church Porch' and 'Vox Ecclesiae, Vox Christi'.

She won in her own lifetime the following that Christian
poets could still command, even to the extent of such critical
exaggerations as could call her 'the most perfect poet that ever,
in the English tongue, linked the highest aspirations of religion
with the most exquisite expressions of poetry'.[38] She was
admired not only by Puseyite sympathizers but by Broad
Churchmen like Kingsley and Ainger. Despite her close
adherence to Anglo-Catholic orthodoxy, she remained wide
enough in her perceptions to offer something to many who
did not share all her beliefs. Perhaps that is another way of
saying that the Oxford Movement could touch the hearts of
those who did not accept all its presuppositions, provided they
were not hopelessly bigoted. She brought under Catholic discipline a strong Protestant individualism: the personal encounter that she desired could be aided but not controlled by
the ecclesiastical system.

She remained close in doctrine to those Tractarian teachings
which she had heard in her formative years. Newman had
passed to another obedience before her own commitment was
complete, but the power of his teaching remained. She was
able to respect his struggle, as one who had herself striven
towards holiness. When he died, not many years before her
own death, she wrote of him in words that are fitting for herself
as well:

> O weary Champion of the Cross, lie still:
> Sleep thou at length the all-embracing sleep:
> Long was thy sowing-day, rest now and reap:
> Thy fast was long, feast now thy spirit's fill.

8
A Plague o' Both Your Houses

For some time he inclined to the Tractarian influence then so prevalent at Oxford, and thought for a while that he had found the help he needed; when lo! again, in an hour of startling conviction, he found that the forms with which he had been so busy building his conscience had as little of the Divine in them as the forms of common worldly society. The re-action followed, and he hated the church which he thought had deceived him.[1]

It was a reaction shared by several of those who had received the Tractarian word with gladness. Like most of the various ways by which men of the nineteenth century slipped from Christianity to agnosticism, the retreat from the Oxford Movement was not a negative thing. The growth of unbelief had many causes; it was as complex as any part of the Victorian situation, characterized by the same earnestness and often expressed in the same kind of language as orthodox faith. The serious doubters were seldom triumphant or ebullient about their new position. The strong moral sense, which had been a factor in their initial opposition to Christianity as it then appeared, made them anxious about the continuance of an ethical system not dependent on supernatural sanctions. They shared with their orthodox contemporaries a lurking fear of the beast in man and of the temptations offered by sentimental humanism divorced from responsibility:

He experienced at last what so long he had denied, that to attempt to separate morality from religion is madness; that religion, reduced to a sentiment resting only on internal emotion, is like a dissolving view, which will change its image as the passions shift their focal distance.[2]

The conclusion reached by Froude's hero Markham Sutherland after his very innocent affair with a married woman was not unique. The retreat from faith tended to be a running skirmish, with both sides loosing and dodging odd shots. The marks which an Evangelical upbringing left on writers as different as George Eliot and Samuel Butler are plain to read; the marks of the Oxford Movement are sometimes indicative of even deeper wounds. That vein of tragedy in the movement which was seen in the rifts caused by secession was present also in the losses. The younger brothers of two of the original Tractarians were among those who became impatient and entered into what at that time seemed complete infidelity.

It would be foolish to try to assess whether close contact with the movement was determinate in the final situation of any individual. There must always be mystery, in the true sense, in the spiritual state. The psychologist and the theologian could each give his reasons why the same heredity and family environment should produce both a cardinal and a strong opponent of formal Christianity. One explanation would not necessarily contradict the other in a question where categories and terms alike are uncertain.

The tensions and final splits were inherent in a movement which itself protested and seemed to innovate yet was seeking to go back and re-establish lost purity: a movement too which strongly emphasized sacerdotal power and ecclesiastical authority while opposing the Roman Catholic claims to hold these things in unique fullness. Those who felt the tension most strongly were those whose own imaginative power later gave verbal expression to what had troubled them. They were among the most enthusiastic supporters in their youth, and their disillusionment was thereby the greater. They came to Tractarianism for many reasons, but two types are outstanding. There were those who came from High Church families and found at Oxford an extension and fulfilment of ideals which they had already learned to value. There were others released from Evangelical homes, taught to value earnestness and deep piety in religion, who sought and found a richer way of bringing these qualities into devotional life. J.A.Froude is typical of the first, Mark Pattison of the second.

The Tractarians began questioning established Anglicanism from within. It was a Frankenstein experiment for some of them and their associates, producing secession to Rome or the drift into doubt – monsters of about equal horror to their contemporaries. By 1845 there were 'forces which were not only leading minds to Rome, but making them Utilitarians, Rationalists, Positivists, and, though the word had not yet been coined, Agnostics'.[3] William Arnold, quoted at the beginning of this chapter, showed how dissatisfaction with the Tractarian position could make an earnest young man feel lost and uncertain. His hero makes the physical retreat that he himself made to India where he tries to grapple with the moral problems of army life. In some ways his lot was easier than that of those who stayed in the land of their birth.

For them the loss was indeed a deep source of suffering. The agonies of Newman in his last months as an Anglican were reproduced in those drifting to doubt, even though both retreats might lead to a new stability. It could not be otherwise in an age when religious allegiance was of such social as well as personal importance. It seemed wicked to leave the national Church, wicked even to doubt and question her tenets. Charlotte Yonge accepted Keble's view that there was sin in doubt itself; those who nourished and developed their doubts often remained troubled by the same teaching. 'Show me if I am wrong,' Markham Sutherland pleads with his friend when doubts afflict him. 'It is easy to be mistaken. But do not tell me it is wicked to have thought all this, for *it is not* – I am certain it is not.'[4] Again, when he sees that his personal questioning will cause him to be cut off from his familiar churchgoing and from all the associations of his youth he cries out: 'God is my witness, nothing which I ever believed has parted from me, but it has been torn up by the roots bleeding out of my heart.'[5]

It is all reminiscent of Newman and Manning, of Henry and Robert Wilberforce. Most moving of all, most indicative of what it all meant, is Froude's appeal for compassion towards those who, like his hero and himself, had finally made the break:

Could you see down below his heart's surface, could you count the tears streaming down his cheeks, as out through some church-door into the street come pealing the old familiar notes, and the old psalms which he cannot sing, the chanted creed which is no longer his creed, and yet to part with which was more agony than to lose his dearest friend; ah! you would deal him lighter measure.[6]

Francis Newman too could find it needful to plead that he should not be shunned by those who differed from him: 'To set up any fixed creed as a test of spiritual character is a most unjust, oppressive and mischievous superstition.'[7] Again, he would defend the rightness of having followed out his questioning and seeing where doubt would lead:

The Will cannot, may not, dare not dictate whereto the inquiries of the Understanding shall lead; and to allege that it *ought*, is to plant the root of Insincerity, Falsehood, Bigotry, Cruelty, and universal rottenness of Soul.[8]

To claim such obligations for the Will was of course just what his brother and the rest of the Tractarians, had done. If they could have looked into the future, would they perhaps have thought that the loss was balanced by the gain in other things that they valued and were accused of denying? Those who learned from them and then departed were among those who pleaded most effectively for love and consideration. Mark Pattison saw the apparent collapse of the Oxford Movement as a liberation of thought at Oxford, and even basically sympathetic modern historians can see the Tractarians are too much detached from the urgency of their time: 'the domination of ecclesiastical subjects and religious beliefs was a real domination; everything else was seen at second hand.'[9] There is enough truth here, even though the social concern shown in Ward's *Ideal* was later to grow and find practical expression in some unexpected associations.

Those who came up to Oxford in the great days of the Tracts came into a fervent, feverish, religious atmosphere – and this at a time when to take religion seriously at all was to invite high temperatures. The picture of indifferent contempt or cold conformism, which the Tractarian apologists were keen to promote, has already been proved exaggerated. Yet the distrust of enthusiasm still made those who were earnest in religion stand out from their fellows. The effect of Oxford was strongest on those young men who were already notably pious – and the depth of piety in the young could be, and still can be, both humbling and disquieting for their elders. Many of them had already felt some of the impact of Tractarianism at home or in school.

In the High Church home of J.A.Froude, the doings of brother Hurrell of course had strong effect. Ideas which had formerly been too much even for the stomachs of staunch High Churchmen now became permissible and even mandatory. 'Transubstantiation was talked of before me as more than possible; celibacy of the clergy and fast days were not only not wrong, but the very thing most needful.'[10] Such strange shifts of emphasis started more fundamental questioning. Francis Newman came from the teaching of clergymen like Walter Mayers, under whose Evangelical influence he had dared even to challenge the sanctity of paternal orders by refusing to copy a letter on a Sunday. Enthusiasm seized him to the degree that novelists loved to satirize; his brother seemed too cold and reserved in faith. He wrote to the young Fellow of Oriel in 1826:

If, as you say, you are not therefore the more inclined to talk of a benefactor because you love him the more; it may be so. I pray God that you may enjoy the riches of his mercy and everlasting consolation, and indeed do not doubt that he thus blesses you: I am sure I do not argue the contrary from your not talking of it. But I am of an opposite temper.[11]

From a fervent or a moderate Evangelical position, one brother was led to increasing concern about the individual moral sense, the other to the task of fitting such doctrines into a more sacramental and sacerdotal system.

Arthur Hugh Clough came from Arnold's liberalism at Rugby, from cheering the author of 'The Oxford Malignants' and the outcome of the Hampden issue. Taught there to question his suppositions, he was led to further questioning at Oxford under the tutorship of Ward and to grudging admission that Newmanism saw not unadulterated evil. Yet it must also be remembered that there were many young men coming up in the early thirties who, like Mark Pattison, were 'in innocent ignorance of all that was brewing beneath the surface – never having so much as heard the name of Keble, or the *Christian Year*'.[12]

The ignorant innocence could not remain untouched for long in a university where the Tracts and their authors were daily talk, where the choice of a new professor could be the trial of party strengths. The religion taught by the Church of England was assumed as absolute truth by the very constitution of the University and her demands on her members. The Thirty-nine Articles had to be subscribed on matriculation, on taking degrees and on certain other occasions. Yet assent to these articles was no longer required for office under the state and men of integrity and respect were openly questioning their validity.

Subscription of the Articles looms large in the realities of the Oxford Movement and in the imaginative writing which issued from it. Dissatisfaction was not the monopoly of any one party or the innovation of the new revival; Thomas Arnold had had 'distressing doubts' at the time of his ordination in 1818. Yet it was the Romanizing movement in Tractarianism which made the articles a prominent issue; the appearance of Tract 90 was a cross-roads for many on the way to Rome or to doubt. Newman himself depicts Charles Reding in *Loss and Gain* coming to find the Articles untenable as he approaches the time for taking his degree and renewing subscription. The attempt of Bateman to give the kind of 'Catholic' interpretation which Newman had offered in Tract 90 is coldly received.

While Anglo-Catholics tried to reconcile the new churchmanship with the old Articles, others were questioning still further and becoming sceptical of more basic teachings. For William Arnold's hero, 'the Thirty-nine Articles stood up as an insuperable barrier'.[13] The requirement of subscription was partly or substantially responsible for the withdrawal from Fellowships of Clough, Francis Newman and J.A.Froude. Their attitude was that which Matthew Arnold described, when the goal of a university free from such demands was nearer attainment:

To profess to see Christianity through the spectacles of a number of second- or third-rate men who lived in Queen Elizabeth's time (and this is what office-holders under the Thirty-nine Articles do) – men whose works one never dreams of reading for the purpose of enlightening and edifying oneself – is an intolerable absurdity . . . it is time to put the formularies of the Church of England on a solider basis.[14]

Despite these tensions and trials, or perhaps rather because of them, the Oxford Movement was in its essentials a movement for the young. Its first leaders were comparatively young men, who could ride about pressing the Tracts on bewildered parish clergymen. Hurrell Froude, and later W.G.Ward, brought gaiety, ebullience – and instability – into the theological issues. It was a movement hostile to the conformist Establishment, questioning the accepted values of contemporary society, reactionary in its appeal but charmed by a romantic nostalgia and the element of 'Charlie over the water-ism' which sent its opponents into paroxysms. It could meet the sensuous and aesthetic needs which Romanticism had stimulated and which the prevailing temper of the age was still starving. Its essence rests not only in the sober portraits of clergymen who were famous for theological argument but also in the Oxford of the thirties and forties with its reading parties of the kind shown in *The Bothie* and 'The Spirit's Trials'. The spiritual anguish was there, but so was the gaiety, the new intimacy of shared revolt.

For a time the unpopularity of Tractarian sympathies was a challenge and a stimulus:

No worldly interests had as yet been threatened with damage, except perhaps the Friday dinner and the Lent second course; the loss of which, being not enough to be painful, became a piquant stimulant and gave edge to appetite.[15]

As things became tougher, more of the fringe adherents were thrown off into conformism or doubt. New ideas and practices could be a bar to advancement, even to ordination – as Keble's curate Peter Young found when he tried to pass from the diaconate to the priesthood. After the debacle of 1845, 'if you were able to describe a man as a Puseyite, he became, *ipso facto* unfit for an public appointment'.[16]

It was the personality of Newman more than any other single factor which had held the movement together. His secession brought with it 'a sense that the past agitation of twelve years was extinguished by this simple act'.[17] While the few faithful ones rallied, there were many who could not endure when the leader was lost. The tributes of those who fell away are the most significant: they make it clear that Newman could draw and hold men who were not committed with all their being to the deeper principles of the movement. His personality, his power of preaching, his natural and graceful authority over young men, are continually praised by those who could not follow him. The excitement of Littlemore could bring out a following of undergraduates after a sermon at St Mary's, attracting the cautious Matthew Arnold and the emotional Mark Pattison.

'While it was in reality only their own great persons which were drawing us all towards them, they unwillingly deceived us into believing it was not their influence but the body's power; and, while in fact we were only Newmanites, we fancied we were becoming Catholics.'[18] The admiration outlived the disillusionment. Froude, who wrote those words, could make another fictional hero speak more deeply of the remembered debt:

In my dark hour I went to Newman. I was with him some hours, laying bare the secrets of my soul to him, and he left me with a feeling for him I never had for man ... Throw away your cant about him; he was the truest and best friend the Church of England held at the hands of Providence, and she has spurned him from her, and set the seal on her own hollowness.[19]

The love endured for years, to be expressed again without the framework of a novel:

The simplest word which dropped from him was treasured as if it had been an intellectual diamond. For hundreds of young men, *Credo in Newmannum* was the genuine symbol of faith.[20]

Newman fared better in the words of the sceptics than in those of most of the Anglicans – and indeed of a section of the Roman Catholics. His brother could overcome emotional as well as theological differences:

My heart smote me on account of one. I had a brother, with whose name all England was resounding for praise or blame: from his sympathies, through pure hatred of Popery, I had long since turned away ... my brother surely was struggling after truth, fighting for freedom to his own heart and mind, against church articles and stagnancy of thought. For this he deserved both sympathy and love. But I, alas! had not known and seen his excellence. But now God had taught me more largeness by bitter sorrow working the peaceable fruit of righteousness; at last when I might admire my brother.[21]

Even Clough, 'Arnoldized' against the spell, could cautiously comment that Newman 'seems to be a very delightful person' and grow to admire some at least of the Tractarian ideas since 'the chief upholders of them are exceedingly good men'.[22]

The attraction of personality was certainly a factor in the progress and retreat of James Anthony Froude. He grew up in the same High Church home that had produced his eldest brother Hurrell, whom he 'adored', but who had treated him badly in childhood. For James had the reputation of being cowardly and lazy; he was sent to Westminster School where the bullying was extreme even for that time, and was threatened with removal to one of the even worse 'Yorkshire Schools' of the kind which Dickens made notorious in *Nicholas Nickleby*. 'The sullen, unhappy boy grew to fear his father and tremble before his father, almost as he had done before his tyrants at the school.'[23] Oxford proved a liberation; believing that he had not long to live, he threw himself into the life of an undergraduate. As the brother of Hurrell, he naturally found himself drawn into the Tractarian movement. For a time it seemed that there would be freedom to make his own life when he met on a reading-party Harriet Bush, the 'Emma Hardinge' whose happy family is wistfully described in 'The Spirit's Trials'. The engagement was soon broken; Froude went for a time to Ireland as tutor to the children of the Church of Ireland incumbent at Delgany in County Wicklow.

The link between Ireland and the Oxford Movement is interesting. There seems to be something symbolic in the occasion of Keble's Assize Sermon when the Irish sees were suffering governmental interference. Ireland was so conveniently near geographically and so remote in other ways. It proved a kind of testing-ground for those Tractarian ideas

which most of its people, whether Protestant or Roman
Catholic, detested. Pusey's reception there has been mentioned. Francis Newman spent some time there and came
under the influence of Darby, founder of the Plymouth
Brethren. Froude, like other Englishmen before and since,
returned with certain revisions in his thinking.

Irish Anglicanism was numerically small but still enjoying
the benefits of establishment. The abuses observable in England – pluralism, non-residence, the wealth of the dignitaries –
were much more striking in Ireland because of the minority
position and the wretched state of the general economy. The
Anglican clergy and laity were mostly very Protestant in face
of the Roman Catholic majority, opposed utterly to the
apparent 'Romanizing' tendencies of the Tracts. Yet the spirit
was less Erastian than in England, the fervour of Evangelicalism less inhibited. Froude was ridiculed by brother Hurrell
for allowing himself to be drawn into such Evangelical circles.
For those whom Oxford had taught to sneer at the Reformers
and shun the name of Protestant, this was a shock. Here too
was the opportunity of seeing Roman Catholicism in action
with the adherence of most of the people: to see it in a more
superstitious and unattractive form than was offered by the
gentlemanly old Catholic English families or the intellectual
vigour of Wiseman.

In short, Ireland was performing her function, happily still
very active, of rubbing down the extremes brought by English
visitors. Froude found something appealing in Irish Protestantism, 'the fruit of the Reformation which we had been
learning at Oxford to hate as rebellion and to despise as a
system without foundation'.[24] Ireland later claimed some of
his historian's attention, but for the moment Oxford did not
release her hold. He was dismissed, amicably enough, for his
defence of Tract 90 and returned to a Fellowship at Exeter
College.

Yet he was changing; the power of Newman was not so
strong now that he had seen the power of Protestantism in a
new situation. He became more critical of the Puseyites, who
seemed too often to be neglecting their college duties in the
pursuit of theological minutiae. Like his fictional hero Edward
Fowler he 'determined to trust himself and not circumstances'.[25]

There were other voices too, and most alluring of them was that of Carlyle. Not for him alone did the pair of sirens, Newman and Carlyle, sing their conflicting songs. Oxford in the forties was receiving the impact of Carlylean thought, all the more strongly for its belated recognition.[26] Not that the conflict was then entirely apparent; both men offered antidotes to the materialism and blind faith in progress. Carlyle had not yet come out strongly against Puseyism, and the medieval ideals of *Past and Present* (1843) were acceptable enough to those already seized with enthusiasm for Hurrell Froude's *Remains*.

For the time being, J. A. Froude could run his ideas in parallel. He bowed to the demands of conformity and took deacon's orders in 1845 as the continuation of his Fellowship required. At Newman's request he undertook to write one of the *Lives of the Saints* which were then issuing under Tractarian auspices. The historical sense received some shocks and the religious sense was the sufferer. What was the real authority for faith? If the spokesmen of a great revival could give their imprint to these dubious legends, what value lay in any 'evidences'? Newman's purpose in the series was to show the continuity of supernatural gifts in post-Apostolic ages. The opposite effect was produced on Froude, who was not disposed to follow the editorial advice to 'rationalize when the evidence is weak'.[27]

The power of Newman over his mind was disappearing even before the secession. According to Thomas Mozley, Froude had always held somewhat aloof from Newman though his caution was not uncomplicated:

Anthony Froude had a great admiration for his father and for his brother, but while he admired he felt oppressed and repelled. The mightier the influence, the more he struggled against it. I believe he felt the same necessity for self-assertion in regard to Newman.[28]

That assessment rings true, though Froude later denied it. He was not the only young man to find in Newman both the attraction and the hostility of a father-figure. He returned to Ireland in 1845, caught smallpox and was devotedly nursed by a peasant family and was again struck by the basic warmth and security of the country despite the unhappy outward circumstances.

This time it was not only the level of churchmanship that came in for questioning. He had learned religious controversy; now he would look more critically at all Christian claims and conclude that 'The Church rests on the history, not the history on the Church'.[29] The Tracts had indeed been leading men to Rome, where their greatest author was now gone, but this was only part of a wider European retreat from the pressures of the age into the security of monolithic Catholicism. The time had come to abandon the leaky ship and take up a career more in tune with the times. Why should he not leave Oxford altogether and study medicine in London?

Because his deacon's ordination could not at that time be resigned, and because it was a bar to almost every other profession, Froude was confronted by the same problem as married clerical converts to Rome. He was in a difficult situation out of which he was precipitated by his own writing. In 1847 he published *Shadows of the Clouds*, containing two stories. The first and longer, 'The Spirit's Trials', was closely autobiographical in its early part. Edward Fowler goes through the same sufferings at home and school as the author, and his engagement is broken by his father's interference. Then the heroine, after accepting and jilting a Casaubon-like clergyman, marries a man she does not love. Edward, suffering from consumption, is trying to regain his health by the seaside when he rescues her little boy from drowning. The result is a deep friendship with her and with her husband, protracted dying made happy by the little boy's presence, and a final commendation of the young couple to each other's love. The second story, 'The Lieutenant's Daughter', tells of the seduction, ruin and suicide of an orphaned girl. Its setting in a dream, which is itself contained in the real memory of smallpox in Ireland, allows the final suggestion that her true history may after all have been happy.

Froude's father is said to have bought and destroyed all the copies of *Shadows of the Clouds* that he could find. The reason may have been the unflattering picture of family affairs in the first story or the outspoken words about prostitution in the second; but there was little hint yet of religious infidelity. Edward Fowler receives Holy Communion on his deathbed. At the time of writing these stories, Froude composed and published an extremely orthodox funeral sermon.[30] The real storm was still to come, and it gathered during another visit to Ireland in 1848. Froude was unhappy, uncertain, wondering whether to settle abroad; he wrote a book that protested against the orthodoxy that was being forced on him.

The Nemesis of Faith again traces some of the autobiographical path. After the impact of Oxford at home and university, Markham Sutherland parts company with his creator and goes to work in a parish. He is touched by the sufferings of the poor, to which churchmen too often seem indifferent, and revolted by the squabbles of factions within the Church. More, he begins to have doubts about the Bible: the Old Testament presents a capricious, revengeful God, the New a doctrine of judgement more harsh than secular systems. No other books satisfy him; even Carlyle 'only raises questions he cannot answer, and seems best content if he can make the rest of us as discontented as himself'.[31] His superiors take his doubts lightly, his moderation makes him unpopular with the extremists who dominate parish life. After an open breach he goes to Italy, where he meets a young married Englishwoman who is unhappy with her husband. Affection grows between them, until their absorption in each other makes them neglect her little girl, who falls out of a boat and dies. Sutherland parts company with Helen, urging her to repentance; he is saved from suicide by the intervention of a convert-priest whom he had admired at Oxford. He becomes a Roman Catholic and goes into a monastery; Helen enters a convent. They both die, apart and unhappy. Sutherland was

. . . sunk down into the barren waste, and the dry sands rolled over him where he lay; and no living being was left behind him upon earth, who would not mourn over the day that brought life to Markham Sutherland.[32]

Which apparently was how Froude was feeling about himself in 1848. *The Nemesis of Faith* tells a sadder story than 'The Spirit's Trials'. Now the love of a married woman leads not to reconciliation and a sainted death but to alienation and loneliness; her child is not saved from the water. The voices of Newman and Carlyle alike are void of help; Christian orthodoxy is found wanting but unaided morality is seen to fail. It was the nadir of Froude's life. For the modern reader the interest is in the accounts of what the Oxford Movement did to contemporaries who were drawn in and then flung out, and in the description of the kinds of doubt which tormented those whose questioning would not cease.

For Froude's contemporaries, the interest was not poignant but scandalous. A copy of the novel was burned by the Sub-rector of Exeter, though in a fit of passion rather than as the public ceremony which rumour soon made from it.[33] Froude himself was inclined to dramatize the situation. 'I have *resigned*,' he wrote to Clough. 'I was preached against Sunday in Chapel, denounced in Hall, and yesterday *burnt* publicly (by Sewell) before two Lectures.'[34] The bravado masked his deeper reaction to what was in fact the crisis of his life. His resignation of Fellowship was the only way of forestalling expulsion. Bishop Phillpotts, as Visitor of the college, approved of what had been done in terms reminiscent of those with which Bishop Wilberforce had written of his brother's secession to Rome. We are again reminded that both Romanizing and infidelity seemed like family affronts and public disgrace:

For the truly venerable Archdeacon [Froude's father] . . . I deeply feel. May God sustain him under one of the heaviest afflictions this world can know – the consciousness of having given birth to one who perverts no ordinary endowments to the corruption of his fellowmen – and the more presumptuous defiance of his God.[35]

Not all churchmen were so lacking in charity. Charles Kingsley courageously befriended Froude at a time when most of his former associates were against him: the occasion from which sprang Newman's *Apologia* was in the making. Froude carried the moral earnestness of his youth into the new situation. He saw himself as a man with a mission, charged with undoing the harm that men like his brother Hurrell had begun. 'Never mind, if the Puseyites hate it,' he wrote after *The Nemesis of Faith* had appeared, 'they must fear it and it *will* work in the minds they have made sick.'[36] The fight with his dead brother continued when he became a successful historian and opposed the extremer Tractarian views about the Reformation. In his outlook he remained nearer to the new liberal churchmen of the fifties and sixties than to the aggressive rationalists.

He renounced his deacon's order when such actions became possible in 1872. By that time he had established his reputation as a historian, though the inevitable attacks on his interpretation were sometimes bitter. Ironically, his dreaded father was in agreement with much in the first two volumes of the *History of England* when they appeared in 1856, and was partly reconciled. Ironically again, Froude lived to be made an honorary Fellow of Exeter College. He wrote in the style of older historians, with the moralism and the emphasis on the power of great individuals which characterized the otherwise opposed Carlyle and Macaulay. He was not in the empirical line of men like Grote, Bury and E.A. Freeman, with the last of whom he carried on a skirmish that lasted while they both lived.

The retreat from orthodoxy of Francis Newman is less directly relevant to the Oxford Movement, since he never professed Tractarian ideals and resigned his Fellowship through his own difficulties with the Articles before the revival was under way. Some interest must attach to his record in *Phases of Faith* (1850) as an antitype of the *Apologia*. It is the story of spiritual change in one who shared the same family background and the same undergraduate environment, with only a few years between, as the future Cardinal. The two brothers moved in different directions from their early Evangelical Anglicanism. Francis resisted John's emphasis on ecclesiastical authority, was forced back to the authority of the Bible and then came to criticize that in turn. At first under the influence of Darby, then on his own initiative, he sought for a Church that could contain spiritual truth while keeping intellectual freedom. In *The Soul* (1849) he considered how spiritual perceptions and desires seem to grow in the individual, whose quest for the Ideal is part of his total growth. Not surprisingly, perhaps, brother John did not read the book; however, he was prepared to condemn it unread as 'a dreadful work, as I am told it is'.[37]

Phases of Faith tells, as the *Apologia* was to tell one day, of adolescent Evangelicalism, of willing early subscription to the Articles at Oxford, of the impact of teaching and theological controversy in the years before the Tractarian revival began.

For Francis, however, the path soon diverged, as he began to have doubts about infant baptism, the Trinitarian doctrine and the attitude of the Anglican hierarchy to social problems. He found St Paul more congenial than the Gospels, which seemed to suffer from 'dislocation'; and the Fathers who changed his brother were for him neither notably moral nor intellectual. He went to Baghdad as a Darbyite missionary, was ostracized by Darby for his doubts about the Trinity and was driven to make his own decision that 'Morality is the end, Spirituality is the means. Religion is the handmaid to Morals'.[38] From there he moved farther and farther from the orthodox, reserving his greatest scorn for the Evangelicals of his youth. He became more critical of Biblical authority; much of what he says would now be accepted by Christian scholars; there is an anticipation of Bultmann in the statement: 'we cannot doubt that the apostles imbibed the logic, like the astronomy, of their own day, with all its defects.'[39] Eventually he cast off most of his old creed, going beyond many agnostics by his criticism of the historical Jesus as a man inclined to be dictatorial and obscurantist.[40] His final credo is idiosyncratic but not contemptible, even though the Christian cannot accept it in its entirety:

Religion was created by the inward instincts of the soul: it had afterwards to be pruned and chastened by the sceptical understanding. For its perfection, the co-operation of these two parts of man is essential. While religious persons dread critical and searching thought, and critics despise instinctive religion, each side remains imperfect and curtailed.[41]

Mark Pattison was just in time for the Oxford Movement, since he went up as an undergraduate in 1832. He is an example of those young men who were drawn deeply into the events of those years and then reacted violently against them. In his later view, the Tracts 'desolated Oxford life and suspended, for an indefinite period, all science, humane letters, and the first stirrings of intellectual freedom which had moved in the bosom of Oriel'.[42] After 1845, clerical dominance declined only to grow again in sinister power in the seventies of the century. Such bitterness deserves a closer search for its causes.

Pattison responds, with the customary Victorian frankness

about spiritual autobiography. His record may well be that of many others, less articulate, who were drawn to the Oxford Movement from Evangelical piety rather than from the recognition of High Church development. 'I began from within,' attracted by the seriousness of these men who cared so much about religion when many were indifferent or coldly conformist. He was drawn closer to their side as the controversy grew more heated:

> I became a declared Puseyite, then an ultra-Puseyite. . . . My reason seemed entirely in abeyance in the years 1840, 1841, 1842; I moved entirely with the party, was loudly prominent in all their demonstrations, and judged of good or bad according as any event or person was docile or otherwise in Newman's tactics.[43]

At the time of Newman's secession, he himself seemed to be heading for Rome. He recited the Breviary and 'once, and only once, got so low by fostering a morbid state of conscience as to go to confession to Dr Pusey'.[44] Pusey, he asserted, later betrayed his confidence.

With the masochism of a man who hates his past self, Pattison recalls how he was a regular visitor at Littlemore and reproduces passages from his journal with a freedom that few of us would care to accord to our youthful effusions in after years (he was in fact nearly thirty when his passion for Newman was strongest). He relates again his scruples and self-accusations with the morbid extremism that young men were often proud to copy from Froude's *Remains*. He remembers the excitement over snippets of information about waverings and secessions, the flirting with Rome, the feverish worship of Newman, the frequent communions, the regular saying of the offices. All that the opponents of the Tractarians hated most was the stuff of Pattison's life.

He believed himself drawn into Puseyism by piety and out again by reason. A visit to France in 1843 shocked him with the credulity of Roman Catholics as he then met them. But were the Littlemore people any less credulous, with their saints' lives? The slow progress towards scepticism began, aided by others who were farther on the same path:

> Went up to Froude, who engaged in writing a novel to expound his views; had long talk with him, with something of confidence on

both sides, though no satisfactory result – a sincere desire on my part to sympathize with his scepticism for the purpose of helping him through it.[45]

Things worked the other way; Froude was nearer to freedom, 'not having had in early youth that profound pietistic impression which lay like lead upon my understanding for so many years of my life'.[46] A female cousin of Pattison's, who seceded from Puseyism to Rome, dissuaded him from following her when he observed her bigotry and fanaticism. Besides, excitement about religion was dying down in Oxford and opinion was more taken up with the railway mania and the revolutionary movements at home and abroad. 'It seemed incredible, in the presence of such an upheaval, that we had been spending years in debating any matter so flimsy as whether England were in a state of schism or no.'[47]

So Oxford returned, in Pattison's view, to sanity. Liberalism held the field and the Puseyites were routed. Pattison, however, tended to see Puseyites under the bed as some people saw Jesuits, and his phobia could disturb the rationality of which he was so proud. Although their power was supposed to have gone, they had a majority in Congregation and in the middle fifties 'the tyranny of the High Church party' was so strong that 'church views were made the test of eligibility to all office or place'.[48] As for Pattison himself, his views broadened; they did not, in his own estimate, really change. He came to the conception of the universal Catholic Church and 'Anglicanism fell off from me, like an old garment, as Puritanism had done before' until eventually 'Catholicism dropped off me as another husk which I had outgrown'.[49] The evolutionary view of faith which Pattison later gave in his contribution to *Essays and Reviews* (1860) was already born.

Pattison is typical of those who entered fully into the Oxford Movement and then were bitter about it for the rest of their lives. Arthur Hugh Clough was one of the young men who came up feeling hostile to the Tractarians and discovered that things were not entirely as he had expected. He came from the conditioning of Rugby; 'the best of all public schools, which are the best kind of schools', he wrote while he was a

boy there.[50] He had experienced the privilege of being one of
Thomas Arnold's cherished pupils: he arrived at the University with an attachment to the broad, comprehensive view of
Christianity, dislike of the 'Oxford Malignants' and a glowing
recommendation from his headmaster. He started very warily
as he eyed the 'Newmanists' from a distance – 'they are very
savage and determined, and such good and pious men to boot'
he noted; nevertheless, they 'have done a vast amount of good'
where the Evangelicals have been ineffective.[51] He could not
resist going just a little nearer to these savage and determined
men; the result is worth quoting as illustrative of the way in
which many outside the movement could see it as a bulwark
against contemporary dangers to faith:

It is no harm but rather good to give oneself up a little to hearing
Oxford people, and admiring their good points, which lie, I suppose,
principally in all they hold in opposition to the Evangelical portion
of society – the benefit and necessity of forms – the ugliness of
feelings put on unnaturally soon and consequently kept up by artificial means, ever strained and never sober. I should think very
likely too their Anti-Calvinistic Views of Justification were ... at
least useful to lead us to the Truth.[52]

Being one of Arnold's favourites could be a handicap as well
as a privilege. 'Arnold's chosen boys felt like young Atlases
carrying a world upon their shoulders.'[53] It was not always
easy for them to come to grips with life when the prop was
taken away, as Arnold's own sons showed clearly enough for
all their brilliance. The hero of *Oakfield* is an epitome of the
conflict between ideal and reality, with the concomitant hesitation about whether to choose detachment or involvement.
Matthew knew the same dilemma:

> We, in some unknown power's employ
> Move on a rigorous line:
> Can neither, when we will, enjoy;
> Nor, when we will, resign.[54]

Clough, who had lacked the stability of the home and had
spent his school holidays almost as an interlude between living,
knew most keenly the feeling of being adrift when the ideals
formed in school appeared untenable yet continued to reproach inaction:

'Tis gone, the fierce inordinate desire,
The burning thirst for Action – utterly;
Gone, like a ship that passes in the night
On the high seas; gone, yet will come again.
Gone, yet expresses something that exists.
Is it a thing ordained, then? Is it a clue
For my life's conduct? is it a law for me
That opportunity shall breed distrust,
Not passing until that pass? Chance and resolve,
Like two loose comets wandering wide in space,
Crossing each other's orbits time on time,
Meet never.[55]   (*Dipsychus* IX 1–12)

Clough was brought into more than casual contact with the Tractarians through W. G. Ward, who was his mathematics tutor. When Clough came up in 1837 Ward, himself only twenty-five, was moving from the influence of Arnold towards that of Newman. One of the many ironies, and in contemporary terms sadnesses, of the movement was that a disciple of Arnold should be the man to bring the Romanizing issue to its crisis. Ward seems to have felt for Clough the type of rather nervous affection, expressing an emotional need, which tutors can develop towards their pupils. In the Long Vacation of 1838 Ward was confiding his religious tensions to Clough and virtually asking for the younger man's support:

I fully trust I may not 'change' if at all till you are prepared to do so too. At the same time with me the current is decidedly setting towards Newmanism at present. I had a long talk with Vaughan of Oriel last night who has thought a good deal of these matters: he says he is perfectly certain of this, that there is no mean between Newmanism on the one side and extremes *far* beyond anything of Arnold's on the other; that Arnold and all Anglican *Protestants* are in a false position.[56]

Clough was rather amused by these febrile confidences and retailed them in letters to old school friends with the detached compassion that marks much of his poetry. His failure to become emotionally involved in the theological situation was like a personal afffront to Ward, who expressed himself in terms that would have caused Kingsley to utter his worst fears about Newmanites: 'I think there will be no need of my making the attempt directly to like you less (in fact I do not see the

217

H

possibility unless I leave Oxford) if I can succeed in shewing it less to you and getting by degrees to see less of you.'[57] Although Ward thought him lukewarm, the rumours carried back to Rugby were that Clough was a decided Newmanist. In fact he was already impatient of the conflicting demands for commitment; England seemed to be torn asunder 'with Newmanism, Romanism, Chartism, and other isms, not forgetting Devilism'.[58]

Years later, Ward blamed himself for Clough's loss of faith.[59] The sceptical temper was in fact developing in the undergraduate years, but certainly Ward struck at much that Arnold had built up without being able to substitute a fatherfigure strong enough to personalize new ideas. The impact of Newman the preacher was never very effective for Clough; and by the time Clough became a Fellow of Oriel in 1842 Newman was seldom in residence. Clough did not share Mark Pattison's enthusiasm for Littlemore.

The doubts and difficulties increased in the early years of his Fellowship. He was unhappy about subscription to the Articles, though from a 'general dislike' rather than from scruples about particular doctrines. His own religious stance seemed ambiguous and unsatisfactory: 'I do not think I am particularly inclined to become a Puseyite, though it is very possible that my Puseyite position may be preventing my becoming anything else.'[60] But Puseyism was perhaps the scapegoat for his malaise about any form of Christianity. He reluctantly signed the Articles but continued to worry about what he had done. Then came the attack on Ward's *Ideal* and the associated attempt to condemn Tract 90.

The affair unsettled Clough still further. What right had these backwoodsmen of Convocation to interpret scholarly statements and press for exactitude where the Church had left things vague? Clough's individualism was insulted and the whole religious position seemed more and more a constriction. He supported Ward out of loyalty and thus clashed with Hawkins, his own Provost. He began to move towards resignation from his Fellowship, impelled largely by the weariness born of theological hatred in which he could feel no part. There were other factors too, probably including the thought of marriage which was impossible for a Fellow at that time.

Clough's departure was protracted: more like the slow step-by-step withdrawal of Newman than the sudden exit of Froude. He confided his doubts to Hawkins, at the same time sensibly trying to enlist the Provost's support in finding new employment. 'Oxford is not the best place for clearing oneself from such troubles,' he admitted. Despite the disagreement about Ward's case, Hawkins showed the best side of his character over Clough. The poor man had seen his college rent by the scandals of a religious party that he did not approve. Writing a testimonial for Clough just after Newman's secession, one of the most helpful things he could say was that he would not have made Clough a College tutor 'if I had not had reason to believe that he was untainted with the principles of the Tract Party'.[61]

Clough cast his net wide: he was attracted to Unitarianism, like many Victorians on the journey away from Christianity. He corresponded with Francis Newman about a post in the new University College in London, which he eventually obtained; at the same time he had thoughts of a Government college in Ireland. He could give the Articles 'only the ordinary negative acquiescence of a layman'; there was no question now of his going on to ordination and keeping his Fellowship, though Hawkins was willing to offer him a lay Fellowship if he would at least sign the Articles without having to teach their doctrine. At the same time, his quiet way of living made some Oxford acquaintances still regard him as a Puseyite.

The formal resignation came in 1848, overtly on account of the Articles. The full truth about his attitude remained obscure; after his death, A.P.Stanley suggested that he was delighted and relieved to get away from Oxford and its religious parties, an idea vigorously countered by R.W.Church. An anonymous correspondent who had known him at Rugby and at Oxford wrote in the High Church *Guardian*:

> The conflict between Dr Arnold's teaching and that of Dr Newman, acting upon a mind overwrought by premature study and thought, and upon a state of health always nervous and susceptible, ended by utterly unsettling his belief.

Others, including Stanley, were inclined to put the blame more squarely on Newman and the consequent disgust with ecclesi-astical authoritarianism.[62]

There can be no doubt that Clough must be reckoned among the castaways of the Oxford Movement, although his involvement was never as deep as that of Froude or of Patti-son. Conjecture is not fruitful; it is enough to suggest that if he had come to Oxford at a time less fraught with controversy he might have developed his Arnoldism into a more orthodox Broad Church position. On the other hand, the sceptical spirit was there and any strong religious party might have swung him away from school Christianity and out into the wilderness. Clough inhabited his own wilderness with much more comfort and ease than many of his contemporaries. *The Bothie of Tober-na-Vuolich* (1849) was partly his valediction to Oxford, and it is not a wholly sad one. The young men on the Highland reading party are serious in discussion but playful in their living; they are more credible and more likeable than the questing under-graduates in *Loss and Gain*. They are critical of conformist religion:

Alas! the noted phrase in the prayer-book,
Doing our duty in that state of life to which God has called us,[63]
Seems to me always to mean, when the little rich boys say it,
Standing in velvet frock by mama's brocaded flounces,
Eyeing her gold-fastened book and the watch and chain at her bosom
Seems to me always to mean, Eat, drink, and never mind others.

(202–7)

The final escape of Elspie and Philip to a new life in New Zealand symbolizes the unfulfilled desire for something better than life had so far provided, the belief that a new start can in fact be made if the right road is found, that was felt by Clough and also in their ways by Arnold and Morris and Tennyson.

Before the new start must come renunciation of the old: Clough achieved one, never quite the other. To the advice of the Tutor, 'the grave man, Adam':

There is a great Field-Marshal, my friend, who arrays our bat-
talions:
Let us to Providence trust, and abide and work in our stations.
This was the final retort from the eager, impetuous Philip.

I am sorry to say your Providence puzzles me sadly;
Children of Circumstance are we to be? You answer, On no wise!
Where does Circumstance end, and Providence where begins it?
What are we to resist, and what are we to be friends with?
If there is battle, 'tis battle by night: I stand in the darkness,
Here in the mêlée of men, Ionian and Dorian on both sides,
Signal and password known: which is friend and which is foeman?
Is it a friend? I doubt, though he speak with the voice of a brother.
Still you are right, I suppose; you always are and will be
Though I mistrust the Field-Marshal, I bow to the duty of order.
Yet is my feeling rather to ask, where is the battle? (IX, ll. 44–57)

The uncertainty was Clough's prerogative as a thinking man;
his personal integrity seemed to rest on it. Like Stephen
Daedalus long after him, he would not serve that in which he
no longer believed. Froude wrote to congratulate him on
getting the London University post 'on your own conditions',
which included not conducting corporate prayers.

They were the only conditions on which Clough could act.
With a Lawrentian 'I don't feel it *here*' he repudiated Arnoldism, Puseyism and then Christianity. It was the Tractarian
approach that was most foreign to him, though for a time he
felt the attraction of its authority. But Newman, echoing in a
different way the tenet of Coleridge, demanded assent shown
through the actions of faith: act as though you believe, and
belief follows – worship, and you come to God. This would
never do for Clough:

Action will furnish belief – but will that belief be the true one?
This the point, you know. However, it doesn't much matter.
What one wants, I suppose, is to predetermine the action,
So as to make it entail, not a chance-belief, but the true one.
Out of the question; you say; *if a thing isn't wrong, we may do it.*
Ah! but this *wrong*, you see – but I do not know that it matters.
('Amours de Voyage', V. ll. 20–5)

His orthodox friends tried to make him believe that it did
matter, working on him as they worked so conscientiously on
agnostic and on Roman converts. He was often on the move,
happiest when forced into an active situation. His ebullient
letters from Rome during the siege of 1849 show that Newman's urging for assent had validity of an unintended kind.

While he worried and thought about faith, seeking for spiritual satisfaction without dogma, he could also be happy and humorous. The pessimism in his poetry is clear to see; he disappointed his contemporaries by his refusal to be poetical in his poetry, his refusal to be either confident or vatic. They were not ready for satire, and the seriously religious did not accept that doubt could be honest or indeed other than sinful. In a partly favourable review of *Ambarvalia*, the critic in the *Guardian* was constrained to take a line which Keble would have taken:

Doubt, it may be urged, is not a Poet's Mood. At all events, states of mind and feelings, however interesting, want to be associated with outward realities, or rather to be expressed in and by them.[64]

He found himself moving farther away from belief, repelled by 'any Church or Chapel and even . . . the family prayers into which circumstances sometimes hurry me'.[65] He desired security but refused commitment; even the nebulous liberalism of Strauss and Bauer could help to move him from orthodoxy but could not satisfy him. The demythologized Christ of the second *Easter Day* gives no more authority for life than the one who 'lies and moulders low' in the first. The apparent hope of 'Say not the struggle' is the work of a man totally rejecting the specific religious categories of his age as much as the satire of *The New Decalogue*. One of the gifts of the Oxford Movement to its disciples was precision in duty and in definition. Some failed to grasp it, and the opponents then as now may say that the precision was grounded on false axioms. But for men like Clough, refusing to take anything as revealed truth, contact with the movement could end only in greater disillusion.

The movement had its castaways, partly because it took religion seriously and asked questions about it which had not been widely asked in England for a long time. Newman, Keble and Hurrell Froude set out in 1833 to question the established position as keenly as any agnostic was to question it. Theirs, however, was the kind of questioning meant to restore truth that had become obscured or neglected. The kind of questioning that led to doubt of religious fundamentals they regarded as sinful in itself and not to be considered. Unfortunately for their cause, the minds of intelligent young men will not usually keep questions running along one channel.

The retreat from all commitments which the movement engendered in some minds contains much that was becoming a commonplace of Victorian agnosticism Tractarian contro versy was only one of the means which caused people to start investigating faith and then end by doubting, often for reasons which neither believer nor unbeliever today would find convincing. Yet in their time they were tragically adequate. The doubts of the Bible set up by new criticism were very damaging in a country where faith was often close to an almost superstitious fundamentalism. 'I am sensible how heavy a clog on the exercise of my judgment has been taken off from me, since I unlearned that Bibliolatry, which I am disposed to call the greatest religious evil of England,' wrote Francis Newman,[66] a sentiment echoed by Froude's hero: 'perhaps the world has never witnessed any more grotesque idol worship than what has resulted from it in modern Bibliolatry.'[67]

The authority of the Bible was not undermined by the Tractarians, although they were against indiscriminate Bible reading. J.H.Newman had a brush with the Bible Society in reality as Markham Sutherland does in fiction. Their interpretation was, in common with the majority of their contemporaries, fundamentalist. The difference was mainly that they took the Bible as proof to support the creeds and the Church rather than as the direct source of doctrine. The Bible was to be interpreted by the Church. Here again the intention was to strengthen faith but the result was sometimes to undermine it. If the Bible was not every man's private oracle but a historical document that needed exegesis, what followed?

For some what followed critical reading was an access of the moral disgust already felt by Paine and later to be stated by Winwood Reade. The God of the Old Testament seemed capricious, revengeful: Sutherland could not understand how a Christian priest could be required to accept such ideas. Even the New Testament only shifted guilt and thus reduced individual responsibility. The doctrine of atonement had helped to produce a society that was content to pass all social problems on to a supernatural plane and to hope that they would be solved in time by another kind of divine plan. 'I felt disquietude that my moral sentiment and the Scripture were no longer in full harmony'[68] – Francis Newman's feeling was shared by Froude and Clough, for both of whom a growing social conscience was associated with the shaking of faith.

Eternal punishment was a particularly difficult doctrine. Maurice lost a Chair in London for questioning it, and Kingsley was censured for the same kind of doubts. Yet the Puseyites held it as firmly as the Evangelicals. 'I could never fear a God who kept a hell prison-house,' declared Froude's hero.[69] A very moderate follower of Tractarian ideas could preach as late as 1856 that the actions and issues of this life meant 'choosing for God or choosing against him: to be ever with Christ or to be ever separated from him'.[70] 'No, Great Unjust Judge,' exclaims Clough through his character who comes to understand where the blame lies for prostitution; 'No, I defy Thee, strike not; crush me if Thou wilt, who deserve it.'[71]

A strong ethical sense, a belief in the seriousness of consequences and the responsibility in personal action, was common to the great Victorian agnostics. It is most acutely expressed by George Eliot but it is plain in those who touched the Oxford Movement. Francis Newman believed that he was more loving and more moral after he had lost the old creed. Froude would test faith by its works. 'The test of orthodoxy is how it affects our conduct . . . the vicious life is not the consequence of the wrong belief, it is more likely the cause of it.'[72] Clough came to scorn claims to know the Will of God which could work miracles on other people and leave for the Christian

In lieu of war and robbing,
Only a little mild stock-jobbing.[73]

Now it is not difficult to understand the moral objections to Christianity as they appeared in the middle of the last century. Those already tending towards withdrawal, often for reasons connected more with clash of personality than with details of dogma, could find apparent justification. The only serious aspects of Protestant Christianity in England were the Evangelical and the Tractarian. Their exponents were earnest about religion; they made demands which invited scrutiny and challenge. The Evangelical, with his emphasis on personal conversion followed by assurance of ultimate salvation through faith alone, could seem to care little for the detailed conduct of the period between conversion and death. The Tractarian, urging a regular sacramental life and obedience to the traditional ordinances of the Church, also seemed to lose sight of practical concern for others. Great men in both parties gave the lie by their examples to these accusations; but there were others for whom they were partially true.

Further, the *odium theologicum* of Oxford in the thirties and forties was enough to disgust men whose cast of mind was of the type that finds dogma uncongenial. The disputes about doctrine, authority and, increasingly in the later years, about ritualism, could bring weariness. There were many like Pattison who came to marvel that such things could occupy intelligent men when the time offered so many other urgencies. If those who called themselves members of the Church of England could dispute so bitterly about the nature of priesthood and the doctrine of the sacraments, surely these things must turn out to be matters of indifference. When Froude's Markham Sutherland starts to ask these questions he is met by evasions, bendings and exceptions to the rules. William Arnold's hero loses patience with even the best among the Tractarians:

I don't the least mean to say that many of these men with their surplice and white-tie fiddle-faddle, were not really excellent men, better men, how often have I felt, than I; the forms which they extol and love may be a help to them but they were not, and never could be, to me; and it would be utterly impossible, when struggling for life and death with such fearful realities as sin and ignorance, to have any true sympathy with those who are ever thrusting to you as the one panacea the shape of a building or the cut of a waistcoat.[74]

These doubters came to look critically at their Church, finding her split and uncertain. They could not stand with those who also saw these things but were prepared to continue to fight to restore lost power. They were impatient for practical showing; for them, better lives were to precede and cause the ideal Church, not to proceed from it. That was the essential of many arguments in common rooms and on reading parties:

Faith and Revolt

I remember insisting to a friend that the essential part of religion was morality. My friend replied that morality was only possible to people who received power through faith to keep the commandments. But this did not satisfy me, for it seemed contrary to fact. There were persons of great excellence whose spiritual beliefs were utterly different. I could not bring myself to admit that the goodness, for instance, of a Unitarian was only apparent. After all is said, the visible conduct of men is the best test that we can have of their inward condition. If not the best, where are we to find a better?[75]

To which the orthodox Tractarian would generally reply that the inward condition and the visible conduct both depended on a right attitude to doctrine and practice as handed down by the Church from Apostolic times.

The middle-of-the-road attitude which polarized Puseyism and German rationalism and counselled steady walking between the two[76] was too tame for the best of the young men who entered the religious debate. They welcomed the ardent claims of the Tractarians; but in time it seemed that these leaders were taking their stand on the authority of a Church that had none. The dilemma drove some to Roman Catholicism, others to various shades of scepticism. They did not believe that a brighter Anglican day would come and they did not wait to see it. In terms of reputation and popularity, both those who fled and those who followed the developing Puseyite line chose a path of sorrow.

9

Last Enchantments

The first twelve years of the Oxford Movement were marked by a deep concern for doctrine and authority. Those who were drawn into involvement at that time found that their religious faith was strengthened and developed, or redirected, or shattered. Even the early years, however, produced the fringe-adherents, drawn in by the aesthetic appeal of ritual or by the excitement of coming closer to the practices of dreaded Roman Catholicism. These factors operated more frequently in succeeding years as the Tractarian teaching became more widely known, not always on insincere or shallow men. The revival became complex in its development and shaded into other aspects of the Victorian scene.

A conflict between forward and backward views of society is characteristic of nineteenth-century thought, but it is not always a conflict between progress and reaction. Both sides could claim to believe in the possibility of improving society and to be working for that end: Disraeli who made political propaganda from his view of the Middle Ages and Kingsley who satirized him for doing it; Hurrell Froude who found better times before the Reformation and his brother who found them after it. Both views could be an emotional retreat from the real pressures of the present. Within this line-up of attitudes, the Oxford Movement was essentially backward-looking. Those things which were proposed to make England a more Christian nation drew their authority as well as their

227

details from the past. The Tractarians themselves looked to the Caroline divines and far beyond them to antiquity; their opponents could see all such appeals as a betrayal of the true Protestant inheritance.

Hurrell Froude was the only one of the early leaders to conceive a strong enthusiasm for the Middle Ages. His restless seeking for the ideal Church led him to medievalism and consequent hostility to the Reformers. His work was not merely escapist or reactionary; he was one of those who taught the Church of England to get away from its historical and geographical insularity and look with wider vision. What he left to the world in his *Remains* did not spring solely from his own brain: it was part of the growing attraction of medievalism which was spreading through society and which became more characteristic of the later Puseyites than it had been of the old Tractarians. By the end of the first decade of Victoria's reign it was a subject for comic parody.[1]

The origins of nineteenth-century medievalism need no detailed discussion here. From its first stirrings at the time of Percy's *Reliques* and Walpole's Gothicism, of the forgeries of Chatterton and Macpherson, it was developed by the Romantic writers until it became a convenient holdall for anything that could chide the present age. If unrestricted individualism was the ailment, medieval collectivism could be produced as the cure; if new factories and schools were ugly, Gothic cathedrals showed how men had built in the old days. The arguments were often specious and historically ill-founded; but the myth was adequate to frame the ideas of great men. Carylyle took a medieval stick to beat the present in *Past and Present*, Ruskin wielded it after him, and William Morris also in his turn.

The Romantic attachment to the Middle Ages, and the Victorian cult which followed, did something to counteract the general bitter hostility to Roman Catholicism. It was not possible to write or paint much on medieval subjects without meeting at least the externals of that Church which was the object of so much scorn. Any reaction in favour of Catholicism was vague and scarcely theological, but in some cases it could go further. Pugin was not the only one to be converted through a process that began with the artistic senses. 'I learned the truths of the Catholic religion in the crypts of the old cathedrals of Europe.'[2] The great esteem in which Walter Scott was held helped not only to raise the status of the novel but also to make men believe that not all was bad outside Protestantism. For this reason he aroused the ire of Borrow and the praise of Keble who could write in 1838:

Whatever of good feeling and salutary prejudice exists in favour of ancient institutions, and in particular the sort of rally which this Kingdom has witnessed during the last three years, not to say the continuance of the struggle at all through the storm of the preceding – is it not in good measure attributable to the chivalrous tone which his writings have diffused over the studies and tastes of those who are now in the pride of manhood? His rod, like that of a beneficent enchanter, has touched and guarded hundreds, both men and women who would else have been reforming enthusiasts.[3]

Keble, however, was in general no medievalist. He was more concerned for the revival of daily services as the Prayer Book enjoined than for changes which could lead to 'mere aesthetic admiration'. His Confirmation poem made Charlotte Yonge think of old square pews and plain windows, though she recorded also that her mentor loved the symbols of saints' days and was not opposed to visual aids to worship.[4] Newman, too, did not follow Froude in finding the note of sanctity in the medieval Church, as he later adduced in his defence: 'I might have said, for instance, that the middle ages were as virtuous as they were believing. I might have denied that there was any violence, any superstition, any immorality, any blasphemy during them.'[5]

Froude differed from the other early Tractarians not only in his medievalism but also in his concern about architecture: the two things were soon to be more often linked. Architecture was a theological issue for those, whether critics or admirers, who did not go too deeply into the realities of the Oxford Movement. There was enough in that movement to make it a rallying-point for many who were discontented with their age for other than dogmatic reasons, and certain aspects of it joined perhaps too easily with what was developing elsewhere. It was natural for Roman Catholic apologists, and for some Anglicans, to look for strength to the undoubtedly Catholic

Middle Ages. It seemed equally natural that the architecture and craftsmanship of that period should reflect Catholic truth, and here came the alliance with the Gothic revival which was already in progress.[6]

At Cambridge the Camden Society turned its attention to the externals that should accompany the revival. Its supporters were anxious to effect a link between the doctrine and the visible manifestation of doctrine, a link which the Tractarians themselves had not been eager to make. J.M.Neale, one of the Society's most able members, declared in 1844: 'It is clear to me that the Tract writers missed one great principle, namely, the influence of aesthetics.'[7] So there emerged the onslaught on fixed pews, the restoration of ruined or desecrated chapels, the establishment of new churches 'decorated as they should be, with candlesticks, ciboriums, faldstools, lecterns, ante-pendiums, piscinas, roodlofts, and sedilia'.[8] It was unfortunate that such things could be made the signs of Catholicism for many who had not fully absorbed the Anglican interpretation of Catholic doctrine, that they sometimes became the play-things of the half-committed and the matter for controversy in which more important matters were lost to sight. 'I never could relish the Cambridge Camden Society and never augured well of it,' Newman wrote, 'though I should now be the first to confess that various excellent Catholics have come out of it.'[9]

Architecture, dragged thus into the theological arena, was already a source of controversy. The 'Battle of the Styles' had been joined between the classicists and the Gothicists and A.W.Pugin had come forward as the principal champion of Gothic. Himself a convert to Roman Catholicism, he designed a number of Anglican churches and became associated with Puseyism. The publication of his *Contrasts* in 1835 had given a source-book for the medievalists, whether theologically inclined or not, to claim that the present age showed a deterioration in design of buildings which betokened a general decline in other respects. The Gothic revival was exercised in other structures besides churches, but it came to be regarded as the fitting expression of those ideals for which the new reformers were striving. There was some point in the supposition, since the Gothic churches and cathedrals had been built for worship which was primarily sacramental, whereas the work of the classical architects in the eighteenth and early nineteenth centuries had been directed towards services in which the sermon was the focus.

Thus the classical churches like Inwood's new St Pancras could seem almost irreverent to the Puseyites. Their opponents were equally dogmatic: 'every Baptist place of worship should be Grecian, never Gothic,' said Charles Spurgeon.[10] The Evangelical Francis Close believed that 'superstition and Church architecture were coeval from the beginning'.[11] However, the divisions were not always clear-cut – Victorian divisions seldom were. Pugin found no favour with the hierarchy of his new communion; he regarded as pagan the Renaissance enthusiasms of Wiseman and fell into angry controversy with Newman and Faber.[12]

In the years immediately following Newman's secession, the theology of the Oxford Movement had thus become inextricably connected with other and more palpable questions. It is not surprising that young men who conceived enthusiasm for Anglo-Catholicism found that their allegiance seemed to involve them in more than religious belief; or that they often came to belief through devious ways and sometimes left it again. Of those who did so, there were some in whom the Oxford Movement might have found a second revival as great as the first and whose dedication might have enriched the Church of England. The undergraduates who in the early fifties formed for a brief time the 'Brotherhood' were united in the acceptance of the new type of Anglicanism. Three of them lived to make notable contributions in the arts.

Richard Watson Dixon was the only one who held firm to the Church of England and the ideal of ordination which the others had shared. It is perhaps significant that he was a convert, the son of a distinguished Methodist minister who had been President of the Methodist Conference. The family Methodism was of the Wesleyan type, feeling closer to the Church of England than to other dissenters, and there does not seem to have been any upheaval when Richard was confirmed at the age of fourteen. At King Edward's School, Birmingham, his headmaster was James Prince Lee who had been a master under Arnold at Rugby: another Clough might have been due to develop, but it was not so. Dixon went up to Oxford in 1852 and entered Pembroke College. In the following January he was joined, at Exeter College, by a schoolfriend called Edward Jones.

Edward Burne-Jones, to give him the name by which he is better known, had advanced further in Puseyism. His letters when he was sixteen already showed an interest in doctrine and particularly in the comparative beliefs of different Christian groups. He was drawn to the High Church side at first by aesthetic appeal which made him revolt against the austerity of the Evangelical worship which his family at that time attended. Frequent holiday visits to relatives at Hereford brought him into the company of John Goss, a young priest who had been at Oxford 'during the soul-searching time of Newman's secession from the Anglican Church'.[13] Still at school, he made himself a strong apologist for the Puseyite side at the time of the Gorham controversy. Oxford, as we shall see, brought some disillusion; but 'there, shoulder to shoulder, stood his life's companion'.[14]

This was the young William Morris, whose love of the Middle Ages was, according to his first biographer, 'born in him'.[15] What was lacking in the environment of an Evangelical home was to some extent supplied by the old churches and country houses which survived within easy reach of his Essex family house. His boyhood showed the beginnings of the self-willed revolt against environment which made a rebel out of what ought, by all probabilities, to have been a typical middle-class Victorian. He went to Marlborough, one of the recently founded schools which were developing after Arnold's example instead of after the cheerful but often brutal anarchism of the old foundations. Here he disliked the new cult of sport, but found opportunities to read his way into a good knowledge of medieval English architecture.

Here too he found a school where the official religion tended towards Tractarianism, though it was in no sense a direct product of the movement. When he left for some private coaching before going up to Oxford his tutor was F.B.Guy, a friend of R.W.Church and himself one of the devoted remnant that had survived the 1845 collapse. In a later memoir, Morris seems to place his coming under 'the influence of the High Church or Puseyite school' at the time of his entry to Exeter College in 1853.[16] The process must in fact have begun considerably earlier, but it burgeoned when he found himself at last in the company of friends who could share his opinions and all that went with them.

The Brotherhood which they formed was a product of the confluence of Anglo-Catholic theology and current beliefs about art; there was, as we shall see, more than this to its foundation and its disintegration, but in its period of enthusiasm the mark of the age was clear. The little group looked forward to the time when they could continue what Oxford had begun, living as a community dedicated to the service of society through religion and concomitant art. It was a natural enough ideal for earnest young men; its particular blend, and its sense of the beneficial power of art, make it local in time.

The idea of ordination was common to them, rather perhaps as an accepted future step than as a vocation to be constantly tested before acceptance. Dixon, who eventually took orders, remembered,

We never spoke of it to one another: and I am sorry to say, for my own part, that it was not contemplated, or kept before the mind. The bond was poetry and indefinite artistic and literary aspirations: but not of a selfish character, or rather not of a selfseeking character. We all had the notion of doing great things for men: in our own way, however: according to our own will and bent.[17]

In the last phrase is told perhaps one reason why the union did not endure. A common interest in poetry and painting, with consciences commonly stirred by Church teaching, brought aspirations of doing something for the world. The firm discipline, the hard logical thought of the Tractarians, was lacking. Each hoped to follow his artistic vocation after ordination, but ordination was not being taken seriously enough to provide the unifying factor. The spirit that governed them came from the most ebullient but least stable of the writers of the Tracts:

Edward [Burne-Jones] hoped to form among his friends a small conventional society of cleric and lay members working in the heart

233

of London, such as that suggested in Hurrell Froude's Project for the Revival of Religion in Great Towns.[18]

For a time, however, there was gaiety and enthusiasm. They met, some half-dozen of them, and sat up in college rooms discussing literature, painting, architecture – and the regeneration of society. They read *Sintram*, whose occultism had its effect later on the painting of Burne-Jones and the poetry of Morris and Dixon. They read and delighted in the author whom *Sintram* had influenced. Morris in particular seems to have been deeply impressed by *The Heir of Redclyffe*, a fact which need not surprise us, though it is not the favourite reading of even idealistic undergraduates nowadays. What Charlotte Yonge learned from Keble was well removed from Hurrell Froude's medievalism, but she was enough of a child of her time to project into novels of contemporary life the fancied ideals of medieval chivalry. Morris found Guy de Morville a good model for imitation.

In fact, Morris seems to have been one of the most devout members of the Brotherhood. He, with Burne-Jones, was regular at daily service – considered to be one of the distinctive marks of a Puseyite. A poem which he wrote at this time is strong in Anglo-Catholic sentiment and symbolism; not, it must be admitted, in many other ways. A few of the opening stanzas are worth quoting to show where his attachment lay when the Brotherhood was still strong and before the more familiar years of socialist activity and writing:

> 'Twas in Church on Palm Sunday,
> Listening what the priest did say
> Of the kiss that did betray,
>
> That the thought did come to me,
> How the olives used to be
> Growing in Gethsemane.
>
> That the thoughts upon me came
> Of the lantern's steady flame,
> Of the softly whispered name.
>
> Of how kiss and words did sound
> While the olives stood around,
> While the robe lay on the ground.[19]

234

Not, one may say, the Morris that posterity knows; yet in imagination, visual sense, sympathy, perhaps not so far removed.

Yet it was not long before the little Brotherhood was breaking up and the dream of an ascetic community of outgoing goodness was shattered. By the third year, new influences were replacing the straight Puseyite devotionalism. 'Art and literature were no longer to be thought of as handmaids to religion, but as ends to be pursued for their own sake, not indeed as a means of gaining livelihood, but as a means of realizing life.'[20] Behind this decision lay on the one hand the reading of Kingsley, whose *Yeast* had competed for popularity with *The Heir of Redclyffe* and triumphed; social service was no longer connected in their minds with Anglo-Catholic asceticism and conventual rules. On the other hand there was Ruskin whose *On the Nature of Gothic* had produced new and exciting ideas about the function of art in society. For Ruskin was no traitor to those who found their ideal in the Middle Ages but he would guide their enthusiasm along new paths. He did not believe that church-building was the highest form of architectural activity; indeed, when he later founded the Guild of St George, he declared that a clergyman had no need of a church at all in order to do his duty.

More to the immediate purpose of the Brotherhood, Ruskin had set out on his own crusade to save the Gothic revival from Catholicism. In his *Notes on the Construction of Sheepfolds* which closely followed the first of *The Stones of Venice*, he in effect exhorted Puseyites and Evangelicals to compound their differences, remember that they were Protestants and not fall into the Roman snare by an aesthetic bait. When Morris and the others read Ruskin's work *On the Nature of Gothic*, 'it seemed to point out a new road on which we should travel'.[21] It was a road away from the Church. Already the abundant energy of Morris was being directed towards the publication of a magazine to promulgate the ideals which had so lately been designed to emerge through a religious community.

Great movements, and little ones too, have their focal points. Causes are complex, but there is often the moment when the beginning or the end is held in time and preserved for the future. The moment for the Brotherhood came in the Long

Vacation of 1855 when Morris and Burne-Jones walked together on the quays of Le Havre and decided not to go on to ordination. They were to leave Oxford as soon as possible; then Burne-Jones would become a painter and Morris an architect. Morris made his apologia and outlined his new creed in a letter to his mother a few months later:

I wish now to be an architect, an occupation I have often had hankerings after, even during the time when I intended taking Holy Orders; the signs of which hankerings you yourself have doubtless often seen. I think I can imagine some of your objections, reasonable ones too, to this profession – I hope I shall be able to relieve them. First I suppose you think that you have as it were thrown away money on my kind of apprenticeship for the Ministry; let your mind be easy on this score; for, in the first place, an University education fits a man about as much for being a ship-captain as a pastor of souls: besides your money has by no means been thrown away, if the love of friends faithful and true, friends first seen and loved here, if this love is something priceless, and not to be bought again anywhere and by any means: if moreover by living here and seeing evil and sin in its foulest and coarsest forms, as one does day by day, I have learned to hate any form of sin, and to wish to fight against it, is this not well too?[22]

The aspirations look forward to Morris's life-work, but there is a familiar note as well. Oxford and the Established Church had been found wanting; the demand for action came to him as it had come to Clough and J.A.Froude in the previous decade. Yet Oxford had given something – the first experience of life and the friendships which had made secession doubly hard for Newman and those who followed him.

Why did the Brotherhood come into being, and why did it break up? Charlotte Yonge and Kingsley and Ruskin had their parts to play, but literary experience alone does not explain all. The causes may be found to lead to the ultimate failure. For this was an association of young men, idealistic and clever, who were high in expectations that were not fulfilled. As schoolboys they had heard of the events at Oxford in the years when the new movement seemed near to extinction. It was a challenge and a hope. Once they came near to the source of those great twelve years, could they not relive the fight and begin to work for the revival that was meeting so much opposition in the country at large? The reality was disappointing and the failure of the Brotherhood was inherent in its formation. When Burne-Jones came up in 1853:

He had believed that help and strength for the life he had chosen must await him in the University which had so lately been the centre of a great religious movement. Newman's simple and lofty exhortations had sunk into his heart, and created there such a belief in the writer as to make even the secession to Rome seem an act upon which it was impossible to pass judgment, and which time alone could shew whether he himself might not feel bound to follow. He had thought to find the place still warm from the fervour of the learned and pious men who had shaken the whole land by their cry of danger within and without the Church. To him it was like a room from which someone he loved had just gone out, and where at every turn he would find traces of his friend. But when he got there the whole life seemed to him languid and indifferent, with scarcely anything left to shew the fiery time so lately past.[23]

The dissatisfaction of one young man with his University proves nothing; but there is no doubt that Oxford in the fifties was in a poor state generally. It was being pushed into the modern world and resisting the process as much as possible. The young men who were content to row and hunt found ample scope, with tolerance for their academic shortcomings. Those who came with higher ideals were liable to pass from incredulity to despair. Dixon was no happier about Pembroke College than Morris and Burne-Jones were about Exeter:

I did not find it in a good state. The Master did nothing in tuition except a Sunday lecture in Greek Testament. There was very little discipline, no social intercourse between the fellows and the undergraduates, and Collections were merely a nominal ceremony.[24]

The evidence does not depend on the members of the Brotherhood alone. In the years following the rout of the Tractarians, Oxford had sunk back into a state comparable to that of England in the early Hanoverian period. Enthusiasm was distrusted and a polite man did not go to extremes in religion. To Mark Pattison, it was a return to sanity, a release from the bitterness and obscurantism of the movement which had for a time engulfed him. Matthew Arnold, no better

friend than Pattison of the Tractarians, was more insightful.
Writing from Oxford when the Brotherhood was in its brief
heyday in 1854 he noted:

The place, in losing Newman and his followers, has lost its
religious movement, which after all kept it from stagnating, and has
not yet, so far as I can see, got anything better.[25]

The passions of the previous decade were outwardly stilled:
the new intellectual ferment of the next decade, beginning
with *Essays and Reviews*, was not yet stirring. Darwin had not
published his findings; Newman and Kingsley had not refought the old battle. The Puseyite strength which was to
reassert itself at Oxford even later in the century was dormant
– many thought it moribund.

While Newman was there, Oxford offered a leader to those
minded for hard theological thinking. Almost every account of
the time, whether hostile or friendly to him, acknowledges his
greatness and his influence over undergraduates. Even from
exile he still spoke. Burne-Jones read his sermons and remembered them: 'he taught me so much I do mind – things that
will never be out of me.'[26] There was no one to take his place
in the Oxford of reality; Pusey was devout and learned and
patiently guiding the movement to wider national influence,
but he lacked Newman's charisma. Burne-Jones at one point
took his religious worries to Charles Marriott, that good man
who now held Newman's old incumbency of St Mary's. The
interview brought 'some relief, but the whole-hearted,
enthusiastic and unenquiring days were gone'.[27]

Inevitably, there were Roman worries in those years when
so many were leaving the Church of England and when questions of authority were being discussed. Burne-Jones went up
with the feeling that he might one day have to follow Newman,
and by 1855, when the Brotherhood was starting to disinte-
grate, one of its members noted sadly that 'Ted is too Catholic
to be ordained'.[28] Both Burne-Jones and Morris conceived a
great regard for the theological writings of Robert Wilberforce,
whose secession in 1854 came near to carrying them over as
well. But it was not long before doubts about authority gave
way to more fundamental doubts of the kind which had
troubled Froude and Clough:

I don't think even if I get through Greats that I shall take my B.A., because they won't allow you not to sign the 39 Articles unless you declare that you are 'extra Ecclesiam Anglicanam' which I'm not, and don't intend to be, and I won't sign the 39 Articles.[29]

Further than all this, the ideals of the Brotherhood revealed tensions which were at the time apparently insoluble. Their social ideals were swept up in the concern about the state of society which was manifesting itself in various ways. There was growing dissatisfaction with the materialism and competition on which an increasingly productive society was developing. The creed of *laissez-faire* seemed intolerable to those who could discern its results in indifference to suffering and abnegation of personal responsibility for society – to the Dickens of *Bleak House* and *Hard Times*, to Carlyle, to Ruskin, to Kingsley, none of whom had any sympathy with Puseyism. The social conscience of the Oxford Movement was not yet developed and Christian Socialism was in Broad Church hands. The days of the Guild of St Matthew and the Christian Social Union were far ahead. The noble work already being done by Tractarian priests in slum parishes grew from simple Christian compassion and was not yet systematized or publicized.

The great idealism of some contemporary thinkers was a contrast to the apparent stagnation of Oxford. Morris was reading *Past and Present* and *The French Revolution* by 1855. Those who were 'united in an ideal conspiracy to reform society by means of beauty'[30] found that their mentors were not theologians but writers who looked to a combination of political remedies with a change of heart coming from individual will rather than the stirrings of divine grace. Puseyism missed some opportunities in the fifties: it may be that the later developments vindicate the need to keep still and reconsolidate at that time. Another failure to hold the older men – which might have resulted from a direct incursion into social problems – would very possibly have been fatal to the revival.

The medieval and archaeological concerns of Anglo-Catholics proved to be false friends. There were many who, captivated by the wider Gothic revival and its artistic possibilities, were drawn into believing that they were in sympathy with a religious movement whose real demands they had never faced. The quiet devotionalism of Charlotte Yonge and Christina Rossetti was a long way from the fussy concern about vestments and ceremonial minutiae. Burne-Jones was reading the old ballads before he developed his Puseyite sympathies and Morris was studying old brasses in the Essex churches at an equally early age. Those who came to Puseyism by way of medievalism seldom found their way to the heart of either. That is a hard saying as applied to William Morris, but it is true. Certainly he had a profound knowledge of medieval archaeology and art, out of which he contributed inestimably to raising the standards of taste in his own time. Yet the Middle Ages were always for him a source of inspiration and justification for the immediate enthusiasm. He did not come to the understanding of medieval theology which, approve or scorn it as we may, is the root of medieval life.

For the Brotherhood, and for others whose names are forgotten, the alliance of medieval and Puseyite strains was not a holy one. It was harmful to their art as well as their peace of mind. The catalogues of basnets and salades in Morris's poetry, the draperies and ornaments of Burne-Jones's paintings, are distractions from the tougher purpose which they both held and often actualized. The externals of medievalism were too easily accepted and depicted, in words or in paint: they could be symbols of concepts which had not been absorbed deeply enough to bear the symbolizing. Religious doctrines which had not been adequately pondered and tested by personal conviction could be comfortably distanced in medieval terms. In a time of uncertainty, lacking great leaders, there was not enough direction of the enthusiasts. No wonder Newman was distrustful of the medieval revival.

Yet the collapse of the Brotherhood was not a disaster. For its most able members there came instead a set of new vocations, a realism less pessimistic than that of Clough and Matthew Arnold. They went their ways, Dixon alone returning to Oxford to prepare for ordination after a short period of trying to become a painter under the tuition of Dante Gabriel Rossetti. Thus he touched the world of the Pre-Raphaelites for whom medievalism was part of the original manifesto and with whom Morris and Burne-Jones became more deeply involved. Their connection changed the nature of that other brotherhood, for Rossetti's friendship with the two young men from Oxford 'virtually marks the break-up of the earlier Pre-Raphaelite movement. From then on, Rossetti's associations were more and more with the younger men.'[31] Neither Morris nor Burne-Jones was formally a member of that movement, but they were associated with it in the public view and they absorbed some of its ideals into their own. Burne-Jones brought new decorative techniques to bear on the romanticized medieval themes. Morris, with his social conscience, took what he needed from Rossetti and applied it to the fierce political struggle of ensuing years. As late as 1880, Morris and Burne-Jones could be associated with the Rossettis, Swinburne and Pater in a general attack on aestheticism.[32]

In the original Pre-Raphaelites the tenuous connection between medievalism and Puseyism was even more marked. If they painted medieval subjects they would depict the types of vestment and ecclesiastical ornaments which the Puseyites were trying to restore to Anglican worship. The religious themes were not entirely accidental. Ford Madox Brown – not an actual member of the movement – had introduced Rossetti to the work of Overbeck and the Nazarenes, whose primitivism in painting was produced in a community on religious lines. Kingsley made one of his frequent blanket condemnations when he scorned the 'meagre eclecticism of the ancient religious schools, and of your modern Overbecks and Pugins'.[33]

The subsequent career of William Morris is not matter for the present study, though its total value to the Victorian age and what came after is only now being fully recognized. The effects of his early enthusiasms remained throughout his multifarious activities. He could still commend himself to churchmen; J.H. Shorthouse thought his medieval treatment superior to that of Tennyson – who had been another hero of the Brotherhood. For Shorthouse, Morris's *Defence of Guenevere*, 'speaking advisedly, is the most wonderful reproduction of the tone of thought and feeling of a past age that has ever been achieved'. Tennyson he finds too modernizing: 'The character of the knights, especially of Lancelot, is precisely that of a modern highly-bred gentleman, with a dash of the Balaclava officer.'[34] Mackonochie of St Alban's, Holborn, later involved in the determined official attempt to suppress ritualism, was an early customer of the firm of decorative artists which Morris founded. Both Morris and Burne-Jones executed work for churches in the later Puseyite tradition which resulted in a great deal of ecclesiastical building and decoration from the sixties onwards.

The medieval strain continued in his Socialism and gave a glow of warmth and colour to the arid squabbles of conflicting groups in which he was almost always the sufferer. Its appearance in his poetry is plain enough, though it had to compete with his love of classical myth and Nordic sagas. It is more significant, as revealing both the insight and the misunderstanding with which he approached the Middle Ages, in the prose works *A Dream of John Ball* (1886) and *News From Nowhere* (1890). The ideal of a dedicated community, small in contrast to the growth of modern social groupings, devoted to the common good and the general betterment of society, survived the decline of orthodox faith. A letter written in 1874 looks back to the years of the Brotherhood and forward to the prose visions:

Suppose people lived in little communities among gardens and green fields, so that you could be in the country in five minutes' walk, and had few wants, almost no furniture for instance, and no servants, and studied the (difficult) arts of enjoying life, and finding out what they really wanted: then I think one might hope civilization had really begun.[35]

He continued to share Pugin's distaste for late Renaissance styles and to urge the medieval. His respect for ancient buildings was salutary in a period when 'restoration' as often as not meant destruction. Sometimes his enthusiasm carried him too far, as when he unsuccessfully resisted in Convocation the decision to deal with the medieval statues on the spire of St Mary's which were simply unsafe as they were. In this, and in other ways, the old loves of the Brotherhood were not deserted. He asked Dixon to conduct his marriage service and the friends met again in 1874, when Dixon found him still 'genial, gentle, delightful'.[36]

For Dixon the road had been closer to the one originally planned. His return to Oxford brought him academic honour when he was awarded the Arnold Historical Essay Prize for his work on 'The Close of the Tenth Century of the Christian Era' – foreshadowing the interest which he later poeticized in *Mano*. During his period as a curate in London he published his first volume of poems, *Christ's Company* (1861), a synthesis – or rather a mixture – of the medieval and Puseyite interests with Pre-Raphaelitism and a growing attachment to Browning. Contemporary opinion regarded these strains as neither productive of good poetry nor suitable for a clergyman:

> His religious feeling is of a morbid and sombre kind; he makes his devotions gloomily, in sackcloth and ashes. His poems display thought; but his reflective powers are obscured by diseased imagination and bad taste.[37]

However, Dixon's subsequent life was tranquil enough. He taught at Highgate and Carlisle and ended his days as a Canon of Carlisle. The poetry which he continued to produce is worth consideration in the light of those early ideals which he had shared with Morris. The work of the latter is better known, and justly so, but Dixon has qualities that are far from negligible. Besides, he retained the Christian faith of his youth, though not a great deal of his poetry after the first volume is explicitly devotional. It is perhaps a symptom of the uncertainties which led them to pursue so many different hares when they were undergraduates that neither Morris nor Dixon ever really acquired the hard craft of poetry. The mental discipline that they might have gained from a real understanding of the Tractarian spirit would also have guided them to a discovery of their unique contributions to poetry. Morris kept poetry as his first love but often strayed away into other modes of expression, and though he rationalized the infidelity as a necessary sacrifice in difficult times, he may have unconsciously realized that he had never quite come to terms with poetry as a commitment.

For Dixon, slighter in talent, the lack of basic strength is more obvious and the amount of direct derivation is painful. He had a gift for observation of nature, minute and accurate, which too often slides away into an attempt at Wordsworthian philosophizing that does not succeed: the poems which have the ominous word 'Ode' in their titles are examples. The opening of 'To Summer' in the volume of *Historic Odes* published in 1864 almost passes belief even in an age when young poets often started by imitating Keats:

> Thou who dost set the prop to crooked arms
> Of apple-trees that labour with their store;
> Who givest sunshine to the nestling farms
> Along the valley, that their roofs may pore
> More placidly upon the open sky. . . .

Yet through the slavish derivation there are heard the faint cries of an original poet trying to get out.

Now Dixon could in fact do much better than this; and he could also have more interesting failures. What has been said about the convenient distancing effect of medievalism is well illustrated by the poem 'Love's Consolation' from the early *Christ's Company*. Here a very commonplace thought is extended in imagery that vaguely suggests an unspecified medieval setting and which also carries Romantic overtones which make the piece 'poetical' in the way that readers in 1861 still generally expected. The following extract will serve to illustrate all this, and something more:

> All who have loved, be sure of this from me
> That to have touched one little ripple free
> Of golden hair, or held a little hand
> Very long since, is better than to stand
> Rolled up in vestures stiff with golden thread,
> Upon a throne o'er many a bowing head
> Of adulators; yea, and to have seen
> Thy lady walking in a garden green
> Mid apple blossoms and green twisted boughs,
> Along the golden gravel path, to house
> Herself, where thou art watching far below,
> Deep in thy bower impervious, even though
> Thou never give her kisses after that,
> Is sweeter than to never break the flat
> Of thy soul's rising, like a river tide
> That never foams.

The mildly amorous suggestions of touching hair and hand could be forgiven a clergyman if they appeared in a setting thus remote. The spiritualized sexual image at the end drew no comment and was almost certainly quite unconscious; but what tensions did the Puseyite praise of celibacy and the derived feelings of guilt lay on young adherents? We may forgive Dixon the split infinitive; after all, Browning produced an almost identical one.

Dixon could do much better with his imagery and with the suppressions that they concealed. The river and the passion return in the simply titled 'Song' from the later *Lyrical Poems* (1887) which can stand more firmly by itself:

> If thou wast still, O stream
> Thou would'st be frozen now:
> And 'neath an icy shield
> Thy current warm would flow.
>
> But wild thou art and rough;
> And so the bitter breeze,
> That chafes thy shuddering waves
> May never bid thee freeze.

One more example must suffice: 'The Wizard's Funeral', which also appeared in *Christ's Company*. Here the imprecise images of Romantic medievalism take on force just because of their imprecision. Yet there is woven with them the horror of Victorian funereal pomp and of a spiritual state in which good and evil mingle without certainty of the final resting-place. William Morris could feel the horror and the occult too, notably in such early poems as 'Shameful Death', 'In Prison' and 'The Haystack in the Floods', but never, I think, did he produce anything of this quality:

> For me, for me, two horses wait,
> Two horses stand before my gate:
> Their vast black plumes on high are cast,
> Their black manes swing in the midnight blast,
> Red sparkles from their eyes fly fast.
> But can they drag the hearse behind,
> Whose black plumes mystify the wind?
> What a thing for this heap of bones and hair!
> Despair, despair!
> Yet think of half the world's winged shapes
> Which have come to thee wondering:

At thee the terrible idiot gapes,
At thee the running devil japes,
And angels stoop to thee and sing
From the soft midnight that enwraps
Their limbs, so gently, sadly fair;
Thou seest the stars shine through their hair.
I go to a mansion that shall outlast;
And the stoled priest that steps before
Shall turn and welcome me at the door.

The break-up of the Brotherhood was not done without pain.

One of the happier events in Dixon's life was his friendship, carried on mainly by correspondence, with Gerard Manley Hopkins whom he had taught for a while at Highgate School. By this time Hopkins was a Roman Catholic and in his Jesuit novitiate. It is a shining light in that age of *odium theologicum*, to which the Tractarians contributed their full share, to read the courteous exchanges between the two priests of different obediences. Their interest was largely in poetry: Hopkins praised Dixon's work but suggested, not unreasonably, that he was a follower of Morris. Dixon would have none of it; by 1881 even the bonds of friendship would not allow him to approve of the way in which Morris had gone: 'His creed, that is, his ideas of life, is to me monstrous and insupportable.'[38] Hopkins returned to the point, however, and noted the modern romanticizing of medievalism common to both poets. By this time Burne-Jones was faring no better: Dixon praises him as a painter but adds: 'I am out of sympathy with him.' Death makes him more charitable to Rossetti – 'one of my dearest friends'.[39]

Dixon, though never an advanced Puseyite, had hardened in the Tractarian line and was inclined to condemn deviations in belief as actual sin. In another way, too, he looked back to the early years of the Oxford Movement, as the loose medievalism of the Brotherhood found more academic expression in a tradition derived from Hurrell Froude. Dixon's *History of the Church of England from the Abolition of Roman Jurisdiction*, on which he worked from 1878 until his death, shows a strong bias against the leaders of the Reformation and a regret for many aspects of the Church of the Middle Ages. It is still of value as an ecclesiastical history; and what Dixon too often failed to achieve in verse he accomplished in prose. He writes clearly, elegantly, evocatively of the age which he describes. His human compassion as well as his theology makes him a critic of events which were popularly esteemed. 'The doings of the Reformation in Ireland were abominable,' he confided to Hopkins. Requesting some information on records of the Jesuit order to help with his *History*, he promised: 'I hope, as I go on, to do some sort of justice to its holy devotion, even if the cause be not wholly my own.'[40]

It was a rare gift of ecumenism for the age, a mastery of the old bigotry against Rome even if agnostics and the unorthodox were still excluded. Dixon is a man who makes the reader wish, foolishly no doubt, that his poetry were equal to his better achievements of personality and execution. Christina Rossetti was acute in her opinion when Dante Gabriel sent her Dixon's poems in 1875:

> Many thanks indeed for bringing Mamma and me acquainted with a poet. She is greatly impressed with the sublime beauty of some part and I with the frequent excellence . . . Do you think the rock, if any, Mr Dixon tends to split on is dryness? [41]

D.M. Dolben (1848–67) owes the memory of his name and work almost entirely to Robert Bridges, who was his contemporary and friend at Eton. It was Bridges too, no adherent of Puseyism in his adult years, who helped to revive Dixon's poetry. Dolben is worth a little consideration, since his writing is not easily obtainable, as an example of the effect of extreme Puseyism on an impressionable youth in the decade after the Brotherhood. It is interesting to see how the externals, and particularly the medievalism, work their fascination as symbols of revolt against the pressures of the age. Dolben, deeply religious from childhood, was caught up in the advance of Oxford Movement ideas and practices after the recession of the fifties.

At Eton both Bridges and Dolben were Puseyites; Bridges did not know, or did not care to recall, how the influence worked on them but suggests that it may have been through *The Christian Year;* this seems too easy an appeal to a famous work. Dolben certainly came under the influence of Euseby Cleaver of St Barnabas, Pimlico, formerly the church of

W.J.E.Bennett and the scene of anti-ritualist riots. Like Morris and Burne-Jones before them they were set on ordination – 'neither of us at that time doubted that our *toga virilis* would be the cassock of a priest or the habit of a monk'.[42] They read Tennyson, Browning and Ruskin; and Dolben developed a liking for the hymns of Frederick Faber, which Bridges did not share.

Dolben's practices were too much for Eton, from which he was quietly removed. English public schools can bear a good deal with equanimity, but a century ago the religious temper was too sensitive to allow the spectacle of a supposedly Protestant boy crossing himself before meals. Even worse, he used to conceal the breakfasts of the boys in his house so that they would communicate fasting; and he used to visit without discrimination Roman and Anglo-Catholic communities in the vicinity of the school. He attached himself to the new Anglican Benedictines and thus came under that strange man Father Ignatius[43] and had the thrill of meeting Pusey himself. At about this time he seems to have been contemplating forming his own community of friends of a kind similar to that planned by the Brotherhood ten years before.

His longed-for going to Oxford, the source of the movement he loved, had to be deferred while he went to read with a private tutor as Morris had done. Like many young Anglo-Catholics, then and now, Dolben displayed an intolerant contempt for the ordinary parochial worship of the Church of England and wrote complaining to Bridges:

> Now to go down to Hereford, and remain there a *year* . . . without Confessor, without any means of more than monthly Communion, without (I must use it) any 'Catholic advantages', this may be a good way to get into Balliol but not, I think, into Heaven. If I were near Oxford, all this would be avoided.[44]

At this time he was increasingly horrified by the desecration of old churches, the ruined shrines, the altar-stones used for paving. He visited the Birmingham Oratory in the hope of seeing Newman, who was away, but was kindly received and did not experience any contempt for his non-Roman monastic habit. 'Dolben's medievalism remained unshaken, and was alienating him more and more from the Church of England'.[45]

If he had gone up to Oxford he would perhaps have taken the path which Morris and Burne-Jones had approached and which Hopkins had recently taken. But he fainted during the matriculation examination and was failed. A short time afterwards he was drowned while bathing.

It is a story that invites conjecture, that most profitless of critical activities. The poetry which he left is all by which we may judge; and it is remarkable enough for a boy, without indicating any certainty of what might have developed. In it is plainly manifested the tensions of following Puseyism at that time, thinly masked as a tension between the classical and the medieval. Dolben loved the classics and could feel the pull of pagan irresponsibility and freedom. His monk Brother Jerome in 'From the Cloister' makes explicit the desire for something outside orthodoxy – the old authors, the myths, the worship of Apollo, 'Dear bright-haired god, in whom I half believe'.

The awareness here of 'Fra Lippo Lippi' is clear, and Dolben is as derivative as one expects a very young poet to be. He was attracted and disquieted by Clough, whose religious fever had been solved in a different way. Dolben was moved to write a reply to Clough's poem in *Ambarvalia* called 'When Israel Came out of Egypt'. Here Clough dismisses the orthodox claims to know God and his Will – and also the confident assertions of complete atheism. Dolben, taking as epigraph Clough's lines

> The clouded hill attend thou still,
> And him that went within,

wrote 'The Eternal Calvary', in which Clough's style and prosody are imitated with less than happy results:

> Not so indeed shall be our creed,
> The Man whom we rely on
> Has brought us thro' from old to new,
> From Sinai to Zion.
> For us He scaled the hill of myrrh,
> The summits of His Passion,
> And is set down upon the throne
> Of infinite Compassion.

249

Clough had also used the hexameter as an English line. Even he was not always highly successful and Dolben's attempt shows how difficult it is to do well. Four lines from 'The Pilgrim and the Knight' will suffice as an example and a warning; but particularly interesting in a bizarre way is the use of classical metre for the familiar medieval subject-matter. The muddle of mid-Victorian allegiances is verbalized:

White are the horses and white are the plumes and white are the
    vestures,
White is the heaven above with pearls that the dawning is scattering,
White beneath the flowerless fields that are hedged with the snow-
    drift,
These are the Knights of the Lord, who fought with the Beast and
    the Prophet.

Yet the brief life of Digby Mackworth Dolben is not a case-history, for all that it reveals of the impact of the Oxford Movement twenty years after Newman had left the Church of England. It is the story of a boy who lived in faith and died before either fulfilment or disillusion could come. Of a boy too who knew what poetry could mean and used it in a truly Romantic way to resolve some of his own conflict. 'He regarded it from the emotional, and I from the artistic side,' Bridges recalled.[46] The emotional release is clear in poems like 'Flowers for the Altar', where a basic and often-stated tenet of Catholic theology is poeticized with the breathless excitement of novelty. The technical words, forbidden currency in Protestant England, are given the similitude of poetic images. There is striving for sensation, but also the genuine sense of new discovery:

> Tell us, tell us, all ye faithful
> What this morning came to pass
> At the awful elevation
> In the Canon of the Mass.
> 'Very God of Very God,
> 'By whom the worlds were made,
> 'In silence and in helplessness
> 'Upon the altar laid.'

Conjecture is profitless – yes, but there must be wonder about what was lost in the death of one who could produce lines like these from 'Good Friday':

> Strong Sorrow-wrestler of Mount Calvary,
> Speak through the blackness of Thine Agony,
> Say, have I ever known Thee? answer me!
> Speak, Merciful and Mighty, lifted up
> To draw those to Thee who have power to will
> The roseate Baptism, and the bitter Cup,
> The Royal Graces of the Cross-Crowned Hill,
> Terrible Golgotha – among the bones
> Which whiten thee, as thick as splintered stones
> Where headlong rocks have crushed themselves away
> I stumble on – Is it too dark to pray?

It was a long line, an often deviating and uncertain line, from Hurrell Froude to that praise of medievalism which became a commonplace of Catholic apologetics, both Roman and Anglican, by the end of the century and on into the next. The myth linked up with some unexpected companions and was shared with men of totally different allegiances. Matthew Arnold knew the power of Oxford 'Whispering from her towers the last enchantments of the Middle Ages'.[47] Little wonder if men for whom Oxford was the source of theological wisdom could indulge also in an uncritical acceptance of the medieval myth. It was an image that could be shared outside Oxford too. The subject of the next chapter felt it as deeply as any, in the aggressively modern life of Birmingham. There too, inspired by his love of the abiding religious tradition and nurtured by his admiration for the poetry of William Morris, he could state what many felt. They were mistaken in some ways, but no source of courage is to be despised, not even

. . . that delightful long-past time when the secular and the religious life walked in amity hand-in-hand – when the king or noble collected within the walled paradise of his home all that the world recollected of learning, or had taught itself of handicraft; and in the midst of the wilderness of waving forest and of wilder men, kept alive the culture and the religion that was to bless an aftertime.[48]

IO

The Zeal of a Convert

The questions which the Tractarians asked about their
Church brought a variety of individual answers. Some were
strengthened by a more disciplined application of old High
Church principles cherished in family tradition; others were
lifted from tepid conformism into a new commitment about
their faith; some were led to believe that true holiness lay only
in Roman Catholicism; others found themselves driven from
questioning to doubt and from doubt to retreat. The movement from Protestant nonconformity to Anglicanism was
less common; there had been little mobility between the
denominations in earlier years, although the revisers of the
Book of Common Prayer in 1662 had inserted an office for
adult baptism partly to deal with the effects of Anabaptist
doctrine. The challenge of authority could be disturbing to
Anglicans but was unlikely to trouble those who dissented
from the principle that apostolic succession was a requisite of
valid sacraments. The rarity of such conversions a hundred
years ago is the first factor in the strange case of Joseph Henry
Shorthouse

That Shorthouse should often have been regarded as in the
newer Anglo-Catholic line, developed under Pusey's leadership, is a tribute to what that line produced in disciplining and
beautifying devotional life. Is it an accurate judgement?
Closer investigation does not place him among those who,
drawn perhaps by the aesthetic appeal of ceremony or the

desire for a more expressive devotional life, accepted the type of Anglo-Catholicism which was making its way particularly in town parishes. It is certain, however, that his personal change and his major literary work owe their being to the Oxford Movement. The rediscoveries and fresh emphases of the Tractarian years gave the Church of England a new image that was not always associated with ritualism.

The career of Shorthouse reveals much about the Church and also about the age. Its pressures and changes, its opportunities for the individual to make more choices about the direction of his life, are reflected in the course that took him to unexpected fame. On a superficial view which would isolate aspects of Victorianism into labelled compartments, his story is improbable. There was no apparent likelihood that a Quaker manufacturer of vitriol, born and still living in Birmingham, should become an apologist of a highly sacramental type of Anglicanism, that he should help to increase interest in the seventeenth-century Church, that he should be concerned in an attempt to relate Platonism and Christianity. Yet it was so, combined with the snobbery, the fear of socialism and the intolerant dismissal of new ideas which the period can also show abundantly. It is all as improbable and as contradictory as the Oxford Movement itself.

To see Shorthouse as a former Quaker is as important as to understand the Evangelicalism of Newman and the Wilberforces. The revival in the Church of England was able to give him what was lacking in his first faith: a deep sacramental sense, without rigid conformity or insistence on details of developed dogma. Similarly Newman had found in Rome the authority and certainty which the Church of his youth would not claim.

The year of Shorthouse's birth, 1834, was the year when the Tracts were beginning to make their influence felt. It was also a time when the Quaker community was sharing with other sections of society the tensions of a new age. The distinctive marks of drab clothing, 'plain speech' and separatism were proving less attractive to the new generation. More serious still was the 'Beacon controversy', which led some of the Evangelical Quakers to deny the primitive belief in the inward light and to seek membership of groups like the Plymouth Brethren.

Shorthouse himself was born into a traditionally conservative Quaker family. He never became entirely free from the constriction of a small and exclusive sect, coupled with parental and grandparental dominance to a degree unusual even at that time. The patriarchal sense ran from the great-grandfather who had founded the chemical works which Shorthouse himself was eventually to inherit. The more influential of his grandmothers was violently against the Church of England and proud in her memory of hearing Wesley preach. Female cousins were the companions of his boyhood; his wife and he knew one another as children. Married life was no escape from the dominance, for the couple were only once away from his father for as much as a fortnight while the latter was alive.[1]

It is not surprising that he found a father image everywhere. He once wrote to the widow of the clergyman who had baptized him that he had three fathers – his real one, the clergyman and the doctor who had saved his life as a child.[2] Add to this that he travelled little, and usually in his parents' company. He never visited Italy, about which he wrote convincingly in *John Inglesant*, and gained most of his impressions by listening to his father talking about it while shaving.[3] He did not go to Little Gidding which also has an important place in the book. The whole situation makes his literary achievement remarkable, his personal progress doubly so. How did he escape the fate of Ruskin? His marriage was happy and enduring, his mind was balanced to the end.

It is impossible to give a sure answer; there are signs that he was not unscathed and that the visionary imaginings of his books provided a necessary relief from tension. Little is recorded about the process which led him to the Church of England: there is none of the agonized self-revelation which characterizes earlier secessions to Rome, for his change was socially less alarming and the period was already more tolerant of individual choice. He and his wife started going to Church and found it congenial; they were baptized together in 1861. After his death his wife wrote: 'More and more my husband felt he could be truly happy only as a baptized member of the church of England.'[4]

The penalty followed a few months later with a severe

epileptic type of seizure which even then was attributed partly to strained relations with his family over the secession. Physical and other nervous causes were also adduced, but it needs little insight to conceive the situation of a parent-dominated young man, brought up in the notion that he was 'not strong' and already suffering from a nervous stammer, who had made such a gesture of independence. It is a credit to all concerned that the effect was not catastrophic.

Some light is thrown on his motives by a letter which he wrote to an unnamed correspondent, a Quaker who was distressed at his secession.[5] He could not help himself, he said; there was overwhelming need to join 'that plan and system of religion which I cannot doubt God has appointed for the world'. The Quaker doctrine of the indwelling of the Word was a great truth, but only a partial one. The Church of England possessed totally what Quakers and other '*so-called* Evangelical Christians' have limited. The Church has the sacraments and organization needed for the true practice of Christianity in this world – 'all that which brings *men as men* absolutely into communion with God'. Primitive Quakerism had died down into a mere sect while the Church of England stood firm as the national Church. True, the visible Church is sadly divided, but the furtherance of unity requires that a man shall attach himself to an outward and visible body of believers. (The argument about possessing totally what others had only in part had been a reason frequently brought forward by Anglican converts to Rome.)

Shorthouse continued with a passage which foreshadows his later excursions into fiction. The immanence of God, the sacramental reference of all experienced phenomena, the deep regard for the Anglican liturgy – all these are contained in *John Inglesant* and in his later novels. His feeling for them goes far to explain his conversion:

We live in a constitution ordained by God which includes all visible things, and everything on earth, belonging to the original creation, both of the world and humanity, is divine and belonging to God. The Prayer-book in this country is the only human ordinance (if it can be called a human ordinance, being nothing but the religion of the Bible arranged as a manual for daily use) that acknowledges this.

He goes on to refer his correspondent to *What is Revelation?* by Frederick Denison Maurice, another influence whose name recurs in the study of Shorthouse. 'I should like thee to read it,' he concludes, with a sudden reversion to the 'plain speech' of Quakerism.

This then is the spirit, and the zeal, which went into the making of *John Inglesant*. Shorthouse started work on the novel in 1866 and continued on and off for ten years, once leaving it aside altogether for nearly two years. Even when it was finished, it remained another four years in manuscript before being privately printed (by a Quaker printer) at the author's expense. It was distributed mostly to his own friends, but a few copies got as far as the reviewers; there were some local notices, and one in the High Church *Guardian*. Shorthouse was encouraged to send it to the venerable firm of Smith Elder, where it was brusquely rejected on the advice of James Payn that it was 'unreadable'.[6] Then Mrs Humphry Ward – improbable midwife for an Anglican novel – gave a copy to Alexander Macmillan. Affected perhaps by the Platonism in which both he and the author were interested, Macmillan decided on publication.

The appearance of *John Inglesant* under that famous imprint in 1881 attracted a good deal of critical attention. Even the *Westminster Review* found space for a brief and mainly favourable notice, although it was not prepared to give the author exalted ideas of his quality:

> Those who expect a historical novel of the brilliantly dramatic kind, which Sir Walter Scott made classic, and which Alexandre Dumas made so delightful, will be disappointed.[7]

The *Saturday Review*, noted for its acerbity in dealing with new books, was both kind and perceptive. Recognizing that Shorthouse had made an important contribution to Anglican fiction, the reviewer noticed a basic weakness in the failure to give fully convincing reasons for the hero's return from Roman to Anglican obedience:

> Inglesant's final declaration in favour of the Church of his birth takes us by surprise instead of developing itself naturally out of his past history, so that we are tempted to quarrel with the last page of the book as inconsistent and out of place, when taken by themselves

[*sic*] they contain one of the most attractive descriptions ever written of the Church of England.[8]

Nevertheless, it was the Anglican tone of the book which won many of its admirers – a sure aid to success in that age of the great man and of partizan religious opinion. The embattled Anglican Gladstone was enthusiastic about it, and was actually to be seen in a photograph 'with the second volume of *John Inglesant* on his knee – the title of the book is quite plain'.[9] Archbishop Trench, arbiter of English style, praised it in words which, if correctly quoted, suggest that his own syntax was momentarily slipping: 'a hasty glance is all which I have had for it yet, but that has made it plain that it is written in rarely good English.'[10]

The critic in the *Spectator* was able to find more profound meaning in the story: 'it mirrors the subtle complexity with which, in actual experience, the proportions of the moral life are blended with the unmoral.'[11] He contrasted Shorthouse's subtlety with the straightforward and uncomplicated morality of Charles Kingsley who, if he had used the story, would have 'had the hero undergo severe punishment for his loyal perjury'. The puzzlement which was to overtake many readers of *John Inglesant* in later years was manifested in another favourable review in *Blackwood's*, whose critic could detect the fact that Shorthouse was not destined to produce anything so important again:

The book altogether is one of the most remarkable that has been written for a long time. . . . We can scarcely guess what is the attitude, any more than what is the purpose of the author, or whether he will have anything more to say to the public, or has written his heart out in this large and singular utterance.[12]

Certainly nothing else that Shorthouse wrote either gained or deserved the fame of *John Inglesant*, which kept its popularity for many years and shed reflected brilliance on his other books. The royal Duke of Connaught read and approved it; in 1889 the *Architect* thought it worth quoting about Italian Renaissance styles.[13] The general adulation is seen in Andrew Lang's dismissive comment: 'By very considerable exertions I managed to avoid the perusal of "John Inglesant".'[14]

The plot, which is long and complex, may be briefly

summarized in its essentials. John Inglesant, child of a family which has kept Roman Catholic sympathies during the turmoil of the sixteenth century, is brought up under Jesuit influence and precipitated into the Civil War on the Royalist side. He undertakes missions for the King which bring him to trial and almost to execution when he falls into Parliament hands and is repudiated by his royal master. After his release he is briefly reunited with his twin brother, just back from a long sojourn abroad and soon to be killed by an Italian villain called Malvolti.

After the murder, Inglesant goes to France where he is tested by the demands of the active and contemplative lives and has his last meeting with Mary Collet whom he had come to love when he visited the Anglican community at Little Gidding. He goes on to Italy, in the service of the Jesuits but bent on revenge for his brother's death. He attends the conclave which elects a new Pope and is then so successful on an errand for his superiors that he is rewarded with a fief and marries an Italian girl. He meets Malvolti but finds himself unable to kill him in cold blood. The episode when Inglesant dedicates his sword in a country church was based on one that Shorthouse found in 'a very old book' and of which he said:

I am quite justified in saying that *John Inglesant* was written to lead up expressly to this one incident, and I do not think it would have been written if I had not chanced upon this beautiful story.[15]

The evidence of this comment is important: the purpose of the novel is to show Christian forgiveness, not exclusively to present the claims of the Church of England.

Later Inglesant sets off to plague-stricken Naples in search of his wife's brother. There he meets Malvolti again, now blind and the devoted member of a religious order that tends the sick. He returns to find his wife dead, goes to Rome where he is involved in the revival and suppression of the Molinists, and is for a time imprisoned. At last he returns to England, to a quiet life and membership of the Anglican Church. In the course of his long pilgrimage he has also incidentally encountered such seventeenth-century worthies as Milton, Cromwell, Hobbes and van Helmont.

The overcrowded plot reflects the preoccupations of a man living in a complex age and himself suffering from the tensions of changed religious allegiance. He chose to write about a time when the Church of England had not gained the security of eighteenth-century conformism, a time when she was challenged by Roman claims and Protestant dissent, when the power of scepticism was seeming to grow to dangerous proportions. Shorthouse of course was not the first to find parallels here with his own time; the men of 1833 had looked to the Caroline divines for justification.

Shorthouse's handling of his material has many virtues. He shows the common Victorian gift for narrative and exciting incident. Like the novelists who turned to the early Church for their apologetic subject, he can draw the reader out of the main theme into an episode of adventure and then back again. If one comes to the book as a reader not too proud and sophisticated to enjoy the kind of thing which Conan Doyle and Rider Haggard were also doing towards the end of the last century, there can be delight in the siege of Chester, the carnival in Florence, the conclave, the trial and condemnation of Molinos. Shorthouse can bring up in all its liveliness the spirit of the seventeenth century.

So well he might, reply the cynics, who point to his direct borrowings from contemporary sources. Ever since Acton – no lover of the Anglican Church – was scornful about the book, Shorthouse has been often abused as a plagiarist who took material which he could not integrate. His sources have been traced in detail and his handling of them has been condemned but also praised.[16] He himself never tried to conceal his reading, and it is rather curious that he has been blamed for doing the sort of research which no one objects to in the novels of Newman, Kingsley, Wiseman and Neale. He loved the seventeenth century and tried to make himself familiar with its details; more particularly, he wanted to evoke for his own age its true spirit:

When, many years ago, I began the book, my principal, perhaps sole object was to endeavour for my own pleasure to realize, if possible, something of the exquisite age-spirit which combined all the finest feelings of our nature, and all the sympathies of our existence, with a certain picturesqueness of tone and result, which seems to me to mark the seventeenth century. That was my first idea. The philosophy and the story developed itself as I went on, but I should have considered myself amply rewarded if I could have succeeded in catching anything of this spirit.[17]

There is no difficulty in explaining the attraction of the age and its characters for him. Molinos the Quietist was an obvious appeal to the former Quaker who was now seeing the Inner Light as only part of a wider and more sacramental system of religion – as Manning and Newman had had to fit their Evangelical presuppositions into Catholicism. 'Throughout the whole course of history few figures seem to me more calm, gracious, and beneficent than that of this Spanish priest.'[18] His love of tradition and dignity went back before his secession and did not leave him in later life. For him, anyone who entered an old church must surely feel 'a sense of the oneness of holy, if vague emotion, with that instinctive and unpremeditated art which is the mere result and reflex of ages of human life'.[19] This was not something he had newly found in the Church of England; rather it had helped to bring him to the Church. As a young Quaker he had written of his reflections in an old country church:

I thought how different a seat there must have been, with that old Crusader beside you, from two hours in the Meeting-House in Bull Street.[20]

The same feeling comes to him in his short story 'The Ringing of the Bells', and the seventeenth century is seen as the great religious age in 'Vestigia':

The seventeenth century may be said to be the key of the nineteenth; and, in more things than many would believe, our thoughts and actions and disputes are but a repetition of the thoughts and actions and disputes of two hundred years ago.[21]

The attraction goes towards explaining why he wrote his first book and why he joined the Church of England. That appeal to basic continuity despite changes of fortune and government was a fundamental appeal for loyal Anglicans in the face of secular attack. The holiness and learning of the Caroline Church was a two-edged sword; it could be wielded against the Erastians who saw the Church as a department of the State and against Romanists who charged Anglicans with never showing the marks of catholicity. We have seen how the early Tractarians, and the old High Churchmen before them, looked for strength and justification to the divines of the late sixteenth and seventeenth centuries. In the early days of the Oxford Movement, and throughout the lives of those first leaders who survived and remained Anglicans, the names often heard were Laud, Taylor, Cosin, Sparrow, Thorndike and Forbes.

For the seceders, this appeal seemed to put Anglicans into a false and limited historicism. Such pride vested in a short period of the past could seem to be a fear of development and a stubborn refusal to consider different opinions.[22] The old High Church and Cavalier tradition which Keble and Hurrell Froude brought to the Oxford Movement was no resting-place for those who were led to researches farther back into history. Some were brought to a distrust of the Reformation and an enthusiasm for medieval Catholicism, others to antiquity and the discovery of a different set of criteria.

What was the effect on Shorthouse, starting his novel over twenty years after Newman's secession and nearly thirty after the publication of Froude's *Remains*? He has tended to be associated with the Anglo-Catholic movement which had developed over those years, without full allowance for the strains and differences in that movement or for its effect on the Church of England as a whole.[23] There is indeed evidence which might suggest that he had taken Froude's path from the Caroline to the medieval. After the passage from 'Vestigia' quoted above, he goes on to praise 'the life of true romance – the life, that is, of everything that is noble and disinterested as opposed to all that is sordid and mean'. But where is this life to be found?

The seventeenth century, though possessing it very much more than the nineteenth century does, certainly possessed it very much less than the fourteenth; and yet most persons, and I among them, would consider the seventeenth century infinitely nobler than the fourteenth. Again, there is no doubt that, as we possess it much less than the seventeenth century did, so there are not wanting thinkers who maintain (as I think mistakenly but who still maintain) that our century is a nobler one than the seventeenth.[24]

This involved and muddled comparison of the possession of the noble and disinterested, which yet may not be the mark of a nobler age, was one in which even the author recognized the 'difficulty'. What it shows principally is that he, like many of his contemporaries, liked to find in the past sticks with which to beat the present. The Romantic love of medievalism has rubbed off on him as it did on some of the Tractarians, on Morris and Tennyson, on Carlyle and Ruskin, despite all their differences. For Shorthouse, the value of Tennyson's medieval world of chivalry was an almost Protestant purity in the Christ-centred religion which Lancelot professes. Such anticipations of the Reformers were to be found even in Malory where:

> So far as I remember, the Virgin Mary is never mentioned once; everywhere the knight is sworn to the service of the Son of God – everywhere His example is set forth for him to follow.[25]

When Shorthouse shows love for the Middle Ages, it is as part of his general love for the old days. Most of it appears in the romantic stories and essays which he wrote when a Quaker, such as 'Chivalry' and 'An Essay which is no Essay'. In his novels, written as an Anglican, he takes the world of the seventeenth century, or of the eighteenth, or of his own day. He was eclectic enough to see the beauty of the saints' legends and to praise the simple faith which they enshrined without feeling compelled to accept the record of miracles: 'we are not by any means obliged to pledge ourselves to the doctrine of the intercession of saints.'[26] With the same eclecticism and tolerance – his enemies might say, the same muddled thinking – he could write with qualified approval of George Borrow for having spoken out

> ... against the attempts of the Popish priests to propagate their religion, and against that school of novels which Scott brought in, the chief characteristic of which is the praise of the Stuarts and of the Catholic or High Church cavaliers. He is no doubt right to a certain extent, and however much we may differ from him in many points, we must all confess that there is much need for out-speaking on the side he takes, and that we should not stifle a man who will speak out what he thinks is true, stoutly and originally, only because we do not agree in all that he says.[27]

All of which suggests that his progress towards the Church of England was no blind following of any Puseyite ritualist line. Another passage of interest is appended to his wife's biographical account. Miss J.D.Montgomery recalls asking him where he would feel most at home, as he so clearly did not belong to the nineteenth century and he replied, laughing: 'In the fourteenth.' Her answer was: 'Yes, because you know so little about it you can imagine according to taste' – which shrewd remark contains a great deal of truth for him and for many enthusiastic medievalists before and since. She adds: 'In truth he was medieval in many ways,' but mentions only a few superficial features.[28] A memoir by an Anglican priest who had known him well says that: 'A man who could not be labelled Low Church or High Church, and was neither a Unitarian nor a Ritualist, was to the average Birmingham citizen in those days an unknown quantity.'[29] Although its polarizings are violent, this remark from a man who presumably understood ecclesiastical terminology is interesting. It may be worth looking more closely at Shorthouse's religious position.

Of his intense devotion to the Church of England after his secession there is no doubt. Both in fiction and in biographical records, it is clear that he loved his new communion and felt no desire for further change. The stability of his faith after 1861, despite the tensions which left their mark on him emotionally and physically, suggests that his decision was not based on aesthetic grounds alone. Many were so drawn, in that age when religious commitment was often far removed from any satisfaction of the senses.[30] This side of worship had its appeal for Shorthouse, but his conversion seems to have followed a path more comparable to that of Newman's towards Rome, allowing for the great differences in the men and their situations. 'His wide reading, especially of the older English divines, made the idea of an historic and national church peculiarly attractive to him.'[31]

He showed the common dislike of the convert for what he has left; he could describe a man as being 'naturally, somewhat in a fog, being a Dissenter'. Again, towards the end of his life, he was regretting 'the universal tendency towards dissenting and Salvation Army methods [which] makes the advocacy of the old-fashioned, moderate, legal Church of England method of supreme value now'.[32] The same love for the moderate and the legal had once impelled him from dissent towards the Church of England. In one of his Quaker essays, after writing admiringly of Milton, he went on:

It is peculiarly characteristic of the age in which Milton lived, and the Puritan sects among which he was brought up, and of those unprofitable and disturbing discussions on things beyond the reach of man's understanding which excited men's minds (and by the attempt to restrain which the Laudian party incurred such a load of obloquy) that Milton, a layman and political tract-writer, seems to feel no diffidence or hesitation in treating of these themes.[33]

This early opinion is a reasonable prologue to *John Inglesant*, with its admiration of structured Catholicism, whether Roman or Anglican, and its hostility to the pretensions of sectaries. Inglesant's encounter with Thorne the Puritan has the ring of personal experience and may well echo some of Shorthouse's arguments with former associates after his secession. The Puritan is treated sympathetically and allowed to have his say without extreme caricature, but in the end there is the revealing comment: 'There was something extremely pathetic in the sight of the human nature in this man struggling within him beneath the force of his Puritanism.'[34]

The Quakers in the book come out rather more attractively. It is true that Inglesant's brother calls them 'an unpleasing sort of people, silent, sullen, and of reserved character' (p. 168), but this is the comment of a fictional creation and echoes the criticism that was usual in the period. The comments in the narration are more sympathetic: Inglesant's reaction to the 'prophesying' of a Quaker woman is far from Johnsonian, for he finds her words strangely in tune with the neo-Platonic mysticism which he has been studying. The Quakers as a whole he thinks 'harmless and sober people, whose blameless lives and the elevated mysticism of their conversation, commended them to him' (p. 185). The arguments, the fidelity to the new communion and the graciousness towards the best of the old, are all reminiscent of *Loss and Gain*.

Certainly Shorthouse owed a great deal to the formative years as a Quaker, a debt comparable to that of Newman to the

Church of England. It was in the Quaker Essay Society that
his first literary effusions were read, and the impression which
they give is very different from the common idea of the
Quakers as grim, unrelaxed and uncultured. The fact was that
Quakerism was changing during his youth, and he was fortunate in finding his place among a particularly enlightened
group. Relaxation of the old severities was coming in the later
fifties, just before his conversion, though there was still opposition among the older people to secular books and particularly to the theatres – opposition manifested as strongly by
some other Protestant groups. In 1862, just after Shorthouse
had become an Anglican, the President of the Friends Reading
Society in his own Birmingham gave very cautious approval to
the reading of novels of the right type, but added that indiscriminate or frequent novel-reading 'is about the most
dangerous employment that can occupy a young person'.[35] It
is clear in *John Inglesant* that Shorthouse was not lacking in
gratitude for what the Quakers had given him, though he saw
it as imperfect just as Newman came to see Anglicanism. One
may question whether or not he was intending a compliment
when, in a later novel, he makes an earnest young agnostic
say: 'I think . . . if I could join any form of faith, I would join
the Quakers. They seem to me to be the most open to all influences of light.'[36]

That Inglesant represents a good deal of Shorthouse's own
private experience is beyond question. His analysis of his
hero's character and motives reads like self-revelation; its
admission of the desire for system and authority points to his
own religious change and is once again strangely reminiscent
of Newman:

> If I have not failed altogether in representing [Inglesant's]
> character, it will have been noticed that it was one of those which
> combine activity of thought with great faculty of reverence and of
> submission to those powers to which its fancy and taste are subor-
> dinated. These natures are enthusiastic, though generally not sup-
> posed to be so, and though little sign of it appears in their outward
> conduct; for the objects of their enthusiasm being generally differ-
> ent from those which attract most men, they are conscious that they
> have little sympathy to expect in their pursuit of them, and this
> gives their enthusiasm a reserved and cautious demeanour. They are

not, however, blindly enthusiastic, but are never satisfied till they have found some theory by which they are able to reconcile in their own minds the widest results to which their activity of thought has led them, with the submission and service which it is their delight and choice to pay to such outward systems and authorities as have pleased and attracted their taste.[37]

After he has been deeply indoctrinated by the Jesuit Sancta Clara, Inglesant visits Little Gidding and finds an unprecedented spiritual satisfaction in the tiny Anglican community which Nicholas Ferrar has there set up. Shorthouse himself never went to the site of the old house, but his book helped to stimulate an interest that was already growing. The pattern of Little Gidding, strictly Anglican and loyalist but keeping the ancient offices and honouring some at least of the conventual principles, was bound to appeal to the more moderate Anglo-Catholics who distrusted the full imitation of contemporary Roman religious orders. Shorthouse did not rediscover the story; biographies of Ferrar were already being written and one of the famous polyglot Bibles produced under his direction was on public exhibition a few years after *John Inglesant* was published.[38] Although his knowledge of Little Gidding was literary and derived, it was convincing to his readers and was, in the opinion of a modern authority on the community, 'in the main very accurate'.[39]

The visits to Little Gidding are more than passing episodes. Inglesant's brief reunion with the dying Mary Collet in Paris comes at a critical time in his fortunes when his destiny is being decided. The memory of her, and of all his former friends in her community, remains with him in Italy and helps to bring him back to his native Church. Even while he is serving the Jesuits, he carries with him the spirit of that group which combined traditional discipline with the freedom of individual decision. He thus impresses the Duke of Umbria: 'in Inglesant he had, for the first time, met a man who, walking to all appearance in the straitest paths of the Catholic Church, seemed to possess a freedom of spirit greater than the Sectaries themselves could boast'.[40]

There is the essential of the attraction which the Church of England held for Shorthouse and for many others: the *via media* to which Pusey and Keble had kept, which Newman had found impossible. Between authority and freedom, Anglicans could believe that they had the best of what extremists falsely polarized. So at last Inglesant turns back to the Church of England and pays it that tribute which is perhaps the best-known part of the book and which bears quoting again both for what it says and as a specimen of Shorthouse at his best:

The English Church, as established by the law of England, offers the supernatural to all who choose to come. It is like the Divine Being Himself, whose sun shines alike on the evil and on the good. Upon the altars of the Church the divine presence hovers as surely, to those who believe it, as it does upon the splendid altars of Rome. Thanks to circumstances which the founders of our Church did not contemplate, the way is open; it is barred by no confession, no human priest. Shall we throw this aside? It has been won for us by the death and torture of men like ourselves in bodily frame, infinitely superior to some of us in self-denial and endurance. God knows – those who know my life know too well – that I am not worthy to be named with such men; nevertheless, though we cannot endure as they did – at least do not let us needlessly throw away what they have won. It is not even a question of religious freedom only; it is a question of learning and culture in every form. I am not blind to the peculiar dangers that beset the English Church. I fear that its position, standing, as it does, a mean between two extremes, will engender indifference and sloth; and that its freedom will prevent its preserving a disciplining and organizing power, without which any community will suffer grievous damage; nevertheless, as a Church it is unique: if suffered to drop out of existence, nothing like it can ever take its place.[41]

That eulogy tells a great deal of what the Oxford Movement was about, and of the tensions which could bring tragedy as well as peace to its followers.

It centres on the gift of that movement to the Church of England, which perhaps above all other aspects affected the lives of individual worshippers. A restoration of the sacramental sense, not as peripheral or subordinated to exposition but as the centre of worship, was the thing that had been most needed in 1833. From that emphasis, with the concomitant claim of a priesthood in Apostolic line, all else may be seen to follow. It was this which went a long way in the process that drew Shorthouse away from Quakerism. He does not seem to have required very frequent celebrations, in the manner of the more 'advanced' Puseyites. Rather was it the reverence of administration and reception, the sense of Divine Presence, that chiefly moved him. At Little Gidding, the sacrament is celebrated only once a month, but with preparation by each communicant and with great devotion. Inglesant receives the elements and contemplates the figure of Christ in the painted window, 'and stillness and peace unspeakable, and life, and light, and sweetness, filled his mind. He was lost in a sense of rapture, and earth and all that surrounded him faded away'. In after times, the memory of that communion 'prevented that craving after the sacrifice of the Mass, which doubtless is one of the strongest of all the motives which lead men to Rome'.[42] Nor was this merely historical romanticizing. In a later novel with a contemporary setting the same mystic unity with the immanent divinity is felt. The celebration again is only monthly, the communicants are generally few, but:

There was a solemn hush and stillness in the air, and over the whole parish, at that particular moment, as though something mysterious and beyond the common was taking place. This was especially the case on fine summer Sundays, after the first service was over when, on ordinary days, boys and young men lingered about the churchyard and the village road. On these first Sundays of the month no one was to be seen. At such times there was a stillness and pause, during which Nature herself seemed to hold her breath, and the yew trees, and the apple orchards, and the rows of stately elms, lay passive and silent in the sunlight glow, and seemed to own and to proclaim a Presence, which was of earth and yet divine, to await the tread of the feet of heavenly messengers, the rustle of angelic wings, the gift of heavenly food that nourishes all conditions and ranks alike.[43]

This deep sacramental sense, involving all natural things in the divine purpose, was a tenet of the Tractarians and especially of John Keble. For Shorthouse it was felt so strongly that he could even accept the medieval notion of the validity of a grass-sacrament if the normal elements were lacking in extremity.[44] The Anglican service gave him a oneness with Christ which he had never experienced before:

The sacrament and Christ feel to me one and the same. At least, the sacrament seems to me the means by which Christ reveals himself to us, through the medium of that, as I call it 'idea of Christ' – the forces that *are* Christ, not were.[45]

Yet he retained some of the Quaker independence and could not accept all the Anglican discipline about communion. He wanted to see an open table, to which all should be admitted without conditions; even the agnostic should participate, to gain more sympathy with religion and a sense of unity with believers.[46]

Thus, except perhaps for that last piece of liberalism, he held the position of those who had received the early Tracts with enthusiasm and then drawn back in face of ritual and Romanist tendencies. It is notable that for years his favourite devotional work was Wilberforce's *Eucharistica*.[47] It was with the voice of an old-fashioned High Churchman that he could say: 'I trace what declension there was in Church life in the eighteenth century to the fact that the *conscience* of the clergy went with the non-jurors.'[48] He shared the High Church sense of historical continuity, of an institution divinely ordained and offering the means of salvation. He had a particular attachment to *The Christian Year* even in his Quaker youth and he continued to read to his wife the appropriate poem for each Sunday. When the sight of one eye had gone, he said: 'I want to know the hymns by heart, so that if I lose my left eye, I shall have them still.'[49]

The appeal to the great Caroline days is also Tractarian rather than Puseyite. 'I thought in *John Inglesant* I wished to indicate the mysticism of the Prayer-Book and the Caroline divines, on the one side *safe*, on the other *infinite*.'[50] In castigating Charles Gore for his 1891 Bampton Lectures, Shorthouse warned such innovators who attacked the principle of Establishment that: 'A cataclysm such as the world never saw is probably at hand.' The Church of England may be destroyed, 'the Church of Hooker, of Jewel, Nowell, Andrews, of Laud, of Sancroft, of Sutton, of Joseph Hall, of Hammond, of Jeremy Taylor, of Leighton, of Patrick, of Comber, and a host more. She may be destroyed but what will take her place!!!'[51]

The relation of Shorthouse's Anglicanism to that of the men who initiated the Oxford Movement was shrewdly noticed by one reviewer of *John Inglesant*:

The book . . . seems to embody in artistic form, views and ideas well known to those who are conversant with what one may call, for want of a better phrase, academic High Churchism. The peculiar religious tone and temper which belonged to the finer and more poetical minds in the Tractarian movement, and which is still noticeable among us both within and without our universities, finds here delicate and beautiful interpretation.[52]

Shorthouse was not much in sympathy with the Puseyite developments after 1845. In *Blanche, Lady Falaise*, he draws a wretched character in Damerle the Puseyite clergyman, who quotes Liddon and Neale, makes much of his missioning among the poor and is proud of accusations of Romanizing. He turns out to be a jilter in the manner of Trollope's Adolphus Crosby and goes completely to the bad through drink. Shorthouse is prepared to defend order and dignity in the Church, but elaborate ritual is displeasing. Like the Tractarians he will appeal to what the Prayer Book ordains and approve of a return to older usage rather than an innovation of new. The old parson in *John Inglesant* who performs and justifies certain ceremonies in celebrating the sacrament remains 'a loyal, honest and zealous advocate, according to his capacity, of the Church of England'.[53] In a contemporary setting, the extent of approval is made more explicit:

The old-fashioned High Church notions of Mr de Foi led him to the observance of many practices, since supposed to be modern innovations, a generation at least before Ritualists, so-called, were heard of. He observed the eastward position at the Holy Communion, he invariably bowed to the altar, and he read morning prayers on Wednesdays, Fridays, and Saints' days.[54]

He had no time for the eclecticism which some Anglo-Catholic clergy practised, or for the assumption of excessive priestly power on the strength of apostolic ordination. He wrote to a cousin in 1899:

I distinguish absolutely between Sacramentalism and Sacerdotalism; they seem to me mutually destructive. So long as the clergy confine themselves to their Sacramental office I look upon them as THE channel of grace. When they depart from this, and act and talk out of their own heads, I pay no more attention to them than I do to laymen.[55]

And in the same year to another correspondent: 'I certainly class the *Pseudo*-Ritualist (*not* such as Bishop Cosin) with the Salvation Army, only more so.'[56] Even affectionate treatment of a good priest can be satirical about one

. . . who had an embroidered altar cloth and wax candles in his church, and services on all Saints' days and holy days, who had all the old pews taken down and replaced with open seats, and who had erected, with the help of his brother, a screen and font of the most 'severe taste'.[57]

The dislike of advanced Puseyism went inevitably with deeper dislike of Romanism. Although the Jesuit in *John Inglesant* is a sympathetic and even attractive character, he is still a plotter and given to those equivocations which rouse Kingsley to wrath. Shorthouse was intelligent enough to be amused by the English tendency to use the word Jesuit as 'a vague and intangible designation, standing in the ordinary English mind merely as a synonym for all that was wicked, base and dangerous'.[58] Yet at last the Jesuits for whom Inglesant works are shown as men willing to resort to suppression of truth and persecution in the maintenance of power.

Shorthouse shared the fear of concealed Papistry which had accompanied the growth of the Oxford Movement from its first years. The presentation of Laud in *John Inglesant* is, as might be expected, admiring and even adulatory; but it is a fault in him that he is too tolerant of those who are Romanists at heart. Thus Inglesant's father can nominate as chaplain:

A graduate of Oxford, a man who was 'ex animo' a papist, and who only wanted a suitable time to declare himself one. The number of such men was very great, and they were kept in the English Church only by the High Church doctrines and ceremonies introduced by Archbishop Laud; affording one out of numberless parallels between that age and the present.[59]

It is admittedly a character, but a sympathetic one who acts as objective narrator of the whole story, who is made to describe her own mother as loving but 'a *Parisienne*, and a benighted Papist'.[60] That Shorthouse's own views were far from ecumenical is made clear in his letters. He can be Kingsleyan both in sentiment and in expression:

271

The charge against the Roman Church is not that her doctrines do not contain the germs of truth, but that having based her system upon the profoundest truths, she has succeeded in making truth itself a lie.

Pure evil, or what we call such, is the stupidest thing in existence – it is only when it allies itself with what is supremely good (as in the Romanist Church) that it becomes really dangerous to the child of God.[61]

It is a pleasant irony that Shorthouse and his wife lived very near the Oratory where Newman was, and that they were attended by a Roman Catholic doctor who also attended there. After Newman was dead, Shorthouse allowed himself a little patronizing pity:

What agonies poor Newman went through when he found himself and all his exalted ideals, and the whole *Romanist* Church in England crushed between the more than brutish hoofs of Italian priest-bishops.[62]

Yet he more than most men ought to have understood the gain as well as the loss in Newman's change, since he had followed a similar path. Newman's novels too must have had some influence on the conception and writing of *John Inglesant*.

In common with most imaginative writers, Shorthouse had little good to say of the Evangelicals. Their puritanical fear of pleasure and their distrust of the cultured intellect made them seem too much like the seventeenth-century sectaries, and probably too much like the older Quakers of his own experience. He did, however, include a very sympathetic portrait of the great Evangelical Simeon in *Sir Percival*, praising him for his urbanity and culture as well as his personal holiness. In truth, he disliked all extremes which tended to narrowness and exclusion. In a discussion of comparative levels of churchmanship, he was content to say simply, 'I am a strong sacramentalist,' and the clergyman who wrote the Preface to his biography described his attitude as 'Broad Church Sacramentalism'.[63]

The phrase may bring us closer to the understanding of Shorthouse. Certain affinities and likenesses already noticed have pointed the way towards it. He was prepared to follow some more recent Anglican developments, even though not in the Puseyite line. Despite his strictures on Gore's Bampton Lectures, he was enthusiastic about parts of *Lux Mundi*. Commenting on Moberley's essay on the Incarnation, he wrote:

It seems to me that the key to the whole mystery of existence lies in these words of the new Oxford school of High churchmen, not that they have discovered it but that they will work (shall I say) this Christian Platonism into the faith of that wonderful Church of England which is now, in all the world, the only fruit of Christianity (so far as thought is concerned) of any vitality or standing in practical existence.[64]

Here Shorthouse was saying a good deal about his own belief and about the way in which the ideas of the Oxford Movement were beginning to expand and link up with other schools. Of the Platonism here mentioned there is ample evidence. It was a tempting line of thought for the Anglican apologist to counter the Aristotelian tendency of official Roman Catholic dogmatics. Hobbes is shown using it in this way in *John Inglesant*, and Inglesant himself learns Platonism from his early teacher and from Henry More the great Cambridge Platonist. He applies it in his argument with Cardinal Rinuccini: 'The cross of Christ is composed of many other crosses – is the centre, the type, the essence of all crosses.'

The controversy between Platonist and Aristotelian, Idealist and Nominalist, was of course no new thing in England or any-where in the Western world, nor was it confined to religious thought. However, the theological controversies beginning in the thirties, and the wider promulgation of Catholic doctrines, had brought Greek philosophy into the religious arena. Short-house was taking part in a dispute which was general but which had a special attraction for him. His desire for the Ideal made people think of him as akin to Spenser; both tried to depict 'the saint who was also a gentleman'.[65] As early as 1871, before he had started work on *John Inglesant*, he was writing earnestly to Matthew Arnold about the Incarnation problem which excited him years later in *Lux Mundi*. The Incarnation seemed to him a realization of the Ideal, which can there-after be realized in every life committed to Christ. The divine principle fails if it remains purely spiritual, as in the conception of the Platonic Socrates; it needs to be made actual in daily life.[66]

In 1880, when he was planning a paper on the Platonism of Wordsworth, he noted with a certain intellectual self-confidence: 'It will be necessary to formulate Platonism, which has never yet been satisfactorily done, and the requisite of which "Jowett" has utterly failed even to perceive, at least *as it seems to me*.'[67] From Wordsworth there was a useful line of thought for Anglicans, as the Tractarians had understood. Even more useful was the later thought of Coleridge, though Shorthouse seems to have been less interested in this. Coleridge had delved into the Cambridge Platonists whom Inglesant admired and had used the Ideal to express the immanence of God in manifestations of this-worldly life.[68] The Coleridgean line, which Charles Marriott alone among the Tractarians had taken really seriously, had found its later Anglican expression mainly through Maurice and the Broad Church school. After a short period of mutual approval, Maurice and the Tractarians had drawn apart; and we have seen what Maurice's disciple Kingsley thought about post-Tractarian developments. Now, however, the successors of both movements were finding more common ground.

Now the ascription to Shorthouse of 'Broad Church sacramentalism' begins to make sense. His interest in Maurice was shown in the letter about his secession which was quoted above. It was natural that he should feel sympathy with one who had moved to the Church of England from Unitarianism and who had written a charitable but telling argument against the Quakers in *The Kingdom of Christ* (1842). Further, Maurice had a deep and passionate love for his chosen communion, although Puseyites often accused him of undermining orthodox churchmanship. Beyond this level of personal feeling and shared experience there were more profound things which Maurice could provide.

Shorthouse expressed the debt most fully in a long review of Maurice's biography.[69] He was particularly approving of the way in which Maurice dealt with the question of baptism, a question which keeps recurring in the vexed theological disputes of the time. It was a matter too which was of interest to a man who had been baptized by his own choice as an adult.

Pusey seemed to Shorthouse to be in error over this: he 'regarded baptism as a change of nature'. By contrast Maurice
'saw in it the coming out of the infant into the first radiance of
a light which had ever been shining for it and for all the
world'. The fact is that, although the baptism issue was one on
which they were most deeply divided, the Puseyites and the
Evangelicals shared a gloomy view about human nature and
the uncurable depravity of unaided man. Shorthouse preferred
the more optimistic Broad Church faith in basic goodness;
grace was something to be cherished and developed rather
than something completely opposed to the natural state.

He goes on to praise Maurice for his work in exposing the
errors of the Oxford Tracts and stoutly defends him against
charges of heresy. He comes back to the theme of Christian
Platonism of which both Wordsworth and Maurice are exponents. Maurice is seen as one of those responsible for the
'wonderful change' in English religious life over the last fifty
years. Years later, he wrote that 'Maurice always absorbed me
so much that I had no time for other Divines (of that class and
time)'.[70] This statement suggests what is probably the truth:
that Shorthouse was not greatly drawn to the Broad Churchmen as a whole but was captivated by the undoubted genius of
their leader. He did, however, share their warm enthusiasm
for life under God, their essential optimism about human
potential and their dislike of extremes in dogmatism. For him,
as for them, fanaticism was a dirty word.

'Culture' and 'fanaticism' are polarities which appear with
almost wearisome frequency in Shorthouse's views on religion. If the dislike of fanaticism puts him with the Broad
Churchmen, the love of culture associates him with the Tractarians. The Oxford Movement, for all its tensions and diver-
gences, was solidly based on respect for intellectual power and
on the values of a cultivated life. This was another way in
which it soon came to be opposed to the Evangelicalism from
which some of its leaders had come and with which its first
efforts had been partly in agreement.

Shorthouse left no doubt about his purpose in this connexion when he wrote *John Inglesant*. The key-words are used in
the Preface, and continually in his correspondence with friends
and critics about the book. Typical of many is the explicit

statement: 'The main interest of my book is to exalt culture against fanaticism of any kind.'[71] Inglesant himself is a model of seventeenth-century culture. He is always well dressed, urbane in manner and conversation, a lover of learning and of the arts. His sincere but balanced Anglicanism is contrasted with the fanaticism of both extremes. Valentine Lee, who takes up the narration at the end of the book, points contemptuously to the errors of the Commonwealth rule:

Methinks that if the Puritans of the last age had known that the same word in Latin means both worship and the culture of polite life, they would not have condemned both themselves and us to so many years of shadowy gloom and of a morose antipathy to all delight.[72]

Shorthouse returned to the theme in *The Little Schoolmaster Mark* (1883–4), a short novel which is really a pair of stories tenuously linked. Disaster overtakes those who rigorously separate their religion and their culture or who despise art in the name of religion. It is not one of Shorthouse's happier productions; his attempt at allegory seems pretentious and contrived. Yet it was a success in his own time and furnished matter for sermons by a popular preacher who wrote asking for interpretation: 'I am very anxious to learn all the lessons of your wonderful story.' Shorthouse replied in terms which do not greatly aid the muddled mind of the modern reader but which do tell us something about his own:

When I wrote it I had before my mind chiefly the study of contrast between the spiritual life and the worldly life, in its most attractive form. It is, however, the distinguishing advantage of fiction that the meaning is not limited to what was in the writer's mind at the time. I should *now* say that the story is the *relation of one of many failures to reconcile the artistic with the spiritual aspect of life*.[73]

The beauty of religion was never far from Shorthouse's perception. He loves to linger over the description of churches and services in *John Inglesant*. The fallen but penitent Puseyite in *Blanche, Lady Falaise*, accuses himself of error in separating religion from the total commitment of living in this world; what annoyed Shorthouse about the Puseyite attitude seems to have been not so much its aestheticism as its puritanical dedication to religion in isolation. How different is the layman de Brie in another novel:

> There could be no doubt that he was a happy man. His disposition was singularly sweet and placid, and he escaped, by an instinctive recoil, everything that was coarse, cruel, or unpleasant. His religion consisted in following the good and the beautiful, and he avoided intuitively the disquieting and difficult aspects both of life and thought. The existence of beauty was to him a safeguard and an asylum from all the attacks of Satan and of doubt. It led him to a Father in Heaven.[74]

Beauty inspires religious aspiration; the particular appearance leads to the divine Ideal. So it seems to have been for Shorthouse himself. Like Pater's Marius, he and his heroes come to wisdom through testing types of faith and also by using the evidence of their perceptions to bring experience. Like Pater, and like Newman too, Shorthouse could evoke the sensory impressions of a past age and use them to teach his own age how to evaluate itself.

Such intensity of feeling, seeking for a divine manifestation in everything, can too easily decline into eclectic and portentous pseudo-mysticism. The cosmic struggle can be contained in a plain narrative, but only by a greater genius than Shorthouse. The later books contain too many apparitions, visions and coincidences. The death of Blanche at the moment when Damerle is converted and reconciled with his wife is a noble attempt to state the idea of substitution and vicarious suffering, but it does not quite succeed.

There was another side to Shorthouse, as there is to all men. For all his exaltations and his frequent romanticizing of the past at the expense of the present, he was riddled with nineteenth-century prejudices. His literary judgements were often capricious; he dismissed Carlyle as lacking in humility, regarded Mrs Sherwood as comparable to Jane Austen and de Maupassant as 'nowhere near her', refused even to read *Robert Elsmere*, though Mrs Humphry Ward had done him a good service, and said of the new naturalism in fiction that he loathed it 'beyond expression'.

He had no patience with socialism or democracy; his attitude is closer to the detachment of the Tractarians from social problems than to the growing concern of Anglo-Catholics in his own time. The sense of order and duly constituted authority was deeply set in his religious allegiance. The mob in *John Inglesant* at the execution in Whitehall has the menacing aspect of the mobs in novels of the forties and fifties, particularly in the early Church stories like *Callista* and *Hypatia*. He was kind though paternalist in running his own business and was friendly enough with his workmen so long as this did not imply 'any nonsense of socialism'. He described in the accents of a Bounderby a meeting which was 'addressed by sundry "intelligent mechanics" – thereby impressing you with a healthy horror of democratic parliaments'.[75]

The attack on Gore was based mainly on the latter's comments about righteous dealing in business and the ethical unsoundness of the profit-motive. The reaction from Shorthouse is interesting as further evidence of his antagonism to the Puseyite wing and also as showing the reflections possible to devout Christians at the end of the nineteenth century:

> Surely Mr Gore must know that buying in a cheaper market than that in which we sell is a distinct law of the providence of God, that if a man acts on this principle he will make money, which he may, and often does, expend in building Pusey houses and other good works dear to Mr Gore's heart, and that if he violates this law of God he will come to the workhouse, and what good he will do to Mr Gore or any one else there, I do not know.[76]

In fact, Shorthouse could be both a prig and a snob. There are touches of the 'silver fork' in the later novels, in the sumptuous apartments of the Count in *The Countess Eve*, of Trefennick in *Blanche*. We feel near to Daisy Ashford when, in the latter book, Damerle knocks at the front door of a grand London house and 'It was opened immediately by three servants'.[77] And we feel near to Mr Pooter in some of Shorthouse's own descriptions of the people he met when he was being lionized for *John Inglesant*.

Yet these things scarcely cloud the main achievement of this improbable defender of Anglicanism. In him the capacity of the revitalized Church of England which grew out of the Oxford Movement is manifested. It could satisfy the need for historical tradition and for a full sacramental life in one who was opposed to the more direct and spectacular Puseyite development. We are back once more with the great twelve years that began the movement. It was directly from the Tractarians that the most powerful artistic and intellectual impulses of Anglo-Catholicism were derived. Shorthouse was one of the many who brought their own limitations into an admittedly imperfect Church, to find that the power and the glory were indeed there.

Appendix I

The Nomenclature of the Movement

The Oxford Movement had its effect on the national vocabulary and was responsible for changes of meaning, neologisms, and a good deal of confusion. It is not easy to delimit precise areas of linguistic usage in a revival that was dynamic both in its internal development and in its social reception. Neither its supporters nor its opponents were entirely consistent in their naming. A linguistic specialist who undertook close research on the problem might collect useful information on the principles of semantic change. Meanwhile, a brief survey of trends may help to illuminate some of the foregoing chapters.

Contemporaries like R.W.Church were sensitively aware of the linguistic features of a movement in which language was used copiously and effectively from the start. Theology was pulled out of the study and into the public arena by 'the conflicts which for a time turned Oxford into a kind of image of what Florence was in the days of Savonarola, with its nicknames, Puseyites, and Neomaniacs, and High and Dry, counterparts of the *Piagnoni* and Arrabiati, of the older strife'.[1] The effect was felt not in Oxford alone but in all places where the new religious extremism divided men into bitter faction. It was felt in the pulpit and the novel, in the daily press and the periodical reviews with 'their party nicknames, given without a shudder at the terrible accusations which they conveyed'.[2]

There was nothing novel in the fact that the nicknames

sometimes came to be accepted by the parties which they had at first designated opprobriously. The same thing had happened to the two political parties, which at that very time were changing their styles from Whig and Tory to Liberal and Conservative. The names which came from outside drove away those first chosen from within. Those who initiated the movement called themselves 'Apostolicals', a name which, according to Blachford, was coined by Hurrell Froude 'because it was connected with everything in Spain which was most obnoxious to the British public'.[3] Froude certainly used the name freely in the early years of the Tracts; and the main emphasis of the first Tracts was on the Apostolic Succession as maintained unbroken in the Church of England. Newman, whose message in the first Tract was this very point, came to look back from his Roman Catholic position and to see this insistence on 'Antiquity or Apostolicity' as a mark of Anglican limitations and to contrast it with the fuller Roman assertion of Catholicity.[4] The name did not win much approval beyond the small circle of those who started the revival. By 1838 Clough could write disparagingly of the 'so-called Apostolical Church Opinions' held by Newman and his disciples.[5]

The name 'Orthodox' was also used in the early years. It did not gain very wide currency, but kept its value among those who remembered the beginning. Church could use it in referring back to the events of 1833, as a contrast with the Evangelicals.[6] Matthew Arnold applied it to the Puseyite opponents of the liberal *Essays and Reviews* in the sixties[7] and Clough could find it a substitute for 'Catholic'.[8] For Charlotte Yonge, the 'Orthodox' were regrettably less fervent about missions than the Evangelicals until the Oxford Movement brought a new sense of commitment.[9] The fact that the name was sometimes used among pre-Tractarian High Churchmen may have prevented its becoming very popular among those who were anxious to push the issues much further.

The association with Oxford of course produced the name by which the movement has come to be best known and by which Church thought fit to describe the events of the great twelve years. Thomas Arnold's article on the 'Oxford Malignants' – probably not his own choice of title – has been mentioned. His early biographer could refer depreciatingly to the

'Oxford School'[10] and J.A.Froude wrote retrospectively of the 'Oxford Movement', the 'Oxford Counter-Reformation' and also of 'the Movement, as it was called'.[11] In 1839 the *Quarterly* carried a largely favourable review of *Tracts for the Times* and Hurrell Froude's *Remains*, with the running head-title 'Oxford Theology' and a reference in the text to the 'Oxford School'.[12]

Four years later, the *Quarterly* was using the term 'Tractarian' and making the common accusation that the movement had started well and been led into Romanizing excesses.[13] The word itself was not new, being recorded in 1824 as describing 'writer, publisher or distributor of tracts'.[14] For R.W.Church it remained a nickname of what should better be called the Oxford Movement.[15] It was certainly in frequent use by the end of the thirties and the notorious publication of Tract 90 seems to have increased its currency. *Punch* used it derisively, first in 1843.[16] 'Decanus' who wrote the pamphlet against Newman's secession *Whose the Loss or Whose the Gain* used it of those whom he thought to be coupled with 'Romanists', varying it once by the form 'Tractites', which certainly sounds more offensive. The name continued in popular use throughout the forties and fifties. William Arnold applied it to events at Oxford in the early forties and Hawkins was able to include in his testimonial to Clough that the latter was 'not of the Tract Party'.[17] Kingsley was full of scorn for a 'Tractarian curate' and able to contrast the Tractarian party with both 'Popery' and 'Protestant'.[18] A general condemnation of the movement published in 1845 was entitled *The Judgment of the Bishops upon Tractarian Theology*. Five years later, Russell was approvingly quoting Arnold's use of the word and adding his own advice not to give preferment to any of the Tractarians.[19] The name was generally hostile, but the sting grew less sharp in time. In 1852 a supporter of the movement could publish *Three Lectures on Tractarianism* and by the late sixties it was sometimes felt necessary to enclose the word in quotation marks.[20]

The word 'Tractarian' then was unfriendly but widely accepted. More opprobrious names circulated, particularly in Oxford, but few of them gained wider currency or endured for so long. Whately, from the archiepiscopal eminence of Dublin, was particularly inventive in devising nicknames for some of his former colleagues and apparently was the begetter of 'Tractite':

A nickname was soon found for them: the word 'Tractarian' was invented, and Archbishop Whately thought it worth while, but not successfully, to improve it into 'Tractites'. Archbishop Whately, always ingenious, appears to have suspected that the real but concealed object of the movement was to propagate a secret infidelity; they were 'Children of the Mist', or 'Veiled Prophets'.

Whately also suggested 'Thugs' and 'Rabbinists';[21] his ingenuity seems to have been greater than his ability to make names stick.

A major change in the fortunes of the movement was reflected in nomenclature. It was inevitable that the leadership of Newman should give a name to his followers: they were 'Newmanists', 'Newmanites', or sometimes 'Neomaniacs'. Such were the usual terms at Oxford when Clough went up in 1836, and for the years immediately following.[22] 'With regard to the Newmanites, I do not call them bad men, nor would I deny their many good qualities,' Thomas Arnold wrote in 1836, trying to be fair before going on to a stern attack.[23] The name was apt, with its recognition of the outstanding power of the leader and with its felicitous suggestion of innovation in religion. Before long, however, it gave place to the name which held popular favour for a long time and became the property of all those in every party who were hostile to the revival.

As Newman withdrew bit by bit from the centre of Oxford life and the charges of secret Romanizing grew, men began to look to Pusey as the head of the movement. Froude was dead, Keble away in a country parish: Pusey was the most notable scholar among the authors of the Tracts. The words 'Puseyism' and 'Puseyite' were in use by 1838 and had become the commonest terms within a few years. By 1843 Clough could ruefully relate that he was suspected of being a Puseyite.[24] The word became a comprehensive term of abuse for any departure from strictly Protestant Anglicanism as early as 1842 and remained such for several decades.[25] Although Newman professed some personal admiration for Pusey in *Loss and Gain*, he wrote to Henry Wilberforce in 1849 about the lack of a deep tradition in 'what *now* is justly called *Puseyism*'.[26] In the same year Froude was expecting the hatred of the Puseyites for *The Nemesis of Faith*.[27] For Elizabeth Harris, Puseyism was the final stop before going over to Rome.[28]

Although Pusey's name ousted both that of Newman and of the Tracts themselves, it never lost a certain slanginess that was disapproved of for formal use. Those whose opposition to the movement was more judicious disliked the rude bandying of names; and they knew that Pusey's personal influence could never equal that which Newman had given. 'When the *Tracts* disappeared in smoke, Tractarian conquered and remained incongruously with posterity. But those without perfect manners continued to use Puseyite.'[29] The attraction of the name was increased by its smooth, feline sound with innumerable opportunities for puns. The name was adapted into the forms of French, German, Italian, Danish and Greek. Pope Pius IX asked an English visitor whether Gladstone were a *Pousséiste*.[30] As far as the general British public was concerned, the heirs of the Tractarians were *Puseyites* and any Anglican practice which seemed in any way Catholic was *Puseyism*.

The name which eventually superseded it and still prevails today had in fact a longer ancestry than its late general acceptance might suggest. In 1840 Bishop Bagot was making inquiries about the 'Anglo-Catholic monastery at Littlemore' a year before the *Library of Anglo-Catholic Theology* was begun. It was soon in vogue among adherents of the movement and began to appear in novels.[31] Newman used it to describe the Caroline theology on which the early Tractarians had based many of their claims and it may well have been his own contribution to the language of the movement.[32] It could still be regarded as a neologism in 1849, when a recent convert to Rome recorded his debt to 'the existence within the English Church of what is sometimes called the Anglo-Catholic school'.[33] It slowly gained favour as a friendly or neutral name and was in general use by the end of the seventies.

Another feature of the movement, in some respects the most interesting linguistically, was the way in which established words changed their meaning. The most notable of these was the epithet *High* as applied to churchmen and their beliefs. The attitude of High Churchmen in the eighteenth and early nineteenth centuries was noted in the first chapter. It was from this tradition that Keble and Hurrell Froude came:

The old-fashioned High Church orthodoxy, of the Prayer Book and the Catechism – the orthodoxy which was professed at Oxford, which was represented in London by Norris of Hackney and Joshua Watson; which vehemently disliked the Evangelicals and Methodists for their poor and loose theology, their love of excitement and display, their hunting after popularity.[34]

When these somewhat negative attitudes acquired a more dynamic message, which was readily accepted by lay families like the Yonges who stood in the same tradition, the idea of being 'High' in religion was naturally associated with the new movement. The transition was noticed by Clough in 1838: the teaching of Newman seemed 'a sort of High-Churchism, with an infusion of Reason and Wisdom'.[35] By the forties, 'High Church' was often used as a synonym of 'Puseyite', with little or no regard for consistency. A friend of W.G.Ward could be described as 'very High Church' in 1841.[36] The special devotions and asceticism of Argemone Lavington are called 'somewhat High Church'.[37] In 1853 Prince Albert could recommend the Prime Minister not to prefer the holders of troublesome new ideas – a discipline which would soon deter 'the most active, ambitious, and talented of the High Church party'.[38]

The change of emphasis in 'High Church' was paralleled in the phrase 'Low Church', which also moved from being primarily descriptive of ideas about the nature of the Church in contemporary society to include matters of doctrine and practice. It became a synonym for 'Evangelical' within the Established Church. Thomas Arnold's letters illustrate the transition. In 1822 he was wishing for a learned periodical that could be 'sincerely Christian . . . neither High Church, nor what is called Evangelical'. When the Tracts were starting to appear in 1833 he grumbled that 'these High Churchmen are far more fanatical and much more foolish than Irving himself'. In 1841, when the controversy over Ward's *Ideal* was raging, he objected to being called 'Low' simply because he opposed the 'High' party at Oxford.[39]

Even the name 'Anglican', which went back to 1635, could

acquire overtones of party. It was in favour among those who had lost enthusiasm for being called Protestants but wanted to stress their opposition to Rome. Ward was sneering at 'Anglican Protestants', including men like Arnold, when he wrote to Clough in 1838.[40] Newman continued after his secession to regard Anglican as a valid title for distinguishing members of the Church of England from both Roman Catholics and nonconformist Protestants; in his controversy with Kingsley he seemed inclined to go further and use it as a synonym of 'Anglo-Catholic' in contrast with Protestant loyalties which his accuser was trying to press upon him.[41] He may have been influenced , whether consciously or not, by the long analysis in *Yeast*, quoted in a previous chapter, of the 'Neo-Anglican' movement.

In 1843 a reviewer in the *Quarterly*, making the customary charge that the Tractarians had moved to a more Romanizing position, instanced their pedantic use of the word 'Catholic' to describe their position, which had previously been applied solely to Romanists – 'though, when more strictness was called for, we talked of the *"Roman* Catholics"'.[42] It may be remarked that popular usage in the twentieth century still mentally attaches the word 'Roman' to the use of 'Catholic'; but the issue was a real one for those who, by 1841, had to decide 'whether or not it was a sham for the English Church to call itself Catholic'.[43] While the nation at last wondered what all the fuss was about, devout women like Charlotte Yonge were at pains to use the word as a contrast with both 'Romanist' and 'Protestant'.[44] Lancelot Smith in *Yeast* argues about the right use of the word with the Puseyite Vicar. Froude's hero Markham Sutherland comes under 'Catholicizing influence' when the Oxford Movement reaches him.[45]

The common usage of supporters of the movement is accurately recorded by Newman in the guise of fiction when White says,

'I have ever been most faithful to the Church of England . . . I have never, indeed, denied the claims of the Romish church to be a branch of the Catholic Church, nor will I.'[46]

Words like 'Romish', 'Romanist', 'Popish' and 'Papist' became important in the controversy. They were freely applied to the supporters of the movement; those which referred to Papal power were considered particularly opprobrious. Francis Newman found both 'Popery' and 'Romanism' in his brother's views long before the secession occurred and the words continued to be hurled at Anglo-Catholics by their most vehement opponents.[47] More scrupulous users of language could contrast Romanism and 'Newmanism', or differentiate it from the 'purely Catholic principle' which a good Anglican should accept.[48]

Although the leaders and followers of the movement were stout in resisting charges of Romanizing, they showed an increasing hostility to being called Protestants. Keble was unhappy about it from the time he wrote Tract 57 and saw the word as descriptive of those to whom faith is 'a matter of feeling rather than a strict relative duty towards the persons of the Holy Trinity'. Later, he disliked the idea of regarding protest as the only answer to Roman Catholic claims; Anglicans were rather 'appellants' to an ecumenical council: 'a protest in any judicial matter supposes the final authority to have spoken.'[49] In 1841 Newman dismissed the new Parker Society as an attempt by 'the Protestants of London' to compete with the *Library of Anglo-Catholic Theology*.[50]

Words became explosive as the controversy grew. The literature of the movement shows a great deal of linguistic interest, ranging from the purely emotive use of words as accepted social smears to the honest attempt at finding out what they really meant. Two essays are worth mentioning in the latter connection and they are full of interest for those who want to see the movement through contemporary eyes; they contain serious linguistic usage by two scholarly men, one inside the movement, the other outside.

Newman's essay 'Prospects of the Anglican Church'[51] appeared in 1839 when the charges of secret Romanism were being made, when he was still the undoubted head of the movement but his doubts were beginning. His language illustrates a good deal of what has been described above, from the start when he says that the Tracts 'were accused in various quarters of tending to Popery'. They contain, however, nothing but 'Catholic doctrines' and 'Catholic truth'. Some of the leading members of the movement 'represent the

High Church dignitaries of the last generation'. Yet there are real difficulties in the way of those who try to state their case:

We have called the other system of opinion Puritanism because we cannot hit upon a fit name for it . . . to call it Evangelical, would be an unlawful concession; to call it Puritan, were to lose sight of its establishment side; to call it Ultra-Protestant, would be to offend its upholders; to call it Protestant, would not be respectful to Protestantism. Anti-Catholic is vague; Anti-Sacramentarian is lengthy. This, indeed, is its very advantage in controversy with the upholders of Catholic principles; that it has a short and glib word ready at hand and may promptly call them 'Papists', while they had [*sic*] no retort courteous to inflict upon it.[52]

He goes on to write of the current of the age as tending to a revival of true Catholicism based on the appeal to antiquity and concludes:

Would you rather have your sons and daughters members of the Church of England or of the Church of Rome? That is the real alternative, if we follow things to their results; and the Romanists feel this. Anglo-Catholicism is a road leading off the beaten highway of Popery: it branches off at last, though for some time it seems one with it. Accordingly they look on the English Church as a fraudulent come-off, as a sort of *cul-de-sac*.[53]

That represents the usage of the leading Tractarian at the height of the movement. Later, when parties were more clearly defined, W. J. Conybeare made one of the most serious efforts to tackle the confusion of nomenclature. His long review of recent religious books contained, as was usual in the ample periodicals of those days, some general reflections about the situation.[54] An opponent of Rome and of extreme Puseyism, he contrives to be judiciously objective in his analysis. The authors whose work he is reviewing are seen as:

Representatives of the three great parties which divide the Church of England. These parties have always existed, under different phases, and with more or less of life. But they have been brought into stronger contrast, and have learned better to understand themselves and one another, during the controversies which have agitated the last twenty years. They are commonly called the Low Church, the High Church, and the Broad Church parties; but such an enumeration is the result of an incomplete analysis.

Each of the three groups contains three subdivisions, showing the basic tenets in their exaggeration, their stagnation or their normal development. Those who have gone to the Low Church extreme may be called 'Puritan' or 'Recordite' – a reference to the Evangelical magazine *The Record*. The main group to which they belong is 'termed Low Church by its adversaries, and Evangelical by its adherents'. The middle group is called 'Moderate, Catholic or Broad Church, by its friends; Latitudinarian or Indifferent by its enemies'.[55]

As for the 'rapid growth of High Church opinions', it was caused by disgust at the extreme Evangelicals (this is historically unfounded). Conybeare points out rightly that the High Churchmanship of 1800 was different from what emerged after 1833. The early Tractarians introduced Caroline principles quite honourably: 'Anglican' shall be the name for the ideas that they promulgated and Samuel Wilberforce can be included among those who keep up the tradition. But unfortunately there grew a more extreme group which can properly be called 'Tractarian', including men like Newman, Ward, Oakely and Phillpotts. Some of them have logically followed their views and gone over to Rome; others, for whom Conybeare has nothing but contempt, have remained as 'Ritualists' following odd practices and wearing odd clothes both in church and outside. They fail to follow the instruction of the Prayer Book to say the daily offices, a job which they leave to junior curates (the regular saying of Morning and Evening Prayer was an important point with the leaders of the Oxford Movement). These extremists are strongest in the dioceses of Exeter, and Bath and Wells, in Scotland and in the colonies. Their habit of calling themselves 'Anglo-Catholic' is to be deplored. As well as them, there remain those whose High Church principles are 'stagnant'; they are the 'High and Dry', a parallel to the 'Low and Slow' of the other extreme.

Conybeare's naming is sometimes idiosyncratic and does not always accord with the evidence of other writers. This proves neither that he was right nor that he was wrong, but that there was a muddle of language which simple men accepted as part of the muddle of opinions and which serious men were trying to disentangle.

Appendix 2
Table of Dates

The following table shows the dates of birth and death of the principal figures mentioned and also their ages at the time of the Assize Sermon in 1833, the secession of Newman in 1845 and the publication of the *Apologia* in 1864.

	born	1833	1845	1864	died
John Keble	1792	41	53	72	1866
Thomas Arnold	1795	38	—	—	1842
E. B. Pusey	1800	33	45	64	1882
J. H. Newman	1801	32	44	63	1890
Nicholas Wiseman	1802	31	43	62	1865
Hurrell Froude	1803	30	—	—	1836
Francis Newman	1805	28	40	59	1897
Henry Manning	1808	25	37	56	1892
Mark Pattison	1813	20	32	51	1884
J. A. Froude	1818	15	27	46	1894
J. M. Neale	1818	15	27	46	1866
A. H. Clough	1819	14	26	—	1861
Charles Kingsley	1819	14	26	45	1875
Charlotte Yonge	1823	10	22	41	1901
Christina Rossetti	1830	3	15	34	1894
R. W. Dixon	1833	0	12	31	1900
William Morris	1834	—	11	30	1896
J. H. Shorthouse	1834	—	11	30	1903

Notes

INTRODUCTION (pp. 1–7)

1 In *Proverbial Philosophy*, third series (1867).
2 Two particularly worthwhile studies are J.E.Baker, *The Novel and the Oxford Movement* (Princeton, 1932) and M.Maison, *Search Your Soul, Eustace* (London, 1961).
3 For further evidence on this and other aspects of the question see P.A.Welsby, 'Anthony Trollope and the Church of England' in *Church Quarterly Review*, vol. CLXIII, no. 347, pp. 210–19.
4 *Bleak House* (1853), ch. 8.
5 Ibid., ch. 30.
6 A.R.Vidler, *The Church in an Age of Revolution* (Harmondsworth, 1961) p. 118.

CHAPTER 1   THE BACKGROUND OF THE MOVEMENT (pp. 9–29)

1 Pope, Epistle IV of *Moral Essays* ('To Richard Boyle, Earl of Burlington'), ll. 149–50.
2 Charles Kingsley, *Yeast* (1850); (all references to Eversley edn, London, 1902), pp. 124–5.
3 Ibid., ch. 17, p. 345.
4 I.Stock, *William Hale White* (London, 1956), p. 63; F.L.Mulhauser, ed., *The Correspondence of Arthur Hugh Clough* (Oxford, 1957), p. 515; W.H.Dunn, *James Anthony Froude* (Oxford, 1961) p. 196.
5 R.B.Martin, *The Dust of Combat* (London, 1959), p. 34.
6 Anthony Trollope, *Autobiography* (1883), ch. 8, referring to *Framley Parsonage*.

7   E.Bellasis, *Memorials of Mr Serjeant Bellasis* (1893), p. 78.
8   The Gunpowder Plot, or rather its detection, was commemorated by a special service in the Book of Common Prayer until 1859.
9   O.Chadwick, *The Victorian Church* (London, 1966), p. 162.
10 Samuel Butler, *The Way of All Flesh* (1903), ch. 28.
11 *Apologia Pro Vita Sua* (1864); (all references to Fontana edn, London, 1959), p. 241.
12 *The Wit and Wisdom of Sydney Smith* (1886), p. 121.
13 Charles Kingsley, *Two Years Ago* (1857), ch. 2; (all references to New Century edn, London, 1908), p. 67.
14 Bellasis, op. cit., p. 19.
15 Henry Fielding, *Tom Jones* (1749), bk 3, ch. 3.
16 The 1851 census gave a total of 7,261,915 in attendance at some place of worship on 30 March in that year, of whom 3,773,474 were at a Church of England service.
17 Hawkins of Oriel to A.H.Clough; F.L.Mulhauser, op. cit., p. 237.
18 Francis Newman, *Phases of Faith* (1850); (all references to 1881 edn), p. 15.
19 F.L.Mulhauser, op. cit., p. 461.
20 J.A.Froude, *The Nemesis of Faith* (1849), pp. 152–3.
21 T.B.Macaulay, 'Gladstone on Church and State', review article in *Edinburgh Review* (April 1839).
22 *Mansfield Park* (1814), ch. 9.
23 The words, spoken in a debate at Cambridge, 'ruffled the young imagination with stormy laughter' (Carlyle, *Life of John Sterling* (1851), ch. 4).
24 *Works* (1850 edn), p. 625.
25 *The Wit and Wisdom of Sydney Smith* (1886), pp. 135–6.
26 N.Sykes, *The English Religious Tradition* (London, 1953), p. 74.
27 C.R.Woodring, *Victorian Samplers* (Lawrence, Kansas, 1952), p. 127.
28 J.S.Mill, *Autobiography* (1873), ch. 2.
29 J.A.Froude, op. cit., p. 17.
30 T.Mozley, *Reminiscences, Chiefly of Oriel College and the Oxford Movement* (1882), vol. 1, p. 273.
31 A.P.Stanley, *Life and Correspondence of Thomas Arnold*; (all references to eighth edn, 1858), vol. 1, p. 255.
32 R.W.Church, *The Oxford Movement* (1891), p. 12.
33 Preface to *St Paul and Protestantism* (1870).
34 O.Chadwick, op. cit., p. 446.
35 T.Mozley, op. cit., vol. 1, pp. 23–4; cf. *Apologia*, p. 173.
36 S.L.Ollard, *A Short History of the Oxford Movement* (London, 1915), p. 141.

37 *Apologia*, p. 168.
38 'Coleridge . . . had taken the simple but all-important step of viewing the Church in its spiritual character as first and foremost and above all things, essentially a religious society of divine institution, not dependent on the creation or will of man, or on the privileges and honours which man might think fit to assign to it; and he had undoubtedly familiarized the minds of many with this way of regarding it, however imperfect, or cloudy, or unpractical they might find the development of his ideas, and his deductions from them' (Church, op. cit., p. 129).
39 Charlotte M. Yonge, *The Castle Builders* (1854), ch. 15; (all references to 1885 edn), p. 187.
40 Anthony Trollope, *The Warden* (1855), ch. 21; (all references to World's Classics edn, London, 1961), p. 262.

CHAPTER 2   TWELVE YEARS (pp. 30–57)

1 'National Apostasy', no. 6 of Keble's *Sermons Academical and Occasional*; (all references to second edn, Oxford, 1848).
2 Charlotte M. Yonge, *Musings over the 'Christian Year'*, etc. (1871), p. clv (hereafter referred to as *Musings*).
3 For the importance of Knox and Jebb in anticipating the *via media* doctrine see Y.Brilioth, *The Anglican Revival* (London, 1925), pp. 45–55, 331–3.
4 J.H.Newman, *Apologia pro Vita Sua*; (all references to Fontana edn, London, 1959), p. 122.
5 William Palmer, quoted in R.W.Church, *The Oxford Movement* (London, 1891), p. 90.
6 He lost his chaplaincy when he opposed the Gorham decision in 1850; a minor casualty of the affair which helped to drive Manning out of the English Church.
7 *Apologia*, p. 124.
8 C.Dawson, *The Spirit of the Oxford Movement* (London, 1933), p. 11.
9 R.H.Froude, *Remains*, vol. 1, p. 438.
10 R.W.Church, op. cit., p. 133.
11 Ibid., p. 215.
12 'Emerson' in *Discourses in America* in *Works* (London, 1903), vol. 4, p. 349. Arnold joins Newman with Emerson and Carlyle as the three great influences on Oxford men at that time.
13 J.H.Shorthouse, *Blanche, Lady Falaise* (1891), p. 31.
14 *Studia Sacra* (1877), pp. 69–78.
15 W.Lock, *John Keble, a Biography*; (all references to ninth edn, 1893), p. 230.

16 *Apologia*, p. 108.
17 H.P.Liddon, *Life of Edward Bouverie Pusey* (1893), vol. 1, p. 139.
18 'Advertisement' to the 'National Apostasy' sermon.
19 No. 4 of *Tracts for the Times*.
20 R.W.Church, op. cit., p. 25.
21 M.Trevor, *Newman: The Pillar of the Cloud* (London, 1962), p. 33.
22 B.A.Clough, *A Memoir of Anne Jemima Clough* (1897), p. 44.
23 R.W.Church, op. cit., p. 98.
24 E.Bellasis, *Memorials of Mr Serjeant Bellasis* (1895), p. 37.
25 G.V.Cox, *Recollections of Oxford* (1868), pp. 302–3.
26 J.C.Shairp, *Studies in Poetry and Philosophy* (1868), p. 278.
27 F.Newman, *Phases of Faith*; (all references to 1881 edn), p. 68.
28 J.A.Froude, *The Nemesis of Faith* (1849), p. 136.
29 *Apologia*, p. 120.
30 *Edinburgh Review* (April 1836). The title appears not to have been Arnold's choice, though there is no evidence that he raised any objection to it. The name of 'malignants' had been given to the Oxford supporters of the Crown by their Puritan opponents during the Civil War.
31 F.L.Mulhauser, ed., *The Correspondence of Arthur Hugh Clough* (Oxford, 1957), p. 42.
32 *Apologia*, p. 89.
33 C.M.Yonge, *Musings*, p. xx.
34 *Remains*, vol. 1, pp. 336, 433.
35 A.P.Stanley, *Life and Correspondence of Thomas Arnold* (1858 edn), vol. 2, p. 111.
36 *Apologia*, p. 166.
37 Ibid., p. 153.
38 Ibid., pp. 139–40.
39 J.A.Froude, op. cit., pp. 122–3.
40 *Apologia*, p. 239.
41 *Life, Letters and Literary Remains of J.H.Shorthouse* (London, 1903), vol. 1, p. 360.
42 C.M.Yonge, op. cit., p. clx.
43 MS. of William Howitt cited in C.R.Woodring, *Victorian Samplers* (Laurence, Kansas, 1952), pp. 215–16.
44 *Apologia*, p. 185.
45 *Remains*, vol. 1, p. 306.
46 *Apologia*, p. 209.
47 F.L.Mulhauser, op. cit., p. 108.
48 *Apologia*, p. 163.
49 M.Church, *Life and Letters of Dean Church* (1895), p. 57.
50 R.W.Church, op. cit., p. 258.

51 Ibid., p. 321.
52 Bellasis, op. cit., which contains a moving account of the occasion, pp. 52–4.
53 R.W.Church, op. cit., p. 336.
54 R.B.Martin, *The Dust of Combat* (London, 1959), p. 71.
55 Mark Pattison, *Memoirs* (1885), p. 212.

CHAPTER 3   A TRACTARIAN PARISH (pp. 58–87)

1 R.W.Church, *The Oxford Movement* (1891), p. 61.
2 C.M.Yonge, *Musings over the 'Christian Year'* etc (1871), p. xxiii. Hereafter *Musings*.
3 W.Tuckwell, *Reminiscences of Oxford*; (all references to 2nd ed 1907), p. 184.
4 Isaac Williams, *Autobiography* (1892), p. 118 note.
5 *The Parochial System*, cited by D.Newsome in *The Parting of Friends* (London, 1966), p. 223.
6 There is a recollected description of such a church in Charlotte M. Yonge's *Chantry House* (1886). The problem of pews comes several times into her novels; so does that of the gallery musicians, most memorably described by Hardy in *Under the Greenwood Tree.*
7 The opening of a new church in the district was attended by Newman and Henry Wilberforce in 1841. E. Bellasis, *Memorials of Mr Serjeant Bellasis* (1893), p. 48.
8 *Musings*, p. viii.
9 Ibid., pp. iii–iv.
10 Ibid., p. i.
11 Ibid., p. v.
12 Tuckwell, op. cit., pp. 292–3.
13 *Life, Letters and Literary Remains of J.H.Shorthouse* (1905), p. 278.
14 A.P.Stanley, *Life and Correspondence of Thomas Arnold*, eighth edn (1858), vol. 1, p. 59.
15 *Studies in Literature* (1891), p. 27.
16 *The Name and Nature of Poetry* (1933), p. 34.
17 F.Mulhauser, ed. *The Correspondence of Arthur Hugh Clough* (Oxford, 1957), p. 85. *Lyra Apostolica* (1836) contained work by Newman and other Tractarian leaders; *The Cathedral* (1838) was by Isaac Williams.
18 O.Chadwick, *The Victorian Church*, pt 1 (London, 1966), p. 68.
19 *Keble's Lectures on Poetry 1832–41* translated by E.K.Francis (Oxford, 1912), vol. 1, p. 68.
20 Ibid., vol. 2, p. 201.

21 R.W.Church, op. cit., p. 57.
22 'Third Sunday after Epiphany.' Keble adds a note from Burnet's *Life of Hale* about care to conceal deep religious feeling lest ill conduct should 'cast a reproach on the profession of it, and give great advantages to impious men to blaspheme the name of God'.
23 *Musings*, p. 53.
24 Ibid., p. 90.
25 W.J.A.M.Beek, *John Keble's Literary and Religious Contribution to the Oxford Movement* (Nijmegen, 1959), p. 11.
26 C.C.Abbott, ed., *The Correspondence of Gerard Manley Hopkins and Richard Watson Dixon* (Oxford, 1955), p. 99.
27 *Musings*, p. 57.
28 *The Heir of Redclyffe*, chs 6, 30; (all references to Everyman edn, London, 1909), pp. 82, 384.
29 *Musings*, p. cxiv.
30 Walter Lock, Introduction to the 1903 edn, p. 21.
31 'Danger of Praise', written in 1842.
32 *Musings*, p. xxxiii.
33 Ibid., pp. 351–3; Keble changed *not* to *as* many years later.
34 Ibid., pp. xxix–xxx.
35 Ibid., p. xix. Keble retained the same tolerant view outside his catechumenal conversations. 'We can but continue [without a General Council] as we are in those points of our creed which other portions of the Church dispute, unless we can be proved to be wrong, not denying their life and catholicity but maintaining our own with submission to the whole Church' (*On Eucharistical Adoration* (1857), p. 178). To an Anglican priest veering towards Rome he wrote: 'I cannot see why we may not acknowledge God's good gifts to another portion of His Church, without in any degree disparaging what He has done, and we trust is doing, for ourselves' (T.W.Allies, *A Life's Decision* (1880), p. 158).
36 G.M.I.Blackburne, Preface to the 1901 edn, p. iii.
37 *Heartsease*, pt 3, ch. 18; (all references to 1859 edn), p. 544.
38 Ibid., ch. 4, p. 392–3.
39 There can be few people who have read all that she wrote; the present writer is not among them. It may be appropriate here to list the titles and dates of some of the most important novels, especially those often mentioned in this chapter: *Abbeychurch* (1844), *The Heir of Redclyffe* (1853), *The Castle Builders* (1854), *Heartsease* (1854), *|The Daisy Chain* (1856), *Dynevor Terrace* (1857), *The Young Stepmother* (1861), *The Trial* (1864), *The Clever Woman of the Family* (1865), *The*

Pillars of the House (1873), *Three Brides* (1876), *Chantry House* (1886).

40 *The Daisy Chain*, pt 1, ch. 19 (1856), p. 183.
41 *The Daisy Chain*, pt 1, ch. 4, p. 39; *The Heir of Redclyffe*, ch. 29, pp. 367–8.
42 *Heartsease*, pt 2, ch. 6, p. 143.
43 *The Daisy Chain*, pt 2, ch. 4, p. 369.
44 *Heartsease*, pt 3, ch. 11, p. 465.
45 See M.B.Reckitt, *Maurice to Temple* (London, 1947), pp. 110–11.
46 Quoted by M.B.Reckitt, loc. cit.
47 *Heartsease*, pt 2, ch. 2, p. 92; it might appear that the baby is baptized again in church when he survives, but the well-instructed author sends him there for the public reception and dedication enjoined by the Prayer Book.
48 *The Daisy Chain*, pt 1, ch. 4, p. 39.
49 *The Heir of Redclyffe*, ch. 22, p. 280.
50 A.P.Stanley, op. cit., vol. 1, pp. 131–2.
51 *Heartsease*, p. 3, ch. 14.
52 *Musings*, p. lxvii.
53 Ibid., p. iv.
54 *The Castle Builders*, ch. 3.
55 Ibid., ch. 18.
56 Ibid., ch. 21.
57 O. Chadwick, op. cit., p. 36.
58 *The Daisy Chain*, pt 1, ch. 26, p. 280.
59 *Letters of Spiritual Counsel*, ed. R.F.Wilson (1880), p. 58.
60 James Woodforde's Diary (19 April 1793).
61 W.Irvine, *Apes, Angels and Victorians* (London, 1955).
62 *The Heir of Redclyffe*, ch. 4, p. 50; Mrs Edmonstone is quoting from *The Christian Year* in the 'trivial round', etc.
63 G. Battiscombe, *Charlotte Mary Yonge* (London, 1943), p. 73.
64 This romance by the German writer de la Motte Fouqué (1777–1843) had a period of considerable popularity in England. For analysis of its relationship to Charlotte Yonge's book, see G. and K. Tillotson, *Mid-Victorian Studies* (London, 1965), pp. 52–4.
65 E.Sichel, *The Life and Letters of Alfred Ainger* (no date), p. 43.
66 Except *The Pillars of the House* her novels are generally weaker after Keble's death in 1866.
67 *The Trial*, ch. 4; (all references to 1874 edn), p. 46.
68 *Christian Remembrancer* (July 1860).
69 J.T.Coleridge, *Memoir of the Reverend John Keble* (1869), vol. 1, p. 64.

CHAPTER 4   THE INDIGNATION OF CHARLES KINGSLEY (pp. 88–114)

1 *Macmillan's Magazine* (January 1864), p. 217.
2 F.L.Mulhauser, ed, *The Correspondence of Arthur Hugh Clough* (Oxford, 1957), p. 312.
3 *Two Years Ago* (1857), ch. 2; (all references to New Century edn, London, 1908, p. 66.
4 Ibid., Introduction. Kingsley was particularly impressed by *Heartsease*. Charlotte Yonge did not reciprocate his admiration and for many years refused to read him.
5 F.L.Mulhauser, op. cit., p. 271.
6 C.C.Abbott, ed., *The Correspondence of Gerard Manley Hopkins and Richard Watson Dixon* (Oxford, 1955), p. 77.
7 *Two Years Ago*, ch. 26, p. 615. The portrayal of anguish could sometimes carry Kingsley into morbidity; it happens in his poetry, where *St Maura* is a notably unpleasant example.
8 *Yeast*, ch. 3; (all references to Eversley edn, London, 1902), pp. 63–4,
9 A.J.C.Hare, *Biographical Sketches* (London, 1895), pp. 80–1.
10 G.Battiscombe, *John Keble* (London, 1963), p. 163.
11 O.Chadwick, *The Victorian Church* (London, 1966), p. 10.
12 U.Pope-Hennessy, *Canon Charles Kingsley* (London, 1948), p. 248.
13 *Two Years Ago*, ch. 10, p. 236; *Yeast*, ch. 4, p. 95.
14 *Christian Remembrancer* (October 1857), p. 394.
15 *Yeast*, ch. 12, p. 225.
16 Ibid., chs 2, 3, 10, pp. 33, 61, 183.
17 He was even prepared to call himself an old-fashioned High Churchman (F.E.Kingsley, *Charles Kingsley: His Letters and Memories of his Life* (1876), vol. 2, p. 162).
18 Grace Harvey in *Two Years Ago*, ch. 4, p. 109.
19 Ibid., chs 10, 18, pp. 230, 443.
20 *Yeast*, ch. 17, p. 344.
21 *Two Years Ago*, ch. 25, p. 651.
22 Newman in his *Apologia* recalled how he had drawn a rosary when a schoolboy of nine: 'I suppose I got the idea from some romance, Mrs Radcliffe's or Miss Porter's; or from some religious picture'; (all references to Fontana edn, London, 1959, p. 97).
23 See, for instance, the famous 'catspaw' cartoon in *Punch*, vol. 19, p. 246; the association of 'Pusey' and 'pussy' was a gift to the Victorian punsters.
24 W.H.Dunn, *James Anthony Froude* (Oxford, 1961), vol. 1, p. 71.
25 S.L.Ollard, *A Short History of the Oxford Movement* (London, 1915) p. 134. What Arnold actually wrote, in a letter dated 30

Notes

October 1841, was: 'My feelings towards a Roman Catholic are quite different from my feelings towards a Newmanite, because I think the one a fair enemy, the other a dangerous one. The one is a Frenchman in his own uniform, and within his own praesidia; the other is the Frenchman disguised in a red coat, and holding a post within our praesidia, for the purpose of betraying it. I should honour the first, and hang the second' (A.P.Stanley, *The Life and Correspondence of Thomas Arnold* (eighth edn. 1858), vol. 2, pp. 245–6.

26 Some notable examples are Anne Howard's *Mary Spencer* (1844) and *Ridley Seldon* (1845); Catherine Long's *Sir Roland Ashton* (1844); Jean Ingelow's *Allerton and Dreux* (1851).

27 C.R.Woodring, *Victorian Samplers* (Laurence, Kansas, 1952), p. 49.

28 Lest it be thought that sanitary reform was a Broad Church exclusive preserve, it is worth recalling that Charlotte Yonge shows an anxious, if not always deeply scientific, awareness of the connection between bad living conditions and disease. It is a perpetual worry for good Dr May and appears in *The Young Stepmother* and *The Three Brides* also.

29 Keble once dealt with an argument about the evidence of geology with the assertion that 'when God made the stones He made the fossils in them', W. Tuckwell, *Reminiscences of Oxford* (second edn, 1907), p. 37.

30 U.Pope-Hennessy, op. cit., p. 193.

31 *Alton Locke*, ch. 10; (all references to New Century edn, London, 1908), p. 123.

32 On different occasions he said that this experience made him 'for years the veriest aristocrat' and 'that sight made me a Radical' (R.B.Martin, *The Dust of Combat* (London, 1959), pp. 28–9). There is no reason to suppose that Kingsley, who was as ambivalent as many of his contemporaries about the 'condition of England question' was dishonest in either statement.

33 Disraeli's influence, as novelist as well as political thinker, is particularly apparent in *Yeast*. For instance: Lancelot's first meeting with Argemone at the ruined chapel, reminiscent of the meeting of Egremont and Sybil; the character of Lord Vieux-bois; Lancelot reflects on *Coningsby* when Tregarva condemns private almsgiving; the likeness between Barnakill and Sidonia – omniscient, garrulous and mysterious.

34 *Yeast*, ch. 6, p. 118.

35 Ibid., Preface to the first edn, 1851.

36 U.Pope-Hennessy, op. cit., p. 139.

37 C.M.Yonge, *Musings over the 'Christian Year'*, etc (1871), pp. xxxiv–xxxv.
38 Ibid., p. lxix; recollections by Frances Wilbraham.
39 W.Robbins, *The Newman Brothers* (London, 1966), p. 141.
40 R.B.Martin, op. cit., p. 240.
41 *Yeast* ch. 7, pp. 129–30; Argemone in this novel may contain characteristics of Froude's wife as well as Kingsley's; the Puseyite Vicar who works against Lancelot may have been partly based on William Cope, the clerical patron of Eversley.
42 Review of *Yeast* in the *Guardian* (7 May 1851), a paper hostile to Christian Socialists as well as to Broad Churchmen.
43 *Yeast* first appeared in serial form in *Fraser's Magazine* during 1848; it was withdrawn when its radical attacks on country landlords began to anger subscribers. When Kingsley revised it for the 1851 edition, from which quotations in this chapter are drawn, he added Lancelot's correspondence with Luke and the portrait of Newman in ch. 14 – 'What a man . . .' – quoted on p. 110 of this chapter.
44 *Yeast*, ch. 11.
45 Ibid., ch. 13.
46 Yonge, op. cit., p. xxii.
47 *Westward Ho!*, ch. 3 (1899 edn), p. 54; cf. the last section of Kingsley's pamphlet in 1864, *What, then, does Dr Newman mean?*
48 R.W.Church, *The Oxford Movement* (1891), p. 259 note 7.
49 *Yeast*, ch. 8.
50 Ibid., ch. 10.
51 Ibid., ch. 17.
52 *Fraser's Magazine* (April 1848).

CHAPTER 5   FROM OXFORD TO ROME (pp. 115–41)

1 C.M.Yonge, *Musings over the 'Christian Year'*, etc. p. xc.
2 *Apologia pro Vita Sua*, Fontana edn (London, 1959), p. 130.
3 *Phases of Faith*, p. 7.
4 *The Nemesis of Faith*, p. 160.
5 Ibid., p. 216.
6 *Via Media of the Anglican Church*; (all references to 1877 edn), vol. 2, p. 408.
7 C.S.Dessain, ed., *The Letters and Diaries of John Henry Newman*, vol. 12, pp. 356–7 (London, 1962).
8 F.L.Mulhauser, ed., *The Correspondence of Arthur Hugh Clough* (Oxford, 1957), p. 182.

9 *Loss and Gain*, p. 240; (all references to Reynard Library edn, ed. G. Tillotson, London, 1957).

10 D. Gwynn, *Cardinal Wiseman* (Dublin, 1950), p. 97.

11 R. W. Church, *The Oxford Movement* (1891), p. 342.

12 M. Trevor, *Newman: The Pillar of the Cloud* (London, 1962), p. 383.

13 'Max O'Rell' (Paul Blouet), *John Bull and his Island* (no date, c. 1885), p. 262.

14 *The Position of Catholics in England* (1851), ed. D. M. O'Connell (New York, 1952), p. 66.

15 R. Stang, *The Theory of the Novel in England* (London, 1959), p. 4.

16 M. Trevor, op. cit., p. 421.

17 F. L. Mulhauser, op. cit., p. 202.

18 E. Bellasis, *Memorials of Mr Serjeant Bellasis* (1893), p. 71.

19 Newman's brothers were Charles (1802–84), and Francis (1805–97), who have appeared in these pages and will do so again. Both of them turned away from orthodox Christianity. It is of some interest that Newman gave his hero and the hero's favourite sister the Christian names of Charles and Mary. His own sister Mary, whom he had loved deeply, had died in 1828.

20 J. Newman. *Loss and Gain* (1848), p. 305.

21 Ibid., p. 297.

22 Thus Campbell, a Cambridge man, is made to condemn Keble's reference to the Roman Catholic Church in *The Christian Year*: 'A poet says, "Speak *gently* of our sister's *fall*"; no, if it is a fall, we must not speak gently of it' (*Loss and Gain*, p. 267).

23 Years later, Newman recalled how he had abstained from all Roman Catholic practices during his last period as an Anglican, 'for I never could understand how a man could be of two religions at once' (*Apologia*, p. 259).

24 *Loss and Gain*, p. 184.

25 The fourth-century followers of Sabellius denied the orthodox teaching about the Trinity and declared that Father, Son and Spirit were only names for the same 'substance' in different manifestations. Francis Newman came to the conclusion that the Evangelicals really had a similar view.

26 *Loss and Gain*, p. 200.

27 Ibid., p. 307.

28 Ibid., p. 116.

29 *Apologia*, p. 330.

30 *Loss and Gain*, pp. 351–2.

31 *From Oxford to Rome: and how it fared with some who lately made the journey*, by a Companion Traveller (1847), p. 109.

32 *Loss and Gain*, pp. 240–1.

33 *Whose is the Loss, or Whose the Gain, by the secession of the Rev Mr Newman, and others? Considered in a lettter to his Grace the Archbishop of Dublin* by 'Decanus' (1846), pp. 3–4.

34 F.L.Mulhauser, op. cit., p. 556.

35 Isaac Williams, *Autobiography* ed. G. Prévost (1892), p. 69.

36 D.Newsome, *The Parting of Friends* (London, 1966), p. 360.

37 E.S.Purcell, *The Life of Cardinal Manning* (1896), vol. 1, p. 233.

38 J.Fitzsimons, ed., *Manning: Anglican and Catholic* (London, 1951), p. 20.

39 Gorham's baptismal views were rather more 'unorthodox' than those of the moderate Evangelicals.

40 D.C.Lathbury, ed., *Correspondence on Church and Religion of W.E.Gladstone* (London, 1910), vol. 1, p. 283.

41 W.Ward, *The Life of John Henry Cardinal Newman based on his Private Journals and Correspondence* (London, 1912), vol. 1, p. 581.

42 *Apologia*, p. 82.

43 Ibid., p. 89.

44 *Essays in Little* (1891), p. 155.

45 *Apologia*, p. 83.

46 W.Robbins, *The Newman Brothers* (London, 1966), p. 21.

47 J.J.Reilly, *Newman as a Man of Letters* (New York, 1925), p. 303.

48 G.W.E.Russell, *Fifteen Chapters of Autobiography* (London, n.d.) pp. 317–18.

49 See 'Newman the Writer' in G. and K.Tillotson, op. cit., *Mid-Victorian Studies* (London, 1965), pp. 239–58.

50 *Apologia*, p. 297.

51 G. and K.Tillotson, op. cit., p. 255.

52 *Athenaeum* (26 March 1864).

53 *The George Eliot Letters 1836–1880*, ed. G.S.Haight (Oxford, 1954–6), vol. 4, pp. 158–9.

54 'Emerson' in *Discourses in America* in *Works* (1903 edn London), vol. 4, pp. 349–50.

CHAPTER 6   THE APPEAL TO ANTIQUITY (pp. 142–69)

1 Charles Kingsley, *Yeast*, ch. 6, Eversley edn (London, 1902), p. 114.

2 William Palmer, *A Narrative of Events connected with the publication of the Tracts for the Times* (1843), p. 44. Palmer had been one of those present at Hadleigh.

3 J.Bromley, *The Man of Ten Talents* (London, 1959), p. 66.

4 D.Newsome, *The Parting of Friends* (London, 1966).

5 A.P.Stanley, *The Life and Correspondence of Thomas Arnold*, 8th edn (1858), vol. 1, p. 213.
6 J.H.Overton, *The Anglican Revival* (1897), p. 92.
7 *Loss and Gain*, p. 231.
8 *Apologia pro Vita Sua*, Fontana edn, p. 199. (London, 1959).
9 Ibid., p. 176.
10 *Loss and Gain*, p. 314.
11 Ibid., p. 306.
12 *Studies in Literature* (1891), pp. 68–9.
13 *The Christian Year*, poems for Monday before Easter, Monday in Easter Week, St Barnabas.
14 C.M.Yonge, *Musings over the 'Christian Year', etc* (1871), p. 329.
15 *Nemesis of Faith*, p. 122.
16 *Fabiola*, Preface; (all references to the Burnes and Oates edn 1895), p. vii.
17 Ibid., Preface.
18 D.Gwynn, *Cardinal Wiseman* (Dublin, 1950), p. 155.
19 *Fabiola*, pp. 156–61.
20 Ibid., p. 218.
21 P. 217. The modern French writer is presumably Victor Hugo, whose *Derniers jours d'un condamné* (1829) had appeared in two separate English translations in 1840; I am indebted to Dr K.E. M.George for this suggestion.
22 *Fabiola*, p. 13.
23 Ibid., p. 70.
24 *Hypatia* (1853) p. 382; (all references to Oxford University Press edn.)
25 Ibid., p. 449.
26 In 1851 Kingsley had been forbidden by Blomfield to preach in London, after complaints about socialism in a sermon preached at St John's, Charlotte Street. The inhibition was removed after the Bishop had read the offending sermon.
27 Kingsley was pleased enough with the title to use it, in the form 'An Old Foe with a New Face' as the heading of ch. 6 of *Two Years Ago*.
28 P. 298. Kingsley's interest in Synesius may have owed something to J.A.Froude, who had admired him on rather different grounds in *The Nemesis of Faith*: 'One remembers the case of Synesius, who when he was pressed to take a bishopric by the Alexandrian metropolitan, declared he would not teach fables in church unless he might philosophize at home' (p. 41).
29 *Blackwood's Magazine* (June 1855), vol. 77, p. 639.
30 *The Times* (8 June 1863); (reporting from the *Spectator*).
31 *Callista* (1855); (all references to Longmans edn, 1890), p. 16.

32 Newman does not explicitly state this, but only, 'If he be the bishop of that name who suffered at Sicca in his old age, in the persecution of Diocletian', etc. This kind of guarded mingling of tradition and fiction, reminiscent of the style of the Oxford *Lives of the Saints*, was one of the things that infuriated Kingsley about Newman.

33 *Callista*, p. 71.

34 Ibid., p. 336.

35 Ibid., p. 16.

36 *Hypatia*, p. 299.

37 *Callista*, p. 42.

38 Ibid., p. 210–11.

39 M.Trevor, *Newman, Light in Winter* (London, 1962), p. 68.

40 *Callista*, p. 317.

41 Anthony Trollope, *The Warden* (1855), ch. 2.

42 Mary Howitt, quoted in C.R.Woodring, *Victorian Samplers* (Laurence, Kansas, 1952), p. 215.

43 Not to be confused with William Palmer of Worcester College, whose *Reminiscences* was quoted above.

44 Some of the best known are 'Jerusalem the Golden', 'The Day of Resurrection', 'The heavenly Word proceeding forth', 'Light's abode, celestial Salem', 'O happy band of pilgrims', 'Brief life is here our portion', 'The day is past and over'.

45 *Theodora Phranza* (all references to S.P.C.K. edn, 1903), p. 206.

46 Ibid., p. 39.

47 Ibid., Preface to first edn.

48 A.P.Stanley, *The Eastern Church* (1861); (all references to Everyman edn), p. 94.)

49 *Loss and Gain*, p. 266.

50 S.Baring-Gould, *The Vicar of Morwenstow* (1899); (all references to 1913 edn), p. 173.

CHAPTER 7   UPHILL ALL THE WAY (pp. 170–97)

1 G.Battiscombe, *Christina Rossetti* (London, 1965), p. 25.

2 On this point, see A.M.Allchin, *The Silent Rebellion* (London, 1958).

3 The theory that she was in love with the poet William Bell Scott is developed, on the whole convincingly, by L.M.Packer in *Christina Rossetti* (Cambridge, 1963).

4 William Dodsworth (1798–1861) was a Cambridge man who moved from Evangelical to Tractarian churchmanship. He was at the Margaret Street Chapel before going to Christ Church. He was one of those who seceded after the Gorham Judgement.

5 *Maude*, written in 1850, published with an Introduction by W. M.Rossetti in 1897.

6 The diocesan court of Bath and Wells condemned the Archdeacon of Taunton, G.A.Denison, for his teaching about the Eucharist. The Puseyite leaders regarded this case as a test of the doctrine of Holy Communion as the Gorham case had been of baptism.

7 *The Family Letters of Christina Georgina Rossetti*, ed. W.M. Rossetti (London, 1908), p. 103.

8 *The Rossetti-Macmillan Letters* ed. L.M.Packer (Cambridge, 1963), p. 120.

9 R.F.Littledale (1833–90) was a graduate of Trinity College, Dublin, and a friend of J.M.Neale. He published a number of doctrinal and apologetic works; his *Plain Reasons for Not Joining the Church of Rome* (1880) sold over 36,000 copies.

10 *Family Letters*, p. 72.

11 'Pros and Cons' in *Churchman's Shilling* (1867), reprinted in *Commonplace and Other Stories* (1870).

12 H.P.Liddon, *The Life of Edward Bouverie Pusey* (1893), ch. 4, p. 212. Pusey was speaking to the Church Union in 1866.

13 Preface to the 'Golden Treasury' selection of her poetry (London, 1904), p. ix.

14 *Parochial and Plain Sermons*, ed. W.J.Copeland (London, 1868) vol. 3, p. 124, 'A Particular Providence as Revealed in the Gospel'.

15 *The Poetical Works of Christina Georgina Rossetti* (London, 1906), p. 460. The other poems referred to are 'Ash Wednesday' and 'L.E.L.'.

16 The legend is traceable to Violet Hunt, *The Wife of Rossetti* (London, 1932).

17 *Family Letters*, pp. 60–1.

18 L.M.Packer, op. cit., p. 154.

19 'Golden Treasury' selection, p. x.

20 *Family Letters*, p. 29.

21 Ibid., p. 164.

22 Ibid., pp. 14, 76.

23 *The Castle Builders*; (all references to 1885 edn), p. 194.

24 *Family Letters*, p. 186.

25 She would not go to receptions or parties during Lent, even to members of her own family.

26 *Sermons during the Seasons from Advent to Whitsuntide* (1848), p. 135.

27 *Sermons Preached in St Saviour's, Leeds* (1845), p. 163.

28 Cf. Hurrell Froude's sermon, 'Knowledge of Duty attainable only by Practising' (*Remains*, vol. 1, pt 1, pp. 95–108).
29 *Family Letters*, pp. 175–6. It is worthy of mention that her agnostic brother William had his own scruples about accepting the dedication of one of her books since he did not share her faith (ibid., p. 193).
30 *Sermons Preached in St Saviour's, Leeds*, p. 163.
31 So great was the importance attached to baptism for the remission of sins, and so difficult the conditions of reconciliation after grave post-baptismal sin, that catechumens would try to postpone baptism until death seemed near.
32 Pusey, *Plain Sermons*, ed. Isaac Williams (1839–48), vol. 3, p. 272.
33 'Golden Treasury' selection, p. xii.
34 *Family Letters*, pp. 25–6.
35 Ibid., p. 51.
36 Newman, *Parochial and Plain Sermons*, vol. 4, p. 233.
37 *Seek and Find* (1879), p. 14.
38 W. H. Hutton, quoted in S. L. Ollard, *A Short History of the Oxford Movement* (London, 1915), p. 205.

CHAPTER 8   A PLAGUE O' BOTH YOUR HOUSES (pp. 198–226)

1 *Oakfield* (1853), vol. 1; (all references to 1854 edn), p. 15. The author, William Arnold (1828–59), was the second son of Thomas Arnold. He went from Rugby to Christ Church, Oxford, thence to India. His death at Gibraltar is the subject of his brother Matthew's poem 'A Southern Night'.
2 J. A. Froude, *The Nemesis of Faith* (1849), pp. 180–1.
3 R. W. Church, *The Oxford Movement* (1891), p. 294.
4 *The Nemesis of Faith*, p. 19.
5 Ibid., p. 26.
6 Ibid., pp. 106–7.
7 *Phases of Faith* (1881 ed.), p. vi.
8 Ibid., p. 167.
9 E. L. Woodward, *The Age of Reform*; (all references to second edn, Oxford, 1962), p. 512.
10 *The Nemesis of Faith*, p. 123.
11 Unpublished letter quoted in W. Robbins, *The Newman Brothers* (London, 1966), p. 26.
12 Mark Pattison, *Memoirs* (1885), p. 30.
13 *Oakfield*, vol. 1, p. 18.
14 *Works* (London, 1903), vol. 13, p. 236.
15 *The Nemesis of Faith*, p. 137.

16 M.Pattison, op. cit., p. 230.
17 Ibid., p. 212.
18 *The Nemesis of Faith*, p. 126.
19 *Shadows of the Clouds* (1847), p. 157.
20 *Short Studies on Great Subjects*, ed. D. Ogg (London, 1963), p. 236.
21 *Phases of Faith*, p. 72.
22 F.L.Mulhauser, ed., *The Correspondence of Arthur Hugh Clough* (London, 1957), pp. 63, 70.
23 *Shadows of the Clouds*, p. 35.
24 *Short Studies*, p. 243.
25 *Shadows of the Clouds*, p. 73.
26 See 'Matthew Arnold and Carlyle' in G. and K.Tillotson, *Mid-Victorian Studies* (London, 1965). Froude's eventual disappointment in Carlyle may be compared with Clough's farewell remark to Emerson: 'Carlyle has led us all out into the desert, and he has left us there' (E.E.Hale, *J. R.Lowell and his Friends* (1898), ch. 9, p. 46).
27 W.H.Dunn, *James Anthony Froude* (Oxford, 1961), p. 77. It may be worth stating here, since the misapprehension still lingers, that Froude did *not* end his work on St Neot with the words: 'This is all, and perhaps more than all, that is known of the life of the blessed St Neot.' The sentence is taken, and misquoted, from another life in the series by Newman and Dalgairns. For the growth and demolition of the error see 'An Injustice to Froude' by M.E.V. (*Notes and Queries*, 2 June 1945), and Dunn, op. cit., pp. 78–9.
28 T.Mozley, *Reminiscences* (1882), vol. 2, p. 29.
29 *Short Studies*, p. 253.
30 W.H.Dunn, op. cit., pp. 105–7.
31 *The Nemesis of Faith*, p. 35.
32 Ibid., p. 227.
33 The Sub-rector was William Sewell (1804–74), an early Tractarian sympathizer who was alienated by the Romanizers of the early forties but remained a staunch and, as the *Nemesis* episode shows, even an aggressive Anglican. *Punch* made great play with the affair: 'To have publicly refuted it would have been wiser than to have publicly burned it' (vol. 16, p. 114). The burning took place in the College hall and was scarcely 'public'.
34 F.L.Mulhauser, op. cit., p. 247.
35 W.H.Dunn, op. cit., p. 227.
36 F.L.Mulhauser, op. cit., p. 251.
37 C.S.Dessain, ed., *The Letters and Diaries of John Henry Newman* (London, 1963), vol. 13, p. 415.

38 *Phases of Faith* (1850), p. 44.

39 Ibid., pp. 89–90.

40 This section was added to the 1853 edn.

41 Pp. 174–5. Francis Newman's later career has little bearing on the Oxford Movement but it touches many points of interest in Victorian society. See Robbins, op. cit., and the excellent chapter by Basil Willey in *More Nineteenth-Century Studies* (London, 1956).

42 All quotations from Pattison are from the posthumous edn of his *Memoirs* (1885).

43 Ibid., pp. 184–5.

44 Ibid., p. 189

45 Ibid., p. 215.

46 Ibid.

47 Ibid., p. 236.

48 Ibid., p. 250.

49 Ibid., pp. 327–8.

50 F.L.Mulhauser, op. cit., p. 9.

51 Ibid., p. 67.

52 Ibid., pp. 71–2.

53 K.Chorley, *Arthur Hugh Clough* (Oxford, 1962), p. 17.

54 *Obermann*, pp. 133–6.

55 *Dipsychus* IX, 1–12.

56 F.L.Mulhauser, op. cit., p. 81.

57 Ibid., p. 86.

58 Ibid., p. 92.

59 Wilfrid Ward, *W.G.Ward and the Oxford Movement* (1889), p. 108.

60 F.L.Mulhauser, op. cit., p. 124.

61 Ibid., p. 166.

62 K.Chorley, op. cit., pp. 103–4.

63 Clough here misquotes from the Catechism, in a way that is still common. The end of the response to the question 'What is thy duty towards thy neighbour?' reads 'To do my duty in that state of life, unto which it *shall* please God to call me'.

64 *Guardian* (28 March 1849).

65 F.L.Mulhauser, op. cit., p. 515.

66 *Phases of Faith*, p. 137.

67 *The Nemesis of Faith*, p. 24.

68 *Phases of Faith*, p. 50.

69 *The Nemesis of Faith*, p. 17.

70 R.C.Trench; see J.Bromley, *The Man of Ten Talents* (London, 1959), p. 119.

71 *Bothie*, IV, ll. 165–6. The line 'No, I defy Thee. . . .!' is found in Clough's corrected copy of 1848.

Notes

72 *Shadows of the Clouds*, p. 159.
73 *Dipsychus*, VI, ll. 156–7.
74 *Oakfield*, vol. I, p. 27.
75 *Short Studies*, p. 241.
76 *The Nemesis of Faith*, pp. 51–2.

CHAPTER 9   LAST ENCHANTMENTS (pp. 227–51)

1 See *Punch*, vol. 12, pp. 126, 267; vol. 13, p. 122.
2 M.Trappes-Lomax, *Pugin* (London, 1932), p. 57.
3 Reviewing Lockhart's *Life of Scott* in the *British Critic* reprinted in *Occasional Papers and Reviews* (1877), p. 67.
4 C.M.Yonge, *Musings on the 'Christian Year'*, etc, pp. v–vi, lxxxvi.
5 *Apologia pro Vita Sua*, pp. 341–2.
6 On this subject see the excellent work by Kenneth Clark, *The Gothic Revival*; (all references to rev. edn, London, 1950).
7 E.A.Towle, *John Mason Neale* (London, 1906), p. 51.
8 *Loss and Gain* p. 263; Newman of course is being satirical.
9 Quoted in D.Newsome, *The Parting of Friends* (London, 1966), p.314.
10 O.Chadwick, *The Victorian Church* (London, 1966), p. 418.
11 Quoted in S.L.Ollard, *A Short History of the Oxford Movement* (London, 1915), p. 228. This was the Dean Close who had said that he would be sorry to trust the author of Tract 90 with his purse. In a later edition of the book quoted he was even more explicit: 'Mediaeval architecture . . . was Popish; was designed and adapted for Mass-Houses, not for reading and hearing of God's Word.'
12 D.Gwynn, *Cardinal Wiseman* (Dublin, 1950), p. 140.
13 *Memorials of Edward Burne-Jones* by G.B–J (Georgina Burne-Jones) (London, 1904), vol. I, p. 39; hereafter referred to as *Memorials*.
14 Ibid., p. 71.
15 J.W.Mackail, *The Life of William Morris* (1899), p. 10 of the World's Classics edn (Oxford, 1950) to which all references in this chapter are made.
16 In a letter which he wrote to the Austrian Socialist Andreas Scheu in 1883.
17 MS. notes used by Mackail; quoted in R.W.Sambrook, *A Poet Hidden* (London, 1962), p. 19.
18 *Memorials*, vol. I, p. 78.
19 J.W.Mackail, op. cit., p. 56.
20 Ibid., p. 63.

21 Morris's Preface to the Kelmscott Press edn of *On the Nature of Gothic* (1892).
22 J.W.Mackail, op. cit., p. 87.
23 *Memorials*, vol. 1, p. 71.
24 D.Macleane, *A History of Pembroke College, Oxford* (1897), p. 460 note.
25 *Works* (London, 1903), vol. 13, p. 51.
26 *Memorials*, vol. 1, p. 59.
27 Ibid., p. 99.
28 Ibid., p. 109.
29 J.W.Mackail, op. cit., p. 85.
30 Robert Bridges, *Three Friends* (Oxford, 1932), p. 113.
31 G.Hough, *The Last Romantics*; (all references to new edn London, 1961), p. 83.
32 'The New Renaissance' by H.Quilter in *Macmillan's Magazine* (September 1880).
33 *Yeast*, ch. 15; (all references to Eversley edn, London, 1902), p. 312.
34 *Life, Letters and Literary Remains of J.H.Shorthouse*, pp. 108–9.
35 J.W.Mackail, op. cit., p. 311.
36 Ibid., p. 313.
37 *Athenaeum* (11 May 1861), p. 629.
38 P. 92. Page references to C.C.Abbott, ed., *The Correspondence of Gerard Manley Hopkins and Richard Watson Dixon*.
39 Ibid., pp. 98, 104, 131.
40 C.C.Abbott, op. cit., pp. 118–20; Hopkins was at this time teaching at the Catholic University in Dublin.
41 *The Family Letters of Christina Georgina Rossetti*, p. 48.
42 P. 10. Page references in this section are to Bridges, op. cit. The life of Dolben reprinted in this book was originally written as a preface to Bridges's edition of Dolben's poetry, published in 1911.
43 J.L.Lyne (1837–1908) revived the Benedictine order in the Anglican Church in 1863 and took the name of Ignatius. In 1870 he founded a community in Wales without proper ecclesiastical authority; after his death the property passed to the Benedictines founded at Caldey by Aeldred Carlyle in 1898.
44 *Three Friends*, p. 77.
45 Ibid., p. 86.
46 Ibid., p. 17.
47 Preface to *Essays in Criticism*, first series (1865).
48 J.H.Shorthouse, *Sir Percival* (1886); (all references to 1894 edn), p. 123.

Notes

1 *Life*, p. 4. Most of the information about Shorthouse as a man is to be found in *Life, Letters and Literary Remains of J.H.Shorthouse*, edited by his widow (London, 1905). The first volume is referred to in this chapter as *Life*, the second as *Remains*. Edmund Gosse in *Portraits and Sketches* (London, 1912) was critical about this work; but he was not very intimately acquainted with Shorthouse and other sources of evidence generally confirm the reliability of Mrs Shorthouse.

2 *Life*, p. 237.

3 Ibid., p. 398.

4 Ibid., p. 64.

5 Ibid., pp. 65–8.

6 James Payn (1830–98) was a prolific novelist and wrote something over a hundred books. He began reading for Smith Elder in 1874.

7 *Westminster Review*, new series, vol. 60, p. 568.

8 *Saturday Review* (9 July 1881), p. 51.

9 *Life*, p. 142.

10 Ibid., p. 107.

11 *Spectator* (25 March 1882) p. 389.

12 *Blackwood's Magazine*, vol. 131, p. 374.

13 *Life*, pp. 169, 274.

14 'Theological Romances' in *Contemporary Review*, vol. 53, p. 815.

15 In a letter dated 28 May 1894, *Life*, p. 329.

16 A severe attack is made by M.Polak in *The Historical, Philosophical and Religious Aspects of John Inglesant* (Purmerend, 1933). The author's indignation at Shorthouse's plagiarisms makes him unable to judge the merits of the novel. There is an idiosyncratic defence of the skill with which Shorthouse used his sources in 'Some Truths about John Inglesant' by W.K.Fleming (*Quarterly Review*, vol. 245, pp. 130–48). A much more sensible assessment is made in 'John Inglesant and its author' by Morchard Bishop (*Essays by Divers Hands*, Royal Society of Literature, vol. 29, pp. 73–87).

17 Letter to Edmund Gosse dated 1 April 1883, *Life*, pp. 190–1.

18 Ibid., pp. 199–200. In 1883 Shorthouse wrote a commendatory Preface to a book of selections from the *Spiritual Guide* of Molinos.

19 *Blanche, Lady Falaise* (1891), p. 10.

20 *Remains*, p. 13.

21 Ibid., p. 207.

Faith and Revolt

22 The latitudinarian Vincent in *Loss and Gain* takes precisely this attitude (p. 154).
23 e.g. 'Shorthouse infused seventeenth-century history with current religious emotions born of Anglo-Catholic mysticism' (C.R. Woodring, *Victorian Samplers* (Laurence, Kansas, 1952), p. 221).
24 *Remains*, p. 222.
25 Ibid., p. 113.
26 'Bede', ibid., p. 96.
27 Ibid., p. 83.
28 *Life*, p. 404.
29 Ibid., p. xiv.
30 Shorthouse's benefactress Mrs Humphry Ward thought that aesthetic attraction would be a major factor in such conversion. Her Dora Lomax is drawn from dissent to Anglo-Catholicism by entering a Puseyite church and discovering 'something in the ordering of the place, in its colours, its scents, in the voice of its priest' (*The History of David Grieve*; all references to 6th edn 1892, p. 163).
31 *Life*, p. 64.
32 Ibid., pp. 363–4.
33 *Remains*, p. 125.
34 *John Inglesant*; (all references to one-volume edn 1883), p. 83.
35 F.J.Nicholson, *Quakers and the Arts* (London, 1968), p. 51.
36 *Sir Percival* (1886); (all references to 1894 edn), p. 154.
37 *John Inglesant*, pp. 63–4.
38 L.Linder, ed., *The Journal of Beatrix Potter* (London, 1966), p. 362.
39 A.L.Maycock, *Chronicles of Little Gidding* (London, 1954), p. 1.
40 *John Inglesant*, p. 260.
41 Ibid., pp. 442–3.
42 Ibid., pp. 59, 62.
43 *Blanche, Lady Falaise*, pp. 171–2.
44 *Sir Percival*, pp. 294–5.
45 *Life*, p. 174.
46 'The Agnostic at Church', *Nineteenth Century*, vol. 11, pp. 650–2.
47 *Life*, p. 358.
48 Ibid., loc. cit.
49 Ibid., p. 386.
50 Ibid., p. 378.
51 Ibid., pp. 304–5; the three exclamation marks, like the frequent italics in these quotations, are Shorthouse's.
52 *Saturday Review*, loc. cit.
53 *John Inglesant*, p. 39.
54 *Sir Percival*, p. 71.

55 *Life*, pp. 372–3.
56 Ibid., p. 365; John Cosin (1594–1672), Bishop of Durham, was a friend of Laud, suffered exile during the Commonwealth, and was one of the revisers of the Book of Common Prayer after the Restoration.
57 'The Fordhams of Severnstoke', *Remains*, p. 373.
58 *John Inglesant*, p. 142.
59 Ibid., p31.
60 *Blanche, Lady Falaise*, p. 4.
61 *Life*, pp. 123, 370.
62 Ibid., p. 365.
63 Ibid., pp. xii, 399.
64 Ibid., p. 308.
65 Ibid., p. xx.
66 Ibid., p. 84.
67 Ibid., p. 129; this paper was read to the Wordsworth Society in July 1881.
68 See W.Schrickx, 'Coleridge and the Cambridge Platonists' (*Review of English Literature*, vol. 7, no. 1, pp. 71–90).
69 *Nineteenth Century* (May 1884).
70 *Life*, p. 371.
71 Ibid., p. 130.
72 *John Inglesant*, p. 434.
73 E.Sichel, *The Life and Letters of Alfred Ainger* (London, no date), p. 221.
74 *The Countess Eve* (1888), pp. 153–4 of 1891 edn.
75 *Life*, p. 136.
76 Ibid., pp. 303–4; Gore was the first Principal of Pusey House, Oxford, which was opened in 1884 to promote Anglo-Catholicism in the University.
77 *Blanche, Lady Falaise*, p. 125.

APPENDIX I   THE NOMENCLATURE OF THE MOVEMENT (pp. 280–89)

1 R.W.Church, *The Oxford Movement* (1891), p. 141.
2 C.Kingsley, *Yeast*, p. 226.
3 R.W.Church, op. cit., p. 54.
4 *Apologia pro Vita Sua*, p. 176 (Fontana edn, London, 1959).
5 F.L.Mulhauser, ed., *The Correspondence of Arthur Hugh Clough* (Oxford, 1957), p. 70.
6 R.W.Church, op. cit., p. 128.
7 *Works*, vol. 13, p. 233.
8 See Clough's *Bothie*, ll. 91–2, which read in the 1863 edn:

Faith and Revolt

All Cathedrals are Christian, all Christians are Cathedrals
Such is the Catholic doctrine;
Clough's corrected copy of 1848 has 'orthodox' instead of
'Catholic'.

9 C.M.Yonge, *Musings over the 'Christian Year'*, etc (1871), p. xl.
10 A.P.Stanley, *The Life and Correspondence of Thomas Arnold* (eighth edn, 1858), vol. 2, p. 7.
11 W.H.Dunn, *James Anthony Froude* (Oxford, 1961), pp. 40, 72; and his essay 'The Oxford Counter-Reformation' in the fourth volume of *Short Studies on Great Subjects*.
12 *Quarterly Review*, vol. 63, pp. 525–72.
13 Ibid., vol. 72, pp. 232–90.
14 S.O.E.D., s.v. 'Tractarian'; unspecified references to the first use of a word are taken from this source.
15 R.W.Church, op. cit., p. vii.
16 *Punch*, vol. 5, p. 181.
17 F.L.Mulhauser, op. cit., p. 166.
18 *Yeast*, pp. 38, 186.
19 S.L.Ollard, *The Oxford Movement* (London, 1915), p. 134.
20 G.V.Cox, *Recollections of Oxford* (1868), p. 302.
21 R.W.Church, op. cit., pp. 132, 159.
22 F.L.Mulhauser, op. cit., pp. 42, 67, 72, 86, 90, 100, 117.
23 A.P.Stanley, op. cit., vol. 2, p. 34.
24 F.L.Mulhauser, op. cit., p. 124.
25 In 1842 Robert Wilberforce's curate was accused of Puseyism when he ordered the bell to be *tolled* and not *rung* for a funeral (D.Newsome, *The Parting of Friends* (London, 1966), p. 280). Archbishop Trench was called a Puseyite for his insistence on the separate voting of the bishops, priests and laity in the new constitution of the Irish Church in 1869 – 'which at the time was a common epithet of abuse and contempt' (J. Bromley, op. cit., *The Man of Ten Talents* (London, 1959), p. 195).
26 W.Ward, *The Life of John Henry Cardinal Newman* (London, 1912) vol. 1, p. 237.
27 'If the Puseyites hate it they must fear it'; Mulhauser, op. cit., p. 251.
28 *From Oxford to Rome*, p. 120; the new convert to Rome says: 'Puseyism is a step in the right direction and therefore to be encouraged and forwarded.'
29 O.Chadwick, *The Victorian Church* (London, 1966), p. 168.
30 S.L.Ollard, op. cit., p. 48.
31 e.g. *Loss and Gain*, p. 216; the 'Anglo-Catholick' community in J.M.Neale's *Ayton Priory* (1843) and the sub-title of Robert Armitage's *Dr Hookwell: or, The Anglo-Catholic Family* (1852).

314

32 Newman used the term to describe the churchmanship of the seventeenth-century English divines in his essay 'The Prophetical Office of the Church' in 1837, a use which antedates by four years the first reference in S.O.E.D.

33 D.Newsome, op. cit., p. 389.

34 R.W.Church, op. cit., p. 61.

35 F.L.Mulhauser, op. cit., p. 70.

36 E.Bellasis, *Memorials of Mr Serjeant Bellasis* (1893), p. 48.

37 *Yeast*, p. 24.

38 S.L.Ollard, op. cit., p. 135.

39 A.P.Stanley, op. cit., vol. 1, pp. 38, 310; vol. 2, p. 259.

40 F.L.Mulhauser, op. cit., p. 81.

41 *Apologia*, p. 86.

42 *Quarterly Review*, vol. 72, p. 244.

43 R.W.Church, op. cit., p. 269.

44 C.M.Yonge, op. cit., pp. 170, 352; also her last work, *Reasons Why I am a Catholic but not a Roman Catholic* (London, 1901).

45 *The Nemesis of Faith*, p. 122.

46 *Loss and Gain*, p. 215.

47 *Phases of Faith*, p. 72.

48 Mulhauser, op. cit., p. 91; C.M.Yonge, *The Castle Builders* (1854); (all references to 1885 edn), p. 224.

49 *On Eucharistical Adoration*; (all references to third edn 1867), p. 176.

50 S.L.Ollard, op. cit., p. 210.

51 The essay was published in the *British Critic* in April 1839 and reprinted as the sixth essay in *Essays Critical and Historical* vol. 1 (1871), from which references below are made.

52 Ibid., p. 293.

53 Ibid., p. 306.

54 'Church Parties' in *Edinburgh Review*, vol. 98 (1853), pp. 273–342; reprinted in *Essays Ecclesiastical and Social* (1856). The Reverend William John Conybeare (1815–57) was a regular contributor to the *Edinburgh*. He attacked Anglo-Catholicism in his novel *Perversion* (1856).

55 'The name *Broad Church* was used by Stanley in one of his sermons about 1847, but W.C.Lake heard it used by A.H.Clough before that' (*Memorials of William Charles Lake, Dean of Durham*, ed. Katharine Lake (London, 1901), p. 35).

Bibliography

In dealing with events which caused as much strong contemporary feeling as those of the Oxford Movement, early accounts and opinions are of unusual interest. Newman's *Apologia pro Vita Sua* (1864) is of the greatest importance, for this reason as for others; but, as was stated in the text of Chapter 5, it is a highly personal account of one man's part. *The Oxford Movement* by R.W.Church (1891) is a partisan but honest account on which all later historians of the movement have extensively drawn. Two men who were deeply involved in the Tractarian years but were critical of later extremes have left their records: Isaac Williams in his *Autobiography*, ed. G. Prévost (1892); and William Palmer in *A Narrative of Events Connected with the Publication of the Tracts for the Times* (1883). Newman's brother-in-law, Thomas Mozley, told his version in *Reminiscences, chiefly of Oriel College and the Oxford Movement* (1882). Mark Pattison's *Memoirs* (1885) have been discussed as a hostile recollection. A work more sympathetic to the Romanizing party is Wilfrid Ward's *W.G.Ward and the Oxford Movement* (1889). There are some objective records in W.Tuckwell's *Reminiscences of Oxford* (1901).

Valuable source-material is reprinted in the following:

Church and Parliament 1828–1860, ed. O.J.Brose (Oxford, 1958).
Religious Controversies of the Nineteenth Century, ed. A.O.J. Cockshut (London, 1966).
The Mind of the Oxford Movement, ed. O. Chadwick (London, 1960).
Anti-Catholicism in Victorian England, ed. E.R.Norman (London, 1968).

Bibliography

MODERN WORKS – GENERAL

J.E.Baker, *The Novel and the Oxford Movement* (Princeton, 1932).
Y. Brilioth, *The Anglican Revival* (London, 1925). [Still an excellent analysis by a sympathetic but detached foreign scholar.]
F.K.Brown, *Fathers of the Victorians* (Cambridge, 1961).
J.H.Buckley, *The Victorian Temper* (London, 1952).
O.Chadwick, *The Victorian Church* (London, 1966).
A.O.J.Cockshut, *The Unbelievers* (London, 1964).
M.Cropper, *Shining Lights* (London, 1963).
C.Dawson, *The Spirit of the Oxford Movement* (London, 1933).
L.Elliott-Binns, *English Thought: the Theological Aspect 1860–1900* (London, 1956).
G.Faber, *The Oxford Apostles* (London, 1933). [Brilliant and lucid, but unsound in analysis of motivations.]
J.Holloway, *The Victorian Sage* (London, 1953).
E.D.H.Johnson, *The Alien Vision of Victorian Poetry* (Oxford, 1952).
E.E.Kellett, *Religion and Life in the Early Victorian Age* (London, 1938).
U.C.Knoepflmacher, *Religious Humanism and the Victorian Novel* (Princeton, 1965).
E.A.Knox, *The Tractarian Movement* (London, 1933).
G.I.T.Machin, *The Catholic Question in English Politics 1820 to 1830* (Oxford, 1964).
M.Maison, *Search Your Soul, Eustace* (London, 1961).
D.H.Newsome, *The Parting of Friends* (London, 1966).
S.L.Ollard, *A Short History of the Oxford Movement* (London, 1915). [Still well worth reading as an overall account, though somewhat uncritical in admiration.]
C.R.Sandars, *Coleridge and the Broad Church Movement* (London, 1942).
W.J.Sparrow-Simpson, *The History of the Anglo-Catholic Revival* (London, 1932).
A.R.Vidler, *The Church in an Age of Revolution* (Harmondsworth, 1961).
B.Willey, *Nineteenth-Century Studies* (London, 1949).
B.Willey, *More Nineteenth-Century Studies* (London, 1956).

MODERN WORKS – BIOGRAPHICAL AND CRITICAL

Thomas Arnold

T.W.Bamford, *Thomas Arnold* (London, 1960).
E.L.Williamson, *The Liberalism of Thomas Arnold* (Alabama, 1964).

Faith and Revolt

F.J.Woodward, *The Doctor's Disciples* (Oxford, 1954) [Arnold's influence on Clough and others.]

A.H.Clough

I.Armstrong, *Arthur Hugh Clough* (London, 1962).
K.Chorley, *Arthur Hugh Clough: the Uncommitted Mind* (Oxford, 1962).
M.Timko, *Innocent Victorian* (Ohio, 1966).

R.W.Dixon

J.Sambrook, *A Poet Hidden* (London, 1962).

J.A.Froude

W.H.Dunn, *James Anthony Froude* (Oxford, 1961).
H.Paul, *The Life of Froude* (London, 1906).
G.P.Gooch, *History and Historians in the Nineteenth Century* (London, rev. edn 1952).

John Keble

G.Battiscombe, *John Keble: a Study in Limitations* (London, 1963).
W.J.A.M.Beek, *John Keble's Literary and Religious Contribution to The Oxford Movement* (Nijmegen, 1959).

Charles Kingsley

G.Kendall, *Charles Kingsley and his Ideas* (London, 1947).
R.B.Martin, *The Dust of Combat* (London, 1960).
U.Pope-Hennessy, *Canon Charles Kingsley* (London, 1948).
H.G.Wood, *Frederick Denison Maurice* (Cambridge, 1950).

William Morris

R.P.Arnot, *William Morris* (London, 1964).
B.I.Evans, *Morris and his Poetry* (London, 1925).
M.R.Grennan, *William Morris: Medievalist and Revolutionary* (Columbia, 1945).
E.P.Thompson, *Morris: Romantic to Revolutionary* (1955).

Francis Newman

W.Robbins, *The Newman Brothers* (London, 1966).

Bibliography

J.H.Newman

J.M.Cameron, *John Henry Newman* (London, 1956).
A.D.Culler, *The Imperial Intellect* (New Haven, 1955).
W.E.Houghton, *The Art of Newman's Apologia* (New Haven, 1945).
F.McGrath, *The Consecration of Learning* (Dublin, 1963)
S.O'Faolain, *Newman's Way* (London, 1952).
M.Trevor, *Newman: The Pillar of the Cloud* (London, 1962).
M.Trevor, *Newman: Light in Winter* (London, 1962).

Mark Pattison

V.H.Green, *Oxford Common Room* (London, 1957).
J.Sparrow, *Mark Pattison* (Cambridge, 1967).

Christina Rossetti

G.Battiscombe, *Christina Rossetti* (London, 1965).
L.M.Packer, *Christina Rossetti* (Cambridge, 1963).
M.Sawtell, *Christina Rossetti: her Life and Religion* (London, 1955).
D.M.Stuart, *Christina Rossetti* (London, 1930).
E.W.Thomas, *Christina Georgina Rossetti* (New York, 1931).
M.Zaturenska, *Christina Rossetti* (New York, 1949).

Nicholas Wiseman

D.Gwynn, *Cardinal Wiseman* (Dublin, 1950).

Charlotte M.Yonge

G.Battiscombe, *Charlotte Mary Yonge* (London, 1943).
G.Battiscombe, ed., *A Chaplet for Charlotte Yonge* (London, 1965).
M.Mare and A.C.Perceval, *Victorian Best-seller* (London, 1947).

Index

Index

Index

Index

Index

Index